SHIPS THAT BUMP IN THE NIGHT

by

Frank Ledwith

ROBERT HALE · LONDON

Robert Hale & Company
63 Old Brompton Road
London, S.W.7

Composed by Specialised Offset Services Ltd, Liverpool
and printed in Great Britain by
Lowe & Brydone Ltd, Thetford

Contents

To the Reader

This might be sub-titled "The Ships and the City I remember". To many Englishmen 'The City' is the old Roman and medieval city of London, 'the square mile', once surrounded by defensive walls, parts of which still remain. Today, its inhabitants are down to less than ten thousand, although hundreds of thousands stream in to work there each day. The City is probably the greatest concentration of financial expertise in the world; but it is many other things besides.

Some things I forget. Others I remember all wrong. This is not a book of careful research, but of carefree affectionate recollection. I have not verified facts and dates: if I am wrong anywhere, please forgive me.

FRANK LEDWITH

1

Debut

I saw St. Mary Axe for the first time on a hot July day in 1924. I was to work there for forty-eight years.

Is there "a divinity that shapes our ends, rough-hew them how we will"? I did not think so then. It seemed blind chance or, rather, a somewhat planless plodding that brought me there.

Picture a solid youth of seventeen, with a good deal of fair hair, wiry and inclined to a spiky untidiness, and most peculiarly clothed. Some passers-by gaped at the clothes, but others smiled at a familiar oddity. I wore an ankle-length coat of dark blue, fitted to the waist and wrist, billowing in the skirt and slit up the front for easier walking. It was set off by bright buttons and by two vertical strips of starched white cotton at the neck, known as 'bands', but worn on top of each other, not alongside like those worn by barristers. Below the coat showed black knee-breeches and bright yellow stockings.

This was the school uniform of Christ's Hospital, based on the customary clothes of apprentices in 1552, when it was founded. At that time, of course, a 'hospital' was a refuge for the old, or for the young who needed help in education, as often as for the sick. The school stood in the City until 1902, and still keeps close links with that community, so that some at least knew what the blue coat signified.

My schoolmasters and my father had agreed that I showed no unusual ability of any kind, and that the obvious course for me was an inconspicuous humdrum job with a pension at the end of it. My best subject had been mathematics, so I was encouraged to study for and sit (while still at school) Part I of the examinations of the Institute of Actuaries, with the idea of getting into life insurance. I failed the examination, but nevertheless had come up from school with appointments arranged with insurance companies.

Jobs were few in 1924, but some people still wanted junior clerks. I trudged round from one great stone building to another. Each street seemed like an oven. I saw company after company, secretary, personnel manager, even a doctor or two for medical examinations. At each the answer, straight or qualified, seemed to be "no". The sixth was The National Mutual Life Assurance Company of Australia in London Wall, a romantically named street but to me just another daunting pile of stone containing a vast hall and echoing corridors. So I trudged on along London Wall, into Wormwood Street, into Camomile Street and into St. Mary Axe.

Another curious street name. A curving narrow street, running from Leadenhall Street northwards to the Houndsditch, now a street but once the ditch outside the medieval wall, into which were thrown dead dogs and other rubbish. Mostly narrow-fronted buildings of four or five storeys with many name plates, painted or of polished brass, in the doorways. A church at the southern end, a few scattered shops, small public houses and restaurants. On the left as I turned south stood a large building fronted in sombre brown marble, with a high doorway each side bearing gilt numbers 28 and 24.

No. 24 St. Mary Axe was the last address on my list. The company was The United Kingdom Mutual Steam Ship Assurance Association Limited (Thos. R. Miller & Son, managers). I had not the slightest idea how different this was from the great life insurance companies I had visited all day. I went in. Shining mahogany doors. A high passage lined with shining tiles, and at the end a lift-shaft. The lift came down, steel gates crashed back and a strange, dwarfed, hunchbacked figure peered out. "Hooja want?", he asked. I began to tell him. "Second", he said, seemed to hook me inside with a gesture of his thumb, clashed the doors shut, heaved on a steel rope and we shot upwards.

In a short time, including a brief interview with a head showing through a hatch, a tense seat on the edge of a chair, and a step across a passage, I was shown into a room to meet the man under and with whom I was to work for many years.

The room was full of sunlight and heat, and I was astonished to see a man sitting with his feet on the desk, coat off, showing his braces. I wondered what ever kind of bohemian outfit this was. But the feet came down, and I saw a compact figure, gleaming black eyes, glossy black hair.

The interview was brief, but surely not as brief as memory suggests. "You think you'd like to work here? Good. How much, Thorp [to the corpulent chief clerk in his square-tailed frock coat]? Five pounds a month? Make it six. You'd better have a copy of the Rules. Get one, will you?" Thorp went out and returned with a grey-covered booklet. "This'll tell your father what it's all about. Start on Monday. No, that's bank holiday. Tuesday." Maybe that is an over-concentration, but after the tedium, the pedestrianism, the solemnity of the day, that is what it seemed. I had a job.

Dawson Miller must be reported more fully later, but the first impression was true — a brisk, humane, considerate person, who regarded a decision as something to be made at once, and a problem as something to be solved instantly, and sooner if possible.

The Rules of the Association went home with me. Neither my father nor I could make any sense of them. We were more impressed by the long list of ships printed at the end. They were ships of many nations, but we were pleased to see a large group whose names all began with the same word, *British Lord, British Lady, British Holly* and so on. The British Tanker Company, under its present name of BP Tankers, still uses this system to name their tankers, large and small.

I went back for my last days at school in Sussex. My father took me to Hope Brothers to buy a conservative grey suit, and I returned to St. Mary Axe on the first Tuesday in August. Beyond the hatch marked 'enquiries' I found an L-shaped office, with windows on the inner sides of the L, and doors through into other rooms at each end of the two arms of the L. Across each of these arms stood two double, high, sloping-topped desks. A rather odd youngish man with a bald head (he had lost his hair in an illness at the age of seventeen) led me across to three high stools set at the nearest desk. "This is mine", he said. "Powley's on holiday, so you can have either of the others. They're both damned hard."

From that moment I was one of the T.R. Miller 'family' and felt that I owned a share in the freehold of St. Mary Axe.

2

The Axe and the Club

'The Axe' was a street of history. The name came, it is said, from an incident of the far past, when some Danish raiders rampaged along the street, broke into the nunnery of St. Mary and ravished and killed many of the nuns. From the favourite weapon of the Danes, the nunnery took the name of St. Mary Axe.

The church at the corner is St. Andrew Undershaft. On the other corner, in the Middle Ages, stood the great may-pole shaft round which the lads and lasses danced on May-day. It was 'the church under the shaft', and it survived the Great Fire of London in 1666. So did St. Helen's, formerly approached by labyrinthine alleys, but now in view of the front windows of our office, near the great tower block of the Commercial Union Assurance Company. Part very old, part Georgian, St. Helen's was the scene of a domestic sidelight of history which always catches my imagination. In 1483 or so, Richard Duke of Gloucester, stayed near by at Crosby Hall, the grand house he hired from the City Alderman, Sir John Crosby. Convinced that the boy prince named as Edward V was a bastard and no true king, he was considering whether to assert his own claim to the throne. His little wife, Anne Neville, went daily to St. Helen's Church to pray that Richard would not assume the throne. She was sure it would lead to his death. Two years later, on Bosworth field, she was proved right when the Crown of Richard III was found on a thornbush.

In St. Andrew's Church there is a bust of John Stow, who published his *Survey of London* in 1600. In it he records how, as a boy, he went each morning from his home in Threadneedle Street to the Minories, outside the Wall at Aldgate, to buy milk from the Minorite Sisters. It cost a halfpenny a quart. Each year there is a memorial service for him, when the Lord Mayor of London attends and places a new quill pen in the stone hand of the statue. He may feel like writing another chapter, who knows?

Beyond St. Helen's one can see the beaver on the

weathervane on the block of offices which was the head-quarters of the Hudson's Bay Company in Bishopsgate. Alongside it is another tiny ancient church, St. Ethelburga's, named for a Saxon princess. In it is a window of stained glass, commemorating the fact that Henry Hudson and his crew took communion there in 1617, before sailing on the voyage which discovered Hudson's Bay.

Samuel Pepys, the great diarist, saw a man hanged in St. Mary Axe for robbing a house in Lime Street. And, if fiction may intrude in history, W.S. Gilbert, the comic operettist, placed his sorcerer John Wellington Wells, "a dealer in magic and spells", in our street. And, of course, George Bernard Shaw named one of his characters, the foundling who grew up to be an armament manufacturer, Andrew Undershaft, from the church on the steps of which he was found as a baby.

The great brown-faced building in which I worked also has its part in history. The black gates lead into the Baltic Mercantile and Shipping Exchange. The offices above are Exchange Chambers. This is, with Lloyd's and the Stock Exchange, one of the three great business exchanges of London. Like Lloyd's, it began in a coffee house. In fact, it betters Lloyd's, for it began in two, the Jerusalem and the Baltic, and later amalgamated. At Lloyd's the shipping men who came talked more of insurance, at the Baltic more of the sale and chartering of ships. Gradually each grew into a business institution. And today, if you want to buy or charter a ship (or an aircraft), or buy a cargo of grain or oilseed, to the Baltic you go, if you are a member, or to a Baltic broker.

The Baltic, already an organised community, erected the present building in 1903, one of the first steel-framed structures in London. Three times during the 1939-1945 war, incendiaries fell on the roof, and an adjoining building was destroyed by high explosive bombs. Battered, it still stood, and (as I saw myself) was a good platform for firemen playing their hoses onto burning buildings on the opposite side of the Axe. The site of that adjoining building was bought by the Exchange for an annexe. When this was built, after the war, Sir Winston Churchill laid the foundation stone. Jack Walker, secretary of the Baltic at the time, told me that enquiries were made as to what kind of cigars the great man liked. Apparently they were very large and very mild, and arrangements were made accordingly. After the ceremony and of course the lunch,

Churchill lit a cigar. Shortly after: "Very good cigar this. [Pause] Do you think I could take another back with me?" The Chairman: "Of course, sir. May we send the box up to Downing Street for you?" Churchill: "That's extraordinarily nice of you. Thank you very much. [Pause] Could you send them up right away?"

And when the building was completed, Her Majesty the Queen came to open it. The banqueting room, 'The Queen's Room', can be divided into two by a panelled wall which, by electric motors, rises from the floor. The Queen was shown the trick of it, and pulled the switch herself. When it had risen four feet or so, she (and everyone) suddenly realised it was barring her off from the assembled company, and she delighted them by waving 'goodbye' over the rising wall.

Much of 'the Axe' of 1924 has gone, and been replaced by new. Sandrock's bakery no longer entices the passer-by with odours of fresh bread and buns. Nor does Mooney's Irish House, with its mingled breath of sawdust, Guinness and Irish whiskeys. The building which I saw burn, with its 'art nouveau' terra cotta façade, was replaced by a simple modern office block. The Express Dairy's tea-shop and the offices above it, including Burdick and Cook's three single-ship companies, the Burdale, Buranda and Dorie Steamship Companies, no longer stands on the corner of Bury Court. The site is part of the new building of the Chamber of Shipping of the United Kingdom, with its gigantic anchor and chain running across the shiny metal and glass front and its insert tobacconist shop. Not to my taste, that building. I'm tempted to go in and ask the time of the next bingo session.

A third of the west side has gone entirely, with part of the Leadenhall Street buildings and most of the winding Great St. Helens, to be replaced by two tower blocks of offices, with a wide space round them. The small tower, for the great and ancient Peninsular and Oriental Steamship Company (incorporated by Royal Charter) is not unpleasant. The Commercial Union tower is stark and grim, except when sunny clouds are reflected on the dark glass, when it is quite lovely. The trees they have planted are a welcome addition to the one great plane tree in St. Andrew's Churchyard. But the winds that blow around these tower blocks have to be felt to be believed. Most days there is something. Often there's far too much. And far too frequently it means a frenzied clutch at hat or skirt, and the casualties in terms of umbrellas blown inside out are enormous.

Despite changes, this is still the centre of the ship-owning community, with the P. and O. on one corner, the British and Commonwealth group on the other side (including Clan Line and the Union Castle Line), S. Livanos, Lykiardopulo (one of the oldest Greek shipping names in the City), Goulandris Brothers, and others. Within a street or two are most of the great British shipowners, many of the Greeks, and London agencies for half the world's shipping. All are represented 'on the Baltic'. It is no wonder the rents are enormously high in this little area, two or three times as high as in New York.

Thos. R. Miller and Son moved into the Baltic building in 1909, from Great St. Helens, only a street away. It took me a little while to find out what they did, but gradually it took shape in my mind. Millers were a partnership which managed three non-profit-making insurance businesses in the interests of shipowners.

The most important was the one I had had on my list. If a seaman or stevedore was injured, or a seaman fell ill, or a ship hit a dock, or cargo was mislaid, and the shipowner had to pay, this produced a claim on the insurance. This was the Protecting and Indemnity Association, usually called the P. & I. Club. Another was the United Kingdom Mutual War Risks Association, which insured British ships and crews against war risks. Quiescent in times of peace, it was suddenly very important if war broke out. The third, called the United Kingdom Freight, Demurrage and Defence Association ('the Defence Club'), was an insurance for the legal expenses incurred when a shipowner got involved in lawsuits. To be exact, the Defence Club was not managed by T.R. Miller then. It was based in Newcastle-on-Tyne, and they were London Agents, but it was moved to London and the management transferred in 1932.

The whole business was so wrapped up in shipping and so closely identified with the shipowners concerned that it was no wonder they referred to it as their 'Club'. And, with all respect to clubs situated elsewhere, there was no better place for a club to have its office than in St. Mary Axe.

The partnership was paid management fees, out of which they provided offices and staff. Originally, the clubs were very cosy domestic affairs, often managed on a spare-time basis by an insurance broker or one of the shipowners. But that was when they were first formed in the eighteen fifties and sixties, to cover a few risks not insurable at Lloyds or with insurance companies. By 1924 they were more solid affairs, with permanent management, but Millers, the United Kingdom P. & I. Club, was by no means the largest.

It is amusing to compare the memory picture of that time with the bustle, on a far larger scale, of today. There were, I think, only ten of us on the staff. Harry Miller, the original 'son' of the firm's name, was more or less retired, so there were two active partners, Dawson Miller and G.H. Vos, assisted by Dawson's cousin, Roy Williamson.

Just inside the door and its counter was a minute telephone 'exchange' with two outside lines and five extensions to different parts of the office. On the low cupboard alongside was a press for copying letters, which were typed with a copying ribbon. You put the letter, a sheet of tissue, and two sheets of wetted blotting paper between two oiled cards, slid the whole set into the press, and spun round the brass handle on top to put the pressure on. If the blotting paper was too dry, the copy on the tissue was too faint to read. If it was too wet, the ink on the letter ran and smudged and might become totally illegible.

I learnt to sit on my stool at the high sloping desk and address envelopes with a steel pen. Rowland and Marwood's Steamship Company, Whitby; The Union Steamship Co. of New Zealand, Wellington; Sir William Reardon Smith and Sons Ltd., Cardiff; Bugsier Reederei und Bergungs A.G., Hamburg; Finska Angfartygs Aktiebolaget, Helsingfors. A certain odour of romance began to creep in, to mingle with the smells of dust, ink and leather. Whenever I could snatch the time I would read the letters which went out. This was about a docker who fell down a ship's hatchway and broke his arm. Another described a leak of seawater into a ship's hold, damaging a cargo of grain.

All kinds of people came into the office to see Mr. Miller or Mr. Vos — shipowners, solicitors, insurance brokers, and many more. One of my jobs was to announce them (my tongue stumbling over the names) and to show them in.

One day there was a real thrill when an ordinary-looking visitor was pointed out to me as Captain Jones of the *Trevessa*. His ship, a 'tramp' vessel which traded wherever her owners could find a cargo, had been owned by the Hain Steamship Company, then based in St. Ives, Cornwall, although their London office was just along the corridor from us. In 1923 the *Trevessa* had sprung a leak in bad weather a few days out from Fremantle after loading a cargo of ore concentrates. The cargo choked the pumps, and the crew had to take to the boats, twenty in one, twenty-four in the other, two ordinary heavy awkward ship's lifeboats. To return to Australia was impossible in the teeth of the trade winds. They had to go on. The Captain, remembering his experiences after being torpedoed a few years earlier, had added to the boat stores all the water and condensed milk they could carry. Through storms and calms they went on, day after day. Soon they lost each other at night, but persevered until one boat made Mauritius and the other Madagascar. Only four had died out of the forty-four. I wish I still had that little paper-back book, expanded from the actual log-books, under the title *1800 Miles in Open Boats*.

I gradually began to appreciate what 'the Club' was. It was more than an insurance company. It was a place where men of the sea pooled their difficulties and where help (both financial and otherwise) was given in sorting things out.

The word 'mutual' was significant. Each club was a non-profit-making company. The shipowners insured were 'members' of the club. Each year a call was made on all the members at an agreed rate, to provide funds to pay for the losses. If this proved not to be enough, as was usually the case, a further call was made, until the books just balanced. It seemed to me an extraordinary but curiously attractive way of doing business. And I was now a part of it.

3

Learning a Trade

What makes up a trade, a craft, a profession, a career? A mass
of detail to begin with; a procession of incidents day after
day, year after year; the rub and polish of human relationships; and, of course, the influence of outstanding personalities. There must, too, be the drive of qualities inside
oneself — ambition, pride, the spirit of competition, the
desire for security, perhaps greed for power and for what
money can buy; ideals too, and, with some people, a single
absorbing purpose.

I remember myself as a fairly carefree youth, but with a
questing mind, avidly interested in most things. My mother
used to say that if I picked up a tram ticket on the stairs, I
read both sides before I moved up a step. When people look
askance at what young people wear today, I remember
ruefully the first suit I bought for myself. Thinking that the
City of London needed cheering up a bit, I found a cheap
tailor who made me a suit in a fearsome purple-brown colour,
with enormously wide trousers, very near the 'Oxford bags'
which then decorated our oldest university. For the first few
weeks I enjoyed the comments, but how heartily sick I got of
that loud suit soon after. And of course I had to wear it to
shreds, since six pounds a month allowed for no waste
anywhere.

Lunches were a problem, even at the low prices of those
days. I think you could get two beef sausages and mashed
potato for seven pence. At first, I regularly lunched with
Maurice Costin, a schoolfellow, who soldiered on to become,
eventually, a director of Price and Pierce, the timber people.
He always chose this dish, purely on economic grounds, and
always made the same comment: "It doesn't satisfy me, but
it takes away my appetite." Towards the end of the month I
was often reduced to buying half a pound of broken biscuits
for twopence at Owen and Randall's, the grocers in Leadenhall Market. I learned long after that the Market is on the site
of the Roman forum, the foundations of which are still
buried beneath it. But to me it was just rows of shops

displaying whole carcases of meat by the hundred, game birds in their plumage, and other exciting things to smell and see.

There were also stationers' shops, where I bought my first pulp magazines, westerns, the *Black Mask* detective magazine which launched Raymond Chandler and Dashiell Hammett into fame, and science fiction. The last-named was in those days considered fit only for office-boys and crackpot scientists, and I was laughed at for predicting that men would be on the moon during my lifetime.

But these are mere lunchtime moments in what was a reasonably hardworking office life. Hour after hour, I indexed various kinds of books, totalled account books (first in pencil, then if it tallied in ink), did all sorts of odd jobs, and ran errands. I still remember the first errand. To the question, "Do you know Lloyd's Avenue?" I answered yes, because I was afraid to confess ignorance, and assumed it was near Lloyd's, then in the Royal Exchange. Off I went and for a long time circled the area, too shy to ask. When I did, I needed the advice of a whole series of guides to get me back to the right place, in quite a different direction. The remarks which greeted me when I returned after an hour spent in getting to and from an office four minutes away cured me of that particular idiocy.

A good part of each morning was spent delivering letters over a radius of half a mile or more, since then a junior's wages rated rather less than postage. I became quite an expert on front doors, back doors, lifts and even fire escapes. After a while I could even cover long distances in rainy weather, going through building after building, with only an occasional dash across a street.

And every afternoon there was the session on the post, addressing and stamping envelopes, inserting the contents and carrying the stuff to the post office.

I had to learn quickly and the hard way some basic things about business relationships. In my first month the one and only shorthand typist asked me, rather brusquely, to copy a letter. I always found her rather terrifying as she marched through the office with her straight-bobbed hair swirling round her ears. That may be the reason why I over-reacted, and said I'd do it when I finished the thing I was doing. 'Words' followed. The lady stalked in to Mr. Vos to complain. I was sent for and told straightly, "It is part of your job to get on with the rest of the staff." I may not always have respected that dictum but at least I have never forgotten it.

After a year 'on the post', as we called it, I was transferred to the filing room to work with (it was never under) Victor Lofts. Dear old Victor. He was not much older than me, and Mr. Thorp, the chief clerk, was at pains to warn us not to 'muck about', advice which we naturally disregarded. Sometimes we did so little during the day that a wild whirl of activity was needed to get the more important work done in the last hour, and thus avoid a carry-over of unfiled papers which could cause trouble next day.

Vic covered up for me when I arrived late. I covered up for him when there was a new issue of shares on the Stock Exchange and he was out early on that mysterious operation known as 'stagging'. On a number of occasions he made small profits by re-selling new-issued shares before he had to pay for them (I hope I understood the process), but then he lost all his winnings on an issue which proved unpopular, and gave it up.

During the General Strike of 1926, we all kept the office going as well as we could. I came up by bicycle and have somewhat painful memories of it, not directly connected with the occasional scenes of violence, the stone-throwing at strike-breaking buses, and in one case a bus set on fire. My great passion was cycle-touring, and I spent every possible day and hour out in the country, either with our cycling club, based in South London, or with a few friends. The Saturday before the strike, I'd taken a header over the handle-bars going down Reigate Hill. Besides the cut on my chin, the road stripped a lot of skin off the backs of my hands and off both knees. Each morning as I started to work and each evening as I started home, the chafing of the bandages was agony, but it soon wore off.

On more than one occasion I saw other members of the cycling club during those weeks, and especially a slim young woman in a grey coat and skirt, in whom I'd been taking more and more interest. One day, I saw her swing neatly across in front of a heavy cart-horse, close enough for him to throw up his head in astonishment.

Alas, not very long after that she quietly but firmly warned me off. That was the time I developed a couple of frown wrinkles over my nose. I did no work at all in the office for three solid days. Vic did all my work as well as his own, although I hardly spoke to him. A loyal friend.

Fortunately, not many months later she changed her mind. An odd sequel was that in later life we rarely celebrated our wedding anniversary. Instead, we have remembered 'the day we parted for ever'.

Victor and I still had a lively time in the filing room. I brought up a set of boxing gloves once, and with Reggie Meyer and Butlin we had a tournament in the lunch hour. Two boxed, one refereed, and one kept a look out for the bosses. Later, the small telephone exchange was shifted into our room, with a girl to work it and also type. This increased the fun. After one altercation with her, we hoisted her onto the top of a tall filing cabinet. Mr. Thorp came through, looking for her, but he never thought to look upwards, and she was sporting enough to keep silent, so he went out baffled.

Although one thinks most of the way-out incidents, we must have got through a lot of hard work. We made it a point of pride, too, to find new ways of keeping the files tidier and better, and of having every letter ready to hand in a flash. We talked endlessly about the subjects dealt with in the files; and one winter we went to evening classes in an attempt to get some more general knowledge about ships, ship management and shipping laws. S.E. Britten lectured on ship management, Stevens on shipping law, and H.A. Turner of the Motor Union Insurance Company on marine insurance. I felt we were bad students, bored in the parts which did not impinge greatly on our daily work, and equally bored with such as did, for those few aspects were more familiar to us than to the lecturers. We therefore tended to prompt, correct and even argue with the lecturer on points on which we had specialized knowledge. Strangely enough (as it seemed to us) the lecturers enjoyed this, and Britten especially used to walk with us to the nearest underground station after class, to draw us out farther. He was later very well known as secretary of the British Ship Adoption Society. This arranges for schools to 'adopt' a ship. 'Adoption' entails correspondence with the officers, displays of material sent to the school by the crew, reciprocal visits to ships and schools, and other things which must liven up geography lessons, and promote interest in the merchant marine. Stevens and Turner became noted lecturers and writers.

This experience helped to underline the very specialized nature of the business we were in. It was a mystery to many, even to men in shipping and marine insurance who ought to understand it. Many years afterwards, in 1954, I was asked to give a paper on it to the Marine Discussion Group of the

Insurance Institute of London. It was reprinted over and over again, and is still in demand twenty years after. The title was "The Place of P. and I. clubs in the Insurance Market". It explained that the marine insurance market consisted of Lloyd's, the companies which insure marine risks, and the P. and I. clubs (ours and others like it). Lloyd's and the companies insure the ships themselves (hull and machinery) and the cargoes they carry. The clubs insure the shipowners' liabilities towards other people. In the course of operating ships, it is only too easy for people and their property to suffer damage or loss. At one time, this was considered ill fortune, and no-one tried to make the shipowner legally liable. However, more and more liabilities have attached to shipowners over the years, as it has been considered necessary for them (and other employers and industralists) to accept more and more responsibility for the effect their activities may have on the public.

In 1924, the aggregate of these liabilities gave the clubs a modest position on the fringe of the insurance market. By 1954, they were a much more important section, and my paper discussed, among other things, the inter-reaction between clubs, companies and Lloyd's, and the varying boundaries of their activities. Today, the clubs are even more prominent, and in certain cases a shipowner may pay as much money for his club insurance as for his hull and machinery cover.

The growth of the clubs, and the spread of the mutual principle into certain further areas of insurance, has sometimes brought acid comments from other insurers. Their fears seem to me to be ill-founded. There are advantages and disadvantages to the mutual system. As long as an insurer, or group of insurers, gives the protection and service which is needed, he has little to fear from competition, at least in the long run. And though there have been minor changes, I do not regret the anecdote I used to end the paper. I was asked to comment on the possibility of P. and I. insurance (shipowners' liabilities) being insured by Lloyd's and the companies. It was the opportunity to say how effectively that market insures ships and their cargoes and to re-tell an old joke. A publican was asked by a customer for a small loan. He replied that it was not possible, as he had a private agreement with the banks — "I don't lend money, and they don't sell beer".

Shortly after this, Victor Lofts was offered a transfer to

the claims department which, of course, meant examining and passing for payment claims against the club by its member shipowners. So I was left in charge of the filing, with an assistant to help. And I also took over another job from Vic, the "owners' records". When the clubs were first founded, every member paid a contribution on the same basis, so much per ton on the tonnage of the ships he insured. By this date (1928) it was already clear that this system was not fair to some. Suppose a ship were to develop a small leak. If she was a 'tramp' ship, carrying bulk cargoes, a few tons of wheat might be damaged. If she was a liner, it was more likely to be valuable manufactured goods which were affected. So, means had to be found to adjust the premiums according to the degree of risk.

The firm had started a check to provide data on this issue. The methods of analysis were crude, and everything was written up in ink in great bound books. I took over this work, and found a new interest and challenge in it. It told me a lot about every individual shipowner we dealt with. There were the liners which carried every sort of product to Australia, New Zealand and Argentina, and brought back frozen meat and butter. There were coasters which did a shuttle service between Manchester and London. There were the Baltic traders which brought in the lumber, and Mac-Andrews' little liners which brought oranges and lemons, nuts and cork from Spain and Italy. There were the tankers which brought crude oil and distributed the refined products, though only on a fraction of today's scale. There were ships which traded only in the Great Lakes of North America or the rivers of South America. Their cargoes and crews, the stevedores who loaded and discharged them, their collisions with piers and with each other, all provided figures which went into these records.

It was all very stimulating. Everything seemed to come under my eye, and I devised new ways of keeping track of it all. In those days, the shipping trade was far from prosperous, and firms like ours, who served the shipowners, were always short of money. But I manoeuvred the chief clerk (Thorp's successor) into authorising our first card index and the first loose-leaf books for the owners' records. More and more information was made available to the partners, so that they could assess the cost of each member more exactly, and with understanding as to what produced the losses.

Then came a further change. Dawson Miller prodded me

once or twice by asking what I intended to do with my life. After cogitation, I went in rather nervously and asked if I could handle some of the correspondence with the members. "Do you think you can?" "I don't know, but I'd like to try." After a few more questions he threw over a letter and told me to think about it, and let him know what ought to be done.

I knew of course from reading the post and the copies of letters for filing that the shipowners, when someone made a claim against them, consulted the club. We would either tell them whether to pay or resist, or write direct to the claimant. Moreover, we had correspondents all over the world paid by the club to help with this work.

The letter was from Ellerman & Wilson Lines' Agency Company Limited in Trieste in Italy. Now, over forty years later, they are still the club's correspondents there. It concerned a ship called the *Wiima*, owned by Mr. Antti Wihuri in Finland, and she had run into and damaged a jetty. Attached to the letter was a short report from the captain, recounting what happened, and a longer one from a surveyor, describing the damage and giving an estimate of the cost of repairs. All this came in for exacting scrutiny.

When it had been sucked dry, back I went into Dawson Miller's room, palms slightly sweaty. He looked up. "Sit down. What do you make of it?" I explained carefully that it all seemed to be plain. Those navigating the ship were at fault, the price seemed to be agreed, and the claim ought to be paid. "And if it's not paid", he asked, "how are they going to make us pay? The ship's far away from Italy by now, and so is the owner." This was something I had not even considered — a situation which not uncommonly developed when one discussed a problem with this man. But we agreed it would be undesirable to force the port authority to press its claim in Finland and that I should tell the shipowner this, and ask his authority to tell Ellerman's to arrange a settlement.

From then on, a steady trickle of 'cases', as we called them, came my way for handling. At first, they were picked out for me by the partners; later I picked out some from the incoming post. Miss Lee, the telephonist-typist, took them down in shorthand and typed them, and all this was in addition to my other work.

I learnt to draw up a 'time-sheet' showing whether a ship had used more or less than the time allowed by the contract for its loading and discharging, and to calculate the 'demur-rage' payable as compensation if it took too long. Bit by bit the mechanics of operating and navigating a ship became clearer in my mind, and the many details of a ship's structure and equipment. And memory began to file away the basics of shipping law, sometimes by direct study of textbook or statute, sometimes by reading the reports and 'opinions' of lawyers, or by discussion with them, for we often had to get their assistance in difficult cases. Mr. Percy Botterell, the impressive frock-coated senior partner of Botterell and Roche, the solicitors along the passage, once listened to me very courteously for a while, only to say when I finished: "Your argument, Mr. Ledwith, is a very attractive one. Unfortunately, in the case of the *Christel Vinnen*, the House of Lords has decided to the contrary."

Inevitably, too, correspondence with claimants (for we often took the burden of this off the shipowners) led to interviews with claimants.

There was a series of claims against different ships for damage to grain cargoes in which the great French trading firm, Louis Dreyfus and Co., were interested. Their head office was (and is) in Paris, and I found a formidable opponent in their London office, which looked after the claims. Often there was doubt, for example, whether cargo was damaged by bad weather (for which the shipowners were not responsible) or through a defect in the ship (for which they were). I would fire off an argument, and back would come a crushing reply. Often deadlock would result. I was not the only one who experienced this, as was shown by the fact that they were often involved in lawsuits over different aspects of their very large business.

After rather too much of this 'won't budge' sort of correspondence, I invited round to our office the man whose initials JR appeared on all their letters. As so often happens, he seemed quite different face to face. Jean Raulin was a Belgian, under middle height, wiry hair in tight waves, silver-rimmed glasses over a big nose. He had a melodious and persuasive voice, and, tough bargainer though he was, to deal with him in person was like facing a rapier of charm rather than the steel mace of his written arguments. I received him at one end of the filing room. We were both at ease at once, reached a compromise on that particular matter, and started a long friendship which lasted until he returned to his beloved Belgium. We never made concessions on what we felt was right, but as far as I remember the only times we ever went to Court or arbitration on a dispute were when we needed an independent authority to decide some point as a precedent for similar cases.

Dawson Miller gave me much freedom. His attitude was, "Come to me or Mr. Vos if you don't know something, or get into difficulty." I did this as seldom as I could, but, when I did apply, I always got drastic, if friendly, criticism. If I took one of my letters in to Mr. Vos to check, he always seemed to be reaching for a pen after reading the first words. It was four years before he passed one of my letters without alteration. Once I had the temerity to point out a split infinitive in his new version. He said, "Yes, I did that for emphasis", thought a moment, and ringed round a few more words, inserting them, too, by an arrow into the middle of the infinitive. Dawson, too, sent back an early letter of mine which I'd peppered with 'inst.', 'ult.', 'your favour' and other things I thought of as business-like expressions. Every one of them was struck out, and across the whole letter was written, "Leave this jargon to the drapers."

So, bit by bit, I learnt my trade, or at least the beginnings of it, but this period needs to be rounded off by a happening which profoundly affected business, as well as life generally.

The slim young woman was more and more a part of everything I did. From St. Mary Axe, a little before six o'clock, I would hurry over to Gracechurch Street and look for a face framed in a cloche hat and a fur collar to appear in the doorway of number 57, where she worked as a shorthand typist for a firm of chartered accountants.

Countless times I saw slender legs swing as she leapt for the tail-board of a moving bus. There were no queues in those days, and in the rush hour the spaces went to the nimblest. If we were together we tried to get a seat at the back, for privacy. London lost something when the upper decks of buses were covered in. On the open top buses the seats were hard, it's true, and slatted to drain away rainwater, but the darkness gave a delightful privacy, especially on a wet night when the tarpaulin was stretched up to our chins.

She shared my passion for cycling. Saturdays, Sundays, bank holidays, weekends, even some evenings we would be out and we got to know almost every road, bridleway and even footpath within riding distance of home. To the attractions of hearty exercise, rural beauty (a twentieth, perhaps, of today's motor-car population to interfere), and a degree of adventure, was added a simple and rather innocent romance. Some of those scenes are still so vivid that I can almost smell and feel them. One evening, particularly, walking and riding uphill near Headley, with Orion enormous over us in the sky.

There were also snatched lunches in crowded City restaurants, where shillings were stretched as far as they would go, but I would occasionally order for her a favourite dessert. She still says I wooed her with talk of P. and I. insurance and peach Melbas.

And so, of course, came the day when we married. A friend of my sister had a house off Brixton Hill, not far from where we lived with our respective families. It was too big for them, and for a friend they would let the three top rooms for only twelve shillings and sixpence (62 of our decimal pence) a week. We conferred with them, did anxious sums which always seemed to forecast a permanent deficit, and decided to take the plunge. Until the unexpected offer, our finances made marriage seem so remote that we'd not even discussed a formal engagement. But now we were engaged, married, honeymooned and settled in to a new home, all in a few weeks.

Strictly, home is no part of a story about St. Mary Axe. In practice, Constance had a great part in the story. I talked to her endlessly about my business life. She often helped me over difficulties. I thought of her as I walked, and even as I worked. And she came to mean much to many of the people I worked with.

So perhaps I may sketch in that December, 1932. Her mother was a widow, who had recently given her eldest daughter a proper white wedding. Curiously enough, the bridegroom and I had both, eight years before, sat for Part I of the Institute of Actuaries Examination at their lovely old half-timbered Staple Hall, off Holborn. Meeting in the street afterwards, we discussed the papers. I was quite certain I had passed, he quite certain he had failed. Both of us were wrong. He went on to pass his finals in a record short time — an all time record, for they have since changed the rules. I went into quite a different sort of insurance. He became in the fullness of time actuary and life manager of the Atlas Assurance, president of the Institute of Actuaries, a vice-president of the Insurance Institute of London, a deputy general manager of the Royal Exchange Assurance. But I never envied him. Whatever it was which put me on a different road might have done so because I would never have made a good life insurance man. Something very different was called for.

Well, the lady's mother was somewhat taken aback at financing two weddings in six months. She was forced to tell us that it was a choice between a white wedding and a reception for the usual guests, and a generous cheque as a wedding present. We unhesitatingly chose the cheque. It still seems remarkable to me that my own preference for complete informality and no fuss was not challenged by the bride, to whom the usual formalities must mean so much. It was a great piece of unselfishness.

We therefore come to a simple church ceremony early on Saturday morning, in a business suit, and a dress and hat, verbal invitations only (notifications, rather), and tea and cake for any relations who came back to the house. In the event, I very much enjoyed it, and went round the church shaking hands with everyone before the bride arrived. In spite of everything quite a crowd came, both families, church and other friends, and people I'd worked with in Boy Scouts and Rover Scouts. And of course many of the cycling club who held up a bicycle as a sort of triumphal arch for us to leave under.

At the bride's home, we changed into our more robust cycling clothes (both of us wore shorts) and set off for a brief honeymoon at a cottage in Surrey. By the Wednesday I was back in St. Mary Axe.

4

Dawson Miller

On a cold but dry day early in 1971 a memorial service for
Dawson Risch Miller was held at St. Helen's Church,
Bishopsgate, just across the road from Thos. R. Miller and
Son's offices in St. Mary Axe. Such affairs tend to be formal
and not of much meaning except to the family of the man
commemorated and his closest friends. The attendance is
usually not large, unless the man is a great public figure, or
high in a very large organization. On this occasion over six
hundred people came. Many said there had been no such
gathering so representative of the City in living memory.

Sir Henry Mance, chairman of Lloyd's, was there, and the
chairman of the Baltic Exchange. Dawson Miller's widow,
known to so many as Rob, was straight and gallant in a
splendid broad-brimmed hat. His brother Cyril read the
familiar verses from Ecclesiasticus in the voice to which so
many judges had listened during his twenty years at the Bar.
The Hon. David Montagu, merchant banker, delivered no
formal address, but the simple tribute of a close friend which
seemed to many both fitting and very moving. British
shipowners, directors and managers were there, row after
row. There were as many Greeks, of whom so many do
business in London. After the service I jotted down the
names of those Greek shipowners who had made a point of
shaking my hand in the crowd. There were thirty-three names
on the list. Shipbrokers and insurance brokers were there,
Lloyd's underwriters, all kinds of business connections and
personal friends, the trainer of Dawson's racehorses, and his
jockey. Six business friends flew over from America for the
service. Others came over from Norway and different parts of
Europe.

Dawson Miller was certainly the greatest P. and I. man of
this century and probably of all times. *Seatrade*, the shipping
journal, called him "a grand old man of the City of London",
but those who knew him will always think of him as young,
right up to the time when he retired at the age of
seventy-eight, and, a few weeks later, died. There was a zest

about him, a spring in his spirit as some men have a spring in their step, and an unexpectedness.

I can think of two men in his own field who matched or surpassed him in some respects, but their best friends would give Dawson the palm in all-round achievement.

J. Stanley Todd of Newcastle-upon-Tyne was a patriarchal figure, but really a survivor from another age. He ruled (directors or no directors!) the North of England P. and I. Association which he managed for an incredible period, until over ninety years of age. In his youth he made historic innovations. As the years went on he was still outspoken, fluent and strong in his opinions, but many of his contemporaries thought him out of touch with changing conditions. The Association was solid enough under his guidance but when he died his sons, already old, were unable to carry on, and there was a management crisis until the directors courageously brought in entirely new blood.

R.D. (Bob) Riley was very different again. He was a great-grandnephew of the John Riley who, in 1854, was co-founder with his brother-in-law, Peter Tindall, of the very first P. and I. club, now well known as the Britannia. His four sons are still engaged in the management. He was a very lovable character, warmhearted and impetuous, and a great athlete. I met him rather violently on one occasion in an association football match between our two firms. Brought up on Rugby football, I believed that if you tackled a man, the idea was to put him down so that he stayed down. Bob came charging down the wing with the ball at his feet. I met him with the point of my shoulder in his solar plexus. Admittedly, he was a tall man, but the referee gave me a lecture while Bob recovered. The point is that he was back in the game at once with undiminished zest. Dawson Miller often deferred to Bob's great knowledge of mutual insurance, and even more to his fantastic memory of past decisions, but the Britannia has not grown to the scale of the Miller Club.

Dawson would not want me to try to assess ways in which he compared with other men, especially those who were good friends and, in some degree, rivals for so long, but I will try to give a few side-lights, more by anecdote than analysis.

First let it be said that he ran the business for some forty-five years, and built it up from one of average standing to being by far the largest, and some say the best in the world, twenty or thirty times the size it had been when he began. It provided insurance for one fifth of the world's merchant shipping.

He was not intended for the City, but for the Navy. After Dartmouth, he worked his way up to the command of the destroyer *Viking* during the 1914-18 war. She was the only destroyer to be fitted, as an experiment, with a 6-inch gun. Since it was not repeated, the experiment must have been unsuccessful. According to him, every time they fired the big gun, the lights went out and the ship had to go back to the dockyard for repairs.

Some years after the war he went to Hamburg and met John T. Essberger, the shipowner. In conversation he found out that Essberger had served in the German navy. Dawson asked if he saw much action. Not much, was the reply, but on one occasion they met an enemy ship which threw such heavy metal across that they thought they would be safer elsewhere, and departed. A comparison of days and times made it reasonably certain that the belligerent ship was the *Viking* and not, as the German thought, a light cruiser like their own. One gathered that this produced some merriment, and that a wet evening was spent on the strength of it. Certainly the two became firm friends, and all the Essberger ships were in due course insured in the Miller P. and I. Club. In fact, they still are.

By 1919, the run-down of the Navy convinced Dawson that his chosen profession held little chance of advancement and virtually no chance of action. He asked his father whether there was an opening for him in the family firm.

The original Thos. R. Miller had been a shipowner and insurance underwriter in Newcastle-upon-Tyne, who moved to London, where he first obtained a share and then the whole of the management of the United Kingdom Club. One of the shipping papers wrote a few years later in the free and easy fashion of the day, "Mr. T.R. Miller is doing a good job in London managing a P. and I. club. He is a lot better at that than he was as a shipowner." One suspects it was not easy to get a suitable person as a club manager. I have seen a copy of the management agreement which T.R. Miller entered into which the club's directors in 1899, when he took his son Harry into partnership, and it is so grossly unfair towards the club and favourable towards the managers that no modern court would give effect to it.

T.R. Miller died in 1916. Harry had another partner, who was ready to retire. Apparently, his reply to Dawson was, "If you can pass the Bar examinations, I'll think about it." (Many club managers were barristers or solicitors, as legal knowledge was a great help in dealing with shipowners' liabilities.) Dawson took this as consent, and sent in his papers to the Admiralty the same day.

H.R. Miller was at times a dour individual. At any rate, we young fellows in the office were rather scared of him. However, before I came on the scene five years later, Harry had said to Dawson, "You take over". It was a staggering achievement for a young man to reach this point, only five years out of the navy. His father kept a room, and with it the right to come in and interfere, but we saw less and less of him until he left completely.

Just after I was made a partner in 1952, the partners gave Dawson a lunch on his sixtieth birthday. Characteristically, he invited his retired partner, G.H. Vos, up from the country to join in, and spent a good part of the lunch singing Vos's praises. He said, "He was the finest partner a man could have. We disagreed on everything, and never quarrelled once." I found out later this was quite untrue. On one occasion, Vos came back from holiday to find that Dawson had reversed a decision he had made, and declined to speak to him for two days. But Dawson obviously thought it was true, or else that in the mood of the moment it didn't matter whether it was true or not. They certainly had been a grand partnership.

He also told us at that lunch about his father handing over control to him. Apparently there were only two pieces of advice given, "Don't accept too much American business, and let Vos handle the directors' meetings and contacts with the directors". With both these precepts he totally disagreed, muttering to himself a naval expression which need not be repeated, and he ignored them, using his own excellent judgment in these as other things.

The lunch, incidentally, was also typical of Dawson. It was in a private room at the Coq d'Or, for years his favourite restaurant. The menu was a classic one: oysters, a saddle of mutton and a cheese soufflé. The wines were carefully chosen and, I was told, were as superb as the food. His old friend, Teddy Jones, of the insurance broking firm associated with Millers', produced at the end of the meal an incredibly antique port. Most of its flavour and body was gone, but they agreed that it had great curiosity value.

He enjoyed good food and drink, thoroughly rather than excessively. Both he and Cyril imported their own choice of French wines and were Chevaliers de Tastevin. After I decided to eschew alcohol, he told me I was missing one of the great pleasures of life. I had to agree, for I was just learning to appreciate good wine, but there were reasons for the decision. He nodded understandingly.

Naturally, my first impressions of D.R.M. were from the point of view of a junior, and mostly concerned his attitude to the staff. He brought into the office a distinct flavour of his naval life. For example, he encouraged us to join the Territorial Army or the Royal Naval Reserve, and gave extra leave to the large proportion of the men who did. At that time this was by no means normal. More generally significant was the way he ran things. He liked everything just so, but provided it was up to his exacting requirements, he left it to you how you did it. He neither noticed nor cared whether you took fifty or seventy minutes for lunch, but woe betide you if you were not there when you were wanted, or a job was not ready at the due time. Then his voice seemed to crack like a whip.

You knew who was captain of the ship but, like a good captain, his care for individuals was endless. He sent for Reggie Meyer and said: "I'm sorry to hear your father has died. I know you are the eldest son. There'll be a lot to see to, so take a week off and do it. Off you go." His first wife left him, a thing often forgotten by those who knew his long and happy second marriage. The newspaper stories were not pleasant. But that very week he called me in and said: "You're getting married, I understand. I'm glad. I am a great believer in marriage. Here is a small present from the partners." It was not the cheque but the gallantry of the statement that made it difficult for me to thank him properly.

Sidney Fowler, now one of the senior partners, Lieut-Commander, R.N.R., and respected as lecturer, arbitrator and justice of the peace, tells how once, as a junior, he fell asleep with his head on his desk. It may have been due to some extra-mural activities the night before. He woke to find his own scratch pad propped up in front of him with the message, written with his own pencil: "See me when you are not quite so busy. D.R.M."

Every Christmas there was a ritual, even when the staff had risen to over two hundred, when he saw each person separately to have a few words with them and present their Christmas bonus. One year, shortly before he died, another partner was with him when he was doing this. In came the little receptionist girl we had at that time, a smart attractive girl who (in those days of mini-skirts and micro-skirts) was said to wear the shortest skirts in the City. After the usual words, he said, "May I be allowed to give you a little advice? Now that you have a little more money, you could buy yourself a longer skirt." She was more amused than confused and more so when he added just before she reached the door, "But I hope you won't."

In the late forties, it came to my ears that some of the young men back from the war, often with wives and babies, were finding it a real battle to live on their salaries. One morning I had the thought to speak to Dawson about it. It was no business of mine, and I was still in some awe of him, but I followed the thought. I need not have been nervous. He thanked me warmly, was obviously concerned, and said he'd see to it. And then he said, "And what about you?" I was a bit off balance, and said something to the effect that I wasn't asking anything for myself, but he did something for me too, anyway.

He seemed just the same with the shipowners and their staffs, and with the club's directors, who are of course chosen from the insured shipowners, and on whose goodwill Millers as the managers depend. In fact, I have known few people who seem so much at ease and behave similarly with people of all kinds, ages, nationalities and backgrounds. I took a shipowner in to him who had a rather unusual problem. "It's like this," he said, "I bought this ship, and to avoid taxation I put all the shares in my daughter's name. Now my son-in-law has quarrelled with me and I can't get the shares back, or any of the profits." Dawson, who had never met the man before, leaned back and looked at him with the lopsided smile which was familiar to so many in the City. "You didn't bring your family up the right way, did you?" he said.

He was very friendly with Walter, the first Baron Runciman, as indeed was Harry Miller before him. Lord Runciman started his working life as deck boy on a sailing vessel, carrying coals to London, and ended it as the owner of a fleet of steamers and motor ships. He was chairman of the club for twenty-eight years. At the end of one directors' meeting we heard a lot of noise from the boardroom, and were told afterwards that the directors had got the peer singing some of the sea shanties they used to sing on the collier brigs, with the other men pounding the table to mark the rhythm. He really was a grand old gentleman and I can clearly picture him coming down the corridor with his pointed white beard and a fresh rose in his buttonhole. After he died his cousin Philip joined the board, and he in turn was followed by Viscount Runciman, who succeeded to both the Runciman peerages. At his first meeting Dawson said to him, "Never had a viscount on the board before. How should I address you, sir?" "I hope you'll call me Leslie", replied the younger man.

'Old Walter' was followed as chairman by Maurice Houlder of the Houlder Line who was canvassed by Dawson on the basis that to accept the chair would guarantee his survival to a ripe old age. He was thoroughly admirable both as chairman and man. His portrait by Sir Gerald Kelly hangs in our boardroom. At seventy-eight he fell off his horse and broke a collar-bone and came up to work with his arm in a splint. And Dawson's prophecy was fulfilled, for he was chairman for twenty years.

Besides his long friendship with men like these, it was an education to watch Dawson leading a board of twenty high-powered shipowners through a long and varied agenda. I am not sure that he was ever refused a request he made to the board. Mostly this was because he mastered every aspect of the business, although doubtless he also knew when and what not to ask.

As the partnership grew, to four, five, six and gradually to fifteen to meet the demands of increasing business, he had to learn a new skill. It was no longer possible to run the business as from the quarter-deck of a small ship of war. When regular partners' meetings were proposed, he grumbled to me about it, and questioned the need. I had to explain that it was embarrassing for us to be asked by a shipowner about a decision, when we did not know he had decided something. But he took the point and, I think, came to enjoy conducting the orchestra, as it were, of those very varied minds round the table at partners' meetings.

He was a remarkable judge of men, and right up to the last we took in new recruits to the firm for him to test and sum up before they could be engaged. Once he wanted to take on a man with a view to a partnership. Several of us objected, on the grounds that he had quite the wrong background. He was a barrister, it was true, and had been legal adviser to the Chamber of Shipping, but for some years he had been farming his family's land in Oxfordshire. We protested, I more loudly than any, but Dawson insisted. Time proved him right again.

When the war came in 1939, he did all he could to get back into the Navy, but fortunately the authorities refused. The merchant navy was just as indispensable if the country was to be fed and supplied, and, if the ships and crews were not insured, there was a good chance that they would not sail. Later, when the air raids came, he was among the first to volunteer to guard the roofs against incendiary bombs, and spent many night hours on the roof of the Baltic Exchange building.

It was in connection with the insurance of ships against risks of war that he first became a spokesman for the British shipowners in negotiations with their government. He was so successful in bridging difference of viewpoint that within a short time negotiations of any kind between these parties were dealt with by him and Martin Hill of the Liverpool P. and I. Club. Most of these had no direct relation to his business. It was a classic example of what he used to tell me and others: "See what help the shipowner needs first, and consider later whether it comes under the insurance."

The effect of this maxim on the minds of people can be seen in the incident when the veteran average adjuster, Gordon Elmslie, detained me in St. Mary Axe for some twenty minutes by a firm grip on my top waistcoat button. His address to me on that occasion, delivered in rolling Edwardian periods, can (like many eloquent speeches) be compressed into one sentence: "The characteristic of your club, Mr. Ledwith, is that it is run for the convenience of the members." I should say (especially as Mr. Elmslie's son still lives, and is a valued friend) that both Dawson and I enjoyed the father's acquaintance, his technical advice on marine insurance and his colourful discourse for a long period of years.

Dawson combined expertise with an inventive mind and a very sensitive touch with people. Despite his father's warning, he developed contacts with the American shipowners on a scale not known before. He devised a new type of limited insurance cover for the special needs of the Yugoslavs. The Germans, former enemies in war, were his firm friends. Captain Herbert Anderson, the Finnish shipowner, used to come to London every year to discuss what premium he should pay for the next year. According to legend, they always tossed a coin as to whether the premiums should go up or down. As to who won depended upon which of them was telling the story.

Dawson's bar training on top of his naval training equipped him well to deal with insurance claims. A Cardiff tramp steamer we insured, the *West Wales*, plodding along in fog, emerged into a gap to find herself in the middle of the Home Fleet, just in time to go smack into the side of HMS *Nelson*. There was nothing much to be said on the question of blame for the collision, but when the Admiralty's claim came in, he attacked it violently, quoting Admiralty regulations and the customary practices when a naval ship was in dockyard hands.

He did much thankless unpaid work for the shipping industry, the committee on this and the council for that. It was not wholly unrecognised. The French was the first government to do so, by appointing him Chevalier of the Legion of Honour for services to the merchant marine. An irreverent friend asked him if it was for services to the French wine industry. Then King Paul of Greece conferred a high honour. Then his own monarch made him a Commander of the British Empire.

To me, no tribute to him can be adequate. Like every man of character, he had his failings. He would sometimes bend a rule to suit circumstances, though his basic integrity was never challenged. He could be testy and obtuse. But I, like many others, owe him a great debt for encouragement, support and generosity and many other things besides. I wish he were still with us, and hundreds of people, I am sure, say the same.

5

A New Ingredient

This chapter can be omitted by those who are not interested in human motives, in the forces which drive one person to achievement and another to destruction or obscurity. Yet it is not basically a chapter of introspection but of adventure. It is the story of how a new ingredient came into my life and affected everything I did, in St. Mary Axe and out of it.

The development began on an evening in the spring of 1933, an evening of mist and moonlight. We were riding home after our regular Saturday outing with the cycling club, through the Surrey lanes, two by two. Constance and I had secured our favourite position among the twenty or so, in second place behind the leaders. One of the two young men in front had a punctured tyre, and stopped with a companion to mend it, and catch up afterwards.

I moved up to ride with the other man in the lead, Eric Sheppard. He was cheerful and fair haired — an average sort of chap. Some four years younger than me (a great gulf at that age). He was not the kind of fellow I took particular notice of, but he started a conversation which kept me riding with him all the way home. Constance (a very new wife) was slightly put out.

Two things he said fascinated me. One was that it was possible for a change to occur in a person's nature. He claimed to have experienced a degree of such change himself, and particularised this, in a matter of fact way. The second was that he was working with a group of people to see if this process could be multiplied sufficiently to change the whole situation in the world. He made a reference to Jesus Christ in a rather everyday sort of manner, but I was prepared to overlook this, as the other things he said were so interesting.

It must be remembered that this was 1933 when Hitler became Chancellor of Germany. The economic situation in Britain was acute. Unemployed were numbered in millions. War or the collapse of civilization seemed equally possible.

Blackshirts and communists fought in the London streets. People's minds, and especially those of the young, were seething.

On top of this, I was making the big adjustment of the newly-married, of sharing the breakfast table, a very limited income, bed, and every thought (or so it seemed) with a woman to whom I was committed for the rest of my life. A lot of it was delightful, but there were undeniable stresses as the adjustments were made. When Eric talked of change, I was immediately aware of certain points at which change in me was urgently desirable.

This was my first touch with those people who were accidentally, and by this time generally, called 'The Oxford Group' and later 'Moral Re-Armament'. Although it is neither necessary nor fitting to go into the whole subject fully here, it may be worth recounting two incidents, both occurring long after, which help to show what kind of new ingredient came into the mixture in 1933.

One was a broadcast by Radio Moscow on its home service in 1952, which said: "For several decades these men have been in the vanguard of the ideological struggle. . . . They have established bridgeheads on every continent and trained teams capable of penetrating the masses with their ideology." A further broadcast on the same service said: "These men substitute for the inevitable class struggle the eternal battle between good and evil. . . . That is the heart of their action whose consequence is nothing less, according to them, than the transformation of the world."

The other incident occurred after Dr. Frank Buchman, the initiator of Moral Re-Armament, died in 1961. The rector of our London parish, the Rev. Donal Browne, preached a sermon about him. He began by saying that in every age of crisis the Church seemed to produce a man to meet the needs of the day. He instanced St. Paul, St. Francis of Assisi and John Wesley and said, "Frank Buchman was such a man". Buchman, like the others, had not only expressed the truths which were needed, but had raised a body of men and women to carry them throughout society.

These can be regarded as two of many facets of something difficult to define, and something which teased and tickled me on that quiet ride homewards. A few days later, Eric and his close friend in the cycling club, Frank Skitch, invited me to a meeting for men in the City of London after work. I knew my wife would be out, so it was easy to accept.

The meeting was held in a long downstairs room, formerly a skittle alley, in Trinity Square, near the Tower of London. It is a blurred memory. There were about forty there, and quite a number spoke, including an office boy and the chairman of a company. The general theme was very much on the lines of what Eric Sheppard had said, but much more varied, of course, with the numerous different approaches of different men. There was talk of activities in many parts of Britain, in Holland, South Africa, and recently in Canada. But the surprise of the evening was the last speaker, Ben Baxter, who had been at school with me. We had not met for nearly nine years.

Afterwards, most of us went over to that ancient inn, the 'Tiger'. Queen Elizabeth was said to have dined there when she was released from the Tower. Upstairs we ate sausages and mash, or bread and cheese, off the billiard table. It was spread with a white cloth, but the high cushions made eating somewhat hazardous. There was a lively rattle of talk, and I made a date to meet Baxter again later.

Constance was still out when I returned. She has often said that she knew as soon as she got in that something had happened to me, because I had a hot drink ready for her. My account of the evening must have been incoherent and rambling, for I only partly understood it all, but I seem to have got the main points quite clear. One was the challenge to absolute moral standards of honesty, purity, unselfishness and love. I must have quoted that because she says, "When I faced those absolute standards, I knew I needed a Saviour." The other main point was that if one wanted it, guidance was available, through one's thoughts, and that it helped the process to write the thoughts down. This also must have got home, because we decided we would get up earlier next morning and to try listening for guidance.

And what happened? Not very much. I jotted down a few words in that day's space in my pocket diary. Looking back, the significant thing is that there was just enough to make it worth trying again next day and the next. It was like the first stages of acquiring a new skill, such as painting or learning to swim. The thrill of success, the drudgery, the disappointments, all had their place.

To me it was a very pragmatic affair of trial and error. For years I had been bitter and cynical about anything to do with religion or the church. At Christ's Hospital, daily attendance at chapel was compulsory and twice on Sunday. Because I missed once, I was confined to the school grounds for most of a summer term. This produced a deep resentment. It may have been this which made me cynical. If so, it seems very petty, but maybe that's in character, too. Anyway, I used to say that I had never met anyone pretending to be a Christian who was not a hypocrite. Of the minister at the church where I helped with the Boy Scouts I said that no-one could be a Christian if he was as fat as that. My mind was closed to almost any normal religious approach.

In our quiet times of listening I sometimes tried to imagine or "feel" what this God (or whatever it was) was like. I remember once a vague thought that it was something like a great tree, living, strong, deeply rooted, and branching out. I still don't know if that was guidance from God, or an idle fancy.

Mostly, the thoughts were mundane, and mingled with thoughts I knew were useless or even wrong. These had to be weeded out. The residue was still worth considering. Some thoughts urged me to confide in Constance all my past and present. This was difficult. It included certain incidents with other girls which I'd felt it would hurt her to know about, and had firmly suppressed. To tell her was painful, but it brought a startling increase in her trust in me, when she felt she knew me fully for the first time.

Other experiences were rather comic. Honesty about our inner feelings included our sharing the fact that each independently had decided that we would never quarrel. And this of course explained those awful silences which had begun to occur, and which had made me fear that our five-months-old marriage was already beginning to crack. We laughed until we felt quite weak. And of course we have known ever since that no solution of a difference can be expected without complete openness between us.

Several times in those first weeks, points came up which puzzled me. I would leave home for the office thinking how good it would be to talk it over with Eric Sheppard or Frank Skitch. Young as they were, they were also trying to find the same way forward as I. Each time, I got on the bus which one of them had boarded at an earlier stop. The first occasion was unremarkable, the second a coincidence, but what were the third, fourth and fifth?

What are the influences which guide our steps and which make our choices for us, or influence us to make them? Why do we go by this road instead of that, pick up this book, encounter this person? A lawyer friend of mine in New York met a girl on a bus. It is true that it took great persistence on his part to meet her a second time, to woo her, and eventually to marry her. But what brought about their first meeting?

The ancient Greeks believed in the workings of Chance as a real and effective force, the Romans in the fates. Talk to people, and you will find that many think something guided them at some point or points in their lives, for example in their marriage. Some believe that there is a pattern which they more or less consciously follow, throughout life.

A man I know spent many years in Papua. He visited the head-hunting tribes, people with a stone age culture, whose language only held a few hundred words. Conversation was made difficult by the fact that most of his western ideas could not be expressed in their language. He asked them if they believed in bad spirits. Oh, yes, everybody knew them. They were very real. Did the bad spirits speak to them? Oh yes, they told men where and how it was easiest to take heads. In their culture, this was a very basic activity. No man was truly a man and no girl would look at him until he had taken a head. A baby or an old woman would do, but it was a social necessity. Also, if you did not listen to the bad spirits, it could mean trouble. They might be angry. Did they believe in a great good spirit? This produced quite a debate, but yes, on balance they did. Would it be good to listen to him? More debate. Why do that, if he would not do you any harm? But on balance, they thought it could be tried. So they sat round in silence for a while. (No making notes here — it was an unknown art, and therefore memory was clearer and stronger.) The visitor turned to the chief and asked if the great good spirit said anything. Oh yes, said the chief, he said to take no more heads, and to tell the chief of the next village that he was his friend. Next day, the visitor saw the chief leaving the village without the equipment which was even more standard in that area than the City man's umbrella and brief-case. He called after him, and the chief turned to say, "I go to the next village." "But why", asked the visitor, "do you go through the bush without spears? The first man you will meet will take your head." The chief replied, "If I go through the bush with spears, how will he know I am his friend?"

A man like that has something to teach the so-called developed nations.

The point where my curiosity got attached to the idea of a plan for life was not in the realm of religion, or metaphysics, or even morals, although a stimulus was given by my sense of need for a great deal more moral order in my own life. When my new friends talked about absolute purity, I knew very well that I was far away from that. There was a lot of frustration, conflict and strain in that area of life. I also had a temper which could go utterly out of control. Twice I nearly killed someone in a rage, and I was haunted by the fear of this, too.

These things produced a sense of need (Henry Drummond once wrote of a man who had every Christian virtue except a sense of need) but the mental process which followed owed more to mathematics. It might even have owed something to my dabbling in science fiction.

It seemed to me that there was a purpose in creation, and a pattern in the universe. If this was so, surely that pattern and plan must extend to every part of the whole, even so tiny a part as an individual person, and to each move and moment which made up each person's life. Time, space, measurement were after all only human inventions, a sort of code which simplified thinking and the procedures based on those thoughts. On the cosmic scale, it could be that our conceptions were all wrong, that the things we felt to be small were large, the ephemeral things of longest effect, and the most trifling were actually the most significant. And equally so in reverse. At least, I was not in a position to say what was important. Maybe everything was important, at least as an essential part of the plan. An incomplete jigsaw puzzle is virtually useless, even if only one part is missing.

The second conclusion was that so complex and complete a scheme must have needed an intelligence to construct it, and it was quite illogical that sentient, intelligent elements in the scheme would be left ignorant of the purpose of the whole. There must be some way in which those elements could find out how to co-operate with and not go against the plan. If, against the background of the master-plan, it did not matter whether I co-operated or not, what was the use of my having intelligence?

It was in this mood that I embarked on daily listening, and on noting the thoughts which came into my mind. Some of them I learnt to cross out or ignore, vagrant thoughts from my sub-conscious, from daydreams, even from the Devil, if there were such a person. If they did not tally with the absolute moral standards, this indicated that they did not qualify. Another useful test was whether they would stand up if told to someone else.

Every day, however, there were some thoughts which seemed to ring true. It was at least possible that they came from what these friends (but not I) called God. Variety, harmony, constructive action were recurring aspects of these thoughts. And often there were thoughts about other people. Although change was a personal thing, it seemed reasonable to let others know that change was possible. I began, therefore, to experiment in this direction with varying results. Some people welcomed it. Some seemed insulted (perhaps I was tactless), some were indifferent (perhaps I was bad at presentation).

Now and then a clear sentence emerged in my mind with arresting effect. One was something like: "Apologise to G.G.D. for your hate for him." I was horrified. George Gordon Didsbury was one of the more senior men in the office, whose job was mainly to deal with personal injury claims by seamen and dockers. At that time the Workmen's Compensation Acts were still in force, and employers had to pay men who were injured at work a proportion of their wages whilst disabled, and certain other compensation. Didsbury dealt with all this for the shipowners we insured.

He was a smallish man, thin, with a rather pear-shaped head, thinning hair, round spectacles below a wrinkled forehead. He smoked a lot and had a racking cough. In the First World War of 1914-18, the Great War as it was called, he had served for a while at sea as a paymaster sub-lieutenant in an armed merchant cruiser, and of this he was very proud.

I caught a glimpse of him on that day of my first interview, screwed round on his high stool, so that he could see what was going on, a somewhat gnome-like figure. He had a characteristic brisk walk, a reputation of being good and exact at his job, and close friendships with a number of men with whom his work brought him in touch. But he could be waspish, sarcastic and revengeful.

He seemed to make it his mission in life to "put me in my place". He continually ordered me about and gave me small jobs to do, although I was not technically under him. It may be that my brashness invited it, but I was unself-critical enough to blame all on him. I thought he considered himself an officer and a gentleman, and me one of the other ranks. Anyway, I resisted his efforts in every possible way. I answered him back, or failed to hear what he said, or wilfully misunderstood. If he insisted that I totalled one of his account books for him, all the totals were mysteriously wrong. After two of the periodic flare-ups we had each complained to Dawson Miller, which only resulted in a cutting rebuke to us both. It was all petty in the extreme.

This staggering thought that I should apologise — it came with the force of a command — produced immediate mental resistance. "It was not my fault," I thought, "Well, it was only partly my fault. Anyway, how could I say something like that in front of other people? We were never alone. G.G.D. would be humiliated by it." I went to work that day with a thoroughly confused mind.

After lunch, I turned the doorknob and swung through into the filing room, to find an unexpected sight. My two colleagues were missing, and the only person in the room was Didsbury, standing with his back to the coal fire, warming his behind. A thought flashed into my mind that here was a great chance, and before I could properly think I blurted out something like, "I wanted to see you. I've hated you, and wished you were dead. I'm sorry and I want things to be different." The effect was, to me, astounding. He gaped for a second, strode out into the room, and gripped me by the hand. I cannot remember what he said. In a few moments, the others came in, and he quickly left, but things were different between us from that moment. He treated me with generosity and friendship. We had our moments occasionally, even one or two violent differences, but the basic relationship remained sound until he died.

It was much later that I assessed those moments adequately. In fact, a nine years' feud was ended in half a minute.

Another thought I found very humiliating. Twice I had had a bicycle stolen from the kerb. My London insurance company was a little put out, so I insured the third machine with a company in Liverpool, not telling them of the previous losses. Then that was stolen too. The company paid. After a number of increasingly squeamish thoughts, I felt I had to write to them, admit my non-disclosure of material facts, and offer to repay the claim. The reply was a little stiff, but declined the repayment: "The Company is well aware of the hazardous nature of the risk." The mortification I felt as an insurance man myself at being in such a position was allayed by relief, as I had no idea where to find the money.

These incidents may seem trivial, but they were necessary. A surgeon once commented that to wash one's hands thoroughly was an essential preliminary, but it was not the operation. More and more I got involved in positive action of various kinds. We were in Oxford during the university's long vacation of 1933, to meet people of all kinds and many lands. One was the secretary of a shipowning company with whom I formed a long friendship. Others were from the great army of the unemployed. A number of them lived in tents in Christ Church Meadows during the conference, to save expense, and came in daily to the meetings. We also camped outside Oxford, partly for economy and partly for the open air and the pleasure of cycling in daily.

One effect of this time was to give body to my intellectual conception that if you could bring change into the lives of enough people, the world would be changed. After I got back to the City, I remember saying to a friend that if we could get a thousand Londoners committed to the idea, each of them would only have eight thousand to deal with. Small groups of us would meet in restaurants or church vestries to plan during the lunch hour, and we were constantly in touch with fresh people, who we thought might join us in the campaign.

Does this seem unrelated to business and the real theme of this book? All I can say is that it coloured and affected everything I did every day. It changed my relationship with every person I met and actually began many of them.

For example, it was to speak of these new ideas that I rang up and asked to see Sir John Niven, a director of Andrew Weir and then chairman of the Baltic Exchange. He was a canny Scot and would not commit himself, but he was also a great gentleman. He invited me to lunch with him on the Exchange, and I still value his courtesy and kindness to a rather raw youth. A far closer relationship was that which developed with Harold Lindley the average adjuster, who was a noted authority on marine insurance. We became fellow-fighters, and intimate friends on a family basis, too. For many years we lunched together twice a week or so, and shared in many moves to advance the moral and spiritual ideas we shared. We must have been a laughable contrast in many ways, for I was by no means a polished character, while he was elegant in mind and person, and of course the Lindley family had a great outreach in the world of shipping and marine insurance. In fact it still has. I learnt much from him.

One other significant development came when some of my new friends held a Bible study session one evening. I joined in 'without prejudice', as the lawyers say. It was on the fifth chapter of St. John's Gospel, about the cripple by the pool who was healed after thirty-eight years of bitter disappointment. To me, the discussion was mildly interesting but did nothing to affect my doubts and reservations. After it was all over, I was sitting quietly by myself, when it was as if a silent voice spoke inside my head: "The force which you have been experiencing when you listen for guidance is the same as that Jesus who healed the cripple by the pool. He is trying to do for you morally what he did for that cripple morally and physically." I knew it was true, just as certainly as two circles are both circular, and many things became clear.

This was the new ingredient, the beginning of change in me and the hope of change in the whole family of mankind. How much it affected the things which followed after, it's impossible to say. But affect them it did.

It may be worth analysing some of the effects of which I'm conscious. The problem is to select from thousands of instances over forty years.

The practice of taking time for listening for guidance each morning, and often discussing over the breakfast table any thoughts which were noted down, has been a stabilising influence to a person of mercurial character. (When I mentioned my ups and downs to a Greek friend, she said, "You must be Greek!" But I used to make my Irish blood an excuse.)

Often I have set out for the day in the City with a clear answer to a problem facing me there. However, the quest for guidance is not like pressing a computer button for an answer. Peter Howard, the sportsman, journalist and playwright, once likened it to a constantly passing shoal of silver fish, of which you might catch what you could. But it takes many forms. It may be a clear intimation or the prompting of a new chain of thought, or even the kind of force which in time moulds character, as a sea-wind sculpts the cliff-top trees, or a river and its tributaries carve out a valley.

At one period I found myself often rewriting my business letters before despatch. A short time of thoughtful silence would reveal that this one was offensive, this showed an undercurrent of bad temper, this one was less than absolutely honest. One day my secretary of those days said, "I do wish you would have second thoughts before you dictate the letters and I type them." Perhaps her remark was a form of guidance too.

One of the staff used to come to me for advice. I gave it to him freely. Then I had the thought, "Next time, ask him what his answer would be to the question." I did this several times, and the knowledge and judgment he showed made me report the matter to the partnership, as this unassuming young man was clearly one on whom we could lay major responsibilities for the future. And we have.

I also found these principles a great support in saying 'no' to the wrong things, however, attractive, and 'yes' to the right ones, however difficult. Decisions of this kind come up constantly in business. One man wants a favour. Another tries to bully, or wheedle, for an advantage. I found I developed a name for being tough in duscussion and negotiation, but not, I hope, too tough. Certainly there was no falling off in the stream of people who came to me for help. Sometimes I was able to recover money, or settle a difficulty, when it was considered hopeless. It did seem to me that at times something outside me was at work.

One incident occurred during a period of major trouble between shipowners and trade unions, both nationally and internationally. I was only marginally involved myself, but I felt deeply that I should take some action. A trade union friend suggested I saw Sir Thomas Yates, then general secretary of the National Union of Seamen, and gave me an introduction. I went down to his office to see him. I had to explain that I had no authority and spoke for nobody, but we had a frank talk and I gave him information which he had suspected but did not know. It broke some of the invisible and unnecessary barriers which so often arise in such a situation. When I returned to the office I thought I had better tell Dawson Miller. When I mentioned the thought of seeing Sir Thomas, he said, "But you can't do that!" I replied that I'd just come back from doing so. Dawson, quickly recovering, said, "Good for you. What happened?" The trouble rapidly diminished in the weeks that followed. I believe my visit helped, but naturally there is no proof of it.

A number of times it seemed right to ignore protocol and go straight to the man at the heart of the situation when there was a difficulty. One such occasion was when a shipowner complained of proceedings brought against him in New York by certain Lloyd's underwriters whose lawyers there had declined to believe the shipowner's written evidence, and made him attend court and produce various private papers, including his income tax returns. The case involved a wrecked ship, and a lawyer had also gone on board the wreck and stolen documents. I complained to senior men at Lloyd's that such operations discredited Lloyd's, even if they were not specifically authorised. In the end the action was settled quite reasonably.

Another time I was asked to a conference of worried men considering how to prise out of the Canadian Government some money outstanding for several years. After listening to the long tale of woe, I had the thought to ask which department of the government was concerned. It was the Ministry of Defence. "It so happens", I said, "that the Minister's son is a student in our office at the moment. Shall I ask him to write to his dad?" I had also met the father, and was not surprised to hear that when his son's letter arrived he acted promptly, indeed eagerly, to end the dispute between two departments which had caused the delay.

These and other incidents exemplified a useful principle, to think out what was right in a situation and then to try to reach it by the shortest route. Another useful principle was to take time to think what was behind someone's action. It could be fear, or greed, or someone's conviction that he is always right. We quite often had someone asking to discuss a just decision which (in our minds) was already made, and would not be altered whatever happened. I realised that often the broker or manager wanted to be able to say to his principal, "I went and argued with them for a solid hour, and they wouldn't budge". And it was not necessarily a waste of time to do this. It could help to build a realistic relationship with both intermediary and principal. In time one could realise the background of emotion and character to a business interview, and handle it accordingly.

The principles I began to learn in 1933 helped in all these things. They are, of course, not confined to certain people, or to a particular point in history. Everyone shares them to a certain extent, if only as part of our racial and cultural inheritance. It is, however, a help to a man like me to have them kept before me, and to make and renew the decision to be guided by them beyond all else.

Another effect is, perhaps, not so general, although it should be. Progressively I found my life integrated into a whole. There was no division into business and private lives. Every factor in life seemed to matter for itself, and fit into every other factor. And the horizons of life widened constantly. I met all types of people, and many nationalities and races. More and more it seemed natural to think of the shop steward and the tycoon, the Asian, African or Australian, as a friend or a potential friend, and indeed as part of a society which would be different from the fractured and creaking structure of the past.

6

War in the Axe

When Neville Chamberlain announced on Sunday, 3rd September 1939, that a state of war existed between the United Kingdom and Germany, I was twenty miles from the City, at Walton-on-Thames in Surrey. It was the universal (but wrong) expectation that in a matter of hours there would be devastating air raids and many thousands of casualties. Arrangements had therefore been made to evacuate as far as possible everyone who did not have to stay in the capital. Not only the children, but most business houses and some government departments scattered themselves right across Britain.

Thos. R. Miller and Son planned to leave a small nucleus in St. Mary Axe, consisting of Dawson Miller, a secretary, and one or two more. For the rest of us, they rented a preparatory school for boys at Walton. The boys had gone further west, hoping to be out of reach of the bombing. Our business needed to be fairly close, but not in the main target area. Housing accommodation was taken for the staff, and often for their families too, at the firm's expense. So one day I was living in South London and working in St. Mary Axe. The next I was living and working in Surrey.

The general arrangement lasted for most of the war, but the City nucleus proved too small, and after four months I had to move back to the Axe, with certain others, to provide proper liaison with the shipowners, the Government, and others.

As with nearly everyone, the outbreak of war meant a great upheaval in our business. A large proportion of our men disappeared overnight, as the Army and Navy reserves were called up for service. James Wright, a solicitor, who had joined the firm a few years before with the promise of a partnership, commanded one of the two Lloyd's companies of the London Rifle Brigade. This was considered an élite part of the Territorial Army. The Lloyd's companies were recruited mainly from the staffs of Lloyd's underwriters and brokers. Sidney Fowler and Henry Brown (now Lloyd's agent in Piraeus) were seamen in the Royal Naval Volunteer Reserve, and a number of others also took off for undisclosed destinations. All their jobs had to be covered by other people.

In addition, the firm's business itself changed overnight, and the War Risks Club suddenly became top in importance. This club insured perhaps a fifth or a sixth of the British merchant navy. The rest was insured with a number of similar businesses, and all worked together as a group.

The world is rarely free of war, and therefore war risks insurance for ships is always needed, but it is usually a skeletal affair. The arrangements continue and small premiums are paid, but claims and other excitements are few. It is a different matter when one's own country is at war, and most or all of the ships are taken over by the Government for war purposes.

This meant that the reinsurance agreement between the British Government and the British war risks clubs was activated. Under this agreement the Government took on 80 per cent of the principal risks (later increased to 96 per cent) against a similar percentage of the premiums. The Government also had the right to decide what premiums should be charged and for what value each ship should be insured. The restriction on values was a guard against the type of profits made by a few shipowners in the 1914-18 war, who insured their ships for very large sums before they were lost.

The merchant ships came under heavy attack from the first, by mine and torpedo. Some of the mines were of types not known before, and losses of ships and men were severe. Immediately after war began, the premium for three months' cover was 160 times the peace-time rate. At the worst period, when losses of ships were so high that Britain and her allies nearly lost the war by interruption of sea-borne communications, the rate was seven times that, 1120 times the peace-time rate.

We had to issue new war-time policies every three months, and collect these premiums. There was also a flood of claims for lost and damaged ships, and for expenses in connection with their crews. Although the work of the P. and I. and Defence clubs dropped off somewhat, all this new work had to be handled by a depleted staff in improvised offices. During three days in December 1939, I prepared, dictated, checked and signed over 200 individual letters on many different subjects, using two typists and for part of the time three.

Except for the blackout, the rationing of food, the worry of all the makeshift arrangements, and of course the work, it was pleasant at Walton-on-Thames. In St. Martin's School, I shared a room with the junior partner, Archie Daukes, a genial man whose real passion was bird-watching. Even in the pressure of those days, he had half an eye for the birds in the trees, on the lawn, and on the red-berried shrub outside our window. After a week, he was very disappointed at only listing nineteen species. But for me the country life lasted four months. Then I was back in St. Mary Axe trudging to the station with Victor Lofts, gasmask on shoulder, carrying the papers which had to pass daily between the two offices, and returning in the blacked-out trains in the evening.

It was often a long day. Our route was through Clapham Junction, the busiest rail junction in Europe. When the air raids began, it was an obvious target for the bombers and our rail line was cut by bomb damage twenty times in the course of the war. We never knew when we left in the morning whether we would go straight through, or transfer to the underground at Wimbledon, or somewhere to buses, or (as happened at times) walk three or four miles. It depended on what had occurred during the night (or nights) before. Our worst journey took four hours from Walton to the City, and three-and-a-half hours home.

One morning, a longer than usual walk took us alongside St. Paul's Cathedral. Some of the textile warehouses there were still burning violently, and in the street outside one of them was a row of firemen playing their jets of water on the front wall. As we passed, we could see the wall swaying, and it was only the force of those jets which, it seemed, kept the whole thing from collapsing across the street on top of us.

Another day, we passed a fair-sized crater in the middle of the roadway in Cornhill, with flames roaring out of a broken gas main. A chatty official told us that the one bomb had also severed a water main, main sewer, electric cables for light, power and telephones, and a hydraulic main.

In the early months of the war, business stopped when there was an air raid warning, and everybody went down into the basements of the buildings, or other shelters. Soon, however, we stopped taking much notice. Daylight air raids were rarely severe. Later in the war, the 'V' weapons produced a different pattern. The V2 rockets arrived with no warning at all. An almighty bang, and it was over. If you heard the bang, you were safe. For those who did not, it was mercifully quick. Our girl telephone operator came to work one morning, still shaken by what she saw the previous evening. Her home-going bus passed a building the front of which had been destroyed by a V2, and looking in she had seen people sitting dead at their desks.

It was the V1 flying bombs which I found peculiarly unnerving. One of the first of these small pilotless aircraft fell near our home in Surrey and the police spent many hours searching for the pilot. Many fell in the City. You heard the mutter of the rocket motor growing steadily louder. If it then got less loud, you breathed out. That one was going to trouble someone else. If it stopped, look out. It was designed for the engine to cut out over the target area. I looked out of my window to see one of them puttering across the sky just north of us, undisturbed by a few anti-aircraft bursts. Then suddenly the sound stopped, one wing dipped, and it dived steeply behind some buildings. A second more, and there was a shattering crash, and a great cloud of smoke and dust. That one cleared us by half a mile. If there was any doubt, there was too much glass around the office for heroism, so I always dived under the desk. More than once I met my secretary doing the same thing from the other side.

During the worst periods of the bombing, the constant loss of sleep made everything seem even worse than it was. Everywhere you looked, you saw grey, strained faces. The damage was great, casualties heavy (though small compared with the mass slaughter of the 1914-18 war in France), and the effect on the nation's war machine was quite substantial. The biggest danger, in my opinion, was none of these, but the steady erosion of the national spirit. If it had gone on much longer, it might just have broken the will to win. It did not, and no one knows how wide the margin was.

Meanwhile, across my desk in St. Mary Axe came the daily reports on the far more intense war at sea. It was strange how comedy sometimes stalked alongside tragedy, although the general impression was of a grim and deadly struggle.

A logbook extract from a tanker discharging spirit at Purfleet read something like this:

1.30 a.m. Parachute mine exploded on foredeck, starting a fire.
2.00 a.m. Ship on fire fore and aft. Shore fire brigade reported on board. Advanced clocks one hour for Summer Time.

A British tramp ship was sunk in one of those homeric battles on one of the convoys to Murmansk. The captain, who survived, wrote a long and colourful report to his owners, with the literary skill of another C.S. Forester. But he ended with a rather false note:

> In case any decorations should be awarded in respect of this action, it occurs to me that you may like to have the names of those who particularly distinguished themselves by their behaviour. I would especially like to mention Chief Engineer Jones, Second Officer Brown, Cadet Robinson, and of course myself.

Other stories had no comic twists to them. One described a small convoy of tankers homeward bound, with an escort of one corvette. No more protection was thought necessary in the Caribbean area, but the Germans had just been able to extend the range of their submarines, and the attack by several of them was the first news of it. Ship after ship was hit and sank, often with all hands. The report came from the senior survivor of the ninth out of the eleven to be lost.

My friend, Harry Macey, was one of the many hundreds who were lost in this six-year battle. He had been a notoriously severe and exacting master in cargo liners, but (before I met him) had heard of and applied the principles of moral rearmament, which made him a much more satisfactory individual. I met him and his wife before the war and corresponded with him as he roamed the seas. In 1938 he retired, and took on a big job in the new Air Raid Precautions organisation. In 1939 he wrote me to say that he had had an insistent thought that his real talents should be put at the country's disposal. Could I help him to get a command? After some thought, I wrote to Capper, Alexander and Co. at 2 St. Mary Axe with the details. A few days later, I had a telephone call from Mr. Charles Alexander, the senior partner, whom I knew a little. He was very much the old style practical shipowner, hard-headed and successful. Sir Frank Alexander, his younger brother, was later chairman of the Baltic Exchange for a number of years, and Lord Mayor of London. Mr. Charles said, "I have received a communication from you regarding a certain Captain Macey. Tell me", and he cleared his throat, "can you guarantee his absolute honesty and sobriety?". Thoughts raced through my mind, but with as much composure and all the faith in Harry I could muster, I gulped and said, "Certainly, Mr. Charles, I'm sure I can."

He got his command. After a year Cappers lost a ship. The master was saved and, as an old servant, was given preference for Harry's ship. However, Charles Alexander recommended him to John Cory and Sons of Cardiff, who appointed him to the *Ramillies*. A few voyages later, she was torpedoed. The chief officer's boat was picked up, but the captain's was not. From the story of the survivors, it seemed likely that he and his men died of cold and exposure. He had served in the earlier war and knew what he was facing when at sixty he decided, in fact begged, to go back.

Here are two more stories, each with a slight touch of the grotesque.

One concerns the 'commodore ship', carrying (though of course a merchant ship) the naval officer in command of a convoy of ships in the North Sea which was heavily attacked by aircraft and E boats. Just as the captain was congratulating himself on having escaped, the chief engineer reported that a large unexploded bomb was rolling about on the second grating (a sort of intermediate deck) in the engine room. They consulted the commodore whose only comment was, "You'd better do something about it." Going below, the captain found a young engineer sitting on the bomb, smoking a cigarette. He explained that this was the only way to keep it still. They rigged tackle, hoisted the bomb out through the engine-room skylight and very carefully rolled it along a plank over the side. As it hit the water, all held their breaths, but it peacefully sank.

The other case was that of the *Catrine* owned by Morel of Cardiff. She set off one or more magnetic mines laid by German aircraft in the Mersey, and suffered considerable damage aft. One item involved the long line of solid steel shafting, probably two feet in diameter, connecting the main engines with the propeller. The force of the explosion had bent the shafting a matter of two-and-a-half inches out of line. While the ship was lying alongside waiting for a drydock, there was an air raid. A bomb pierced the deck and the shaft tunnel, and burst on top of one of the bearings carrying the shafting. We sent a surveyor, Denis Crump, to Liverpool to check on the repairs, as the war risks club would have to pay for them. He was present when the shafting was taken out and tested on a lathe ashore. After the bomb explosion, it was precisely straight again. "But", said the survey report, "the shipowners declined to accept this as constituting a permanent repair."

A case Dawson Miller dealt with himself and which appealed to him greatly, was the celebrated case of the *San Demetrio*. Later, many saw the story in the feature film of the same name. Others read about it in the epic poem called "The Jervis Bay", by the Australian poet Michael Thwaites. I knew Michael when he was a sub-lieutenant, R.N.V.R., serving in minesweepers. He told me that he had shown the manuscript to John Masefield before publication. My personal view is that his poem surpasses even Masefield, and it is one of the few poems I read again and again, each time with deep emotion.

The *San Demetrio* was a tanker owned by Eagle Oil Company, a concern later merged with the Shell fleet. She was one of a convoy attacked near the Azores by a German 'pocket battleship', one of the most dangerous war machines which ever put to sea, carrying very powerful guns. Times were hard on the North Atlantic then, and the only escort for this convoy was H.M.S. *Jervis Bay*, an old passenger-cargo liner well known on the Australian run, which had been hurriedly converted with a few guns into an armed merchant cruiser. When the Germans appeared over the horizon, the *Jervis Bay* at once attacked her head-on. She had no hope of even causing damage, as she was hopelessly out-ranged, unless her opponent concentrated on the merchant ships entirely until she was close. With her small guns and thin old plates she offered herself as target. A few salvoes destroyed her, and several of the convoy were also sunk, but the delay bought by the *Jervis Bay* helped most of them to escape.

The *San Demetrio* was hard hit, set on fire, and had to be abandoned by her crew. Next morning one of the boats saw a ship on an otherwise empty ocean. They rowed towards her and recognised her as their own vessel. The heavy waves had damped down and perhaps extinguished the fire. What were they to do? There were eight men in the boat, led, I think, by the second officer, and they decided to see how things were on board. They brought the boat alongside, a dangerous task in the big sea running. One man leapt for and climbed a trailing rope, and helped the others on board. The deck gushed oil from fractures as the ship flexed with the waves, but they got her under control and started the engines. With heroic toil the small group eventually brought ship and cargo into the Clyde. They lived mainly on potatoes, boiled with a steam line from the engines, as the oil made it too dangerous to light cooking fires.

The first abandonment of the ship ended their contract of employment. Legally, therefore, they had the status of volunteer salvors. Dawson and the Company worked together to help the men recover a generous salvage award, which we as the war risks insurers paid.

The P. and I. side of the business also had different characteristics in time of war. Some parts of it declined. The German and later the Italian members were enemies, and all communication with them was severed. Other parts increased. Sometimes we found ourselves acting for our own or an allied government which was for the time being a shipowner. At others we'd be acting with a shipowner in a dispute with a government. Masses of highly secret information came across our desks, especially in connection with convoys and the deployment of ships. We knew all about radar years before there was anything in the newspapers.

My personal situation as regards the war was rather a borderline one. In past years, I had (like many others) been drawn to pacifism. However, I soon became convinced that even war could be a lesser evil than some evils, and in such a situation there was no doubt in my mind that the lesser evil must be chosen, however reluctantly. But in 1939, where did my duty lie? I was 32, by no means too old to fight, but my age and especially my work put me in a reserved occupation. I could not be called up by the authorities, by their own rules, but I could, if I wished, volunteer. I gave this much thought in those quiet hours in the early morning. Rather against my inclination, I stayed where I was.

As the war lumbered on, there were indications that the decision was a right one. More and more of the men and women of the firm volunteered or were called up. The role of merchant shipping in national survival, quite apart from winning the war, became more and more apparent. The Government considered taking over our functions, but decided against it. Either they thought we could do it better or, more likely, they had too many other things to think about. Still, human nature being what it is, I often found myself longing to be more directly involved in the hazards of the war, although I also was often very thankful that I was not.

The other thing I was convinced of was that war or no war, soldier or civilian, there was still the need for the convictions and principles I had learnt some years before. In fact, I offered to help keep running the London headquarters for the work of Moral Re-Armament after most of the men there were called into the armed forces. This entailed living and sleeping there, out of office hours, for some three years, with only limited visits home.

To guard against the frequent use of incendiary bombs in air raids, fire watchers were organised, with equipment to extinguish the bombs, or limit their effect. I took my part in this for the Baltic Exchange building, and also at M.R.A. headquarters in Berkeley Square. This entailed a shortage of sleep but it called for patience more often than courage.

Field Marshal Lord Wavell wrote that war was made up of long periods of intense boredom, punctuated by short periods of intense fear. I was lucky in my Baltic Exchange fire-watching squad. First, it included the chef of the restaurant on the Exchange, so that our meagre rations were sometimes brightened a little by a Welsh rarebit or a herring which he produced from somewhere. Second, it included a bowls enthusiast, who brought up a set of woods. There was no turf for a bowling green that I knew of but we moved back the tables in the Baltic dining room, and played bowls on the carpet. The science of the game, if anyone does not know, depends on the right use of 'bias', the weight on one side of each wooden ball making it follow a slightly curving course as it is rolled towards the target 'jack'. Our waiting periods were passed very happily in this way. The pile of the carpet had the peculiar effect of producing a permanent bias, always drawing the line of the wood towards the kitchen. And there was much argument as to whether it was legal (or ethical) to send your wood straight up the seam in the carpet, thus cancelling out all bias.

By good luck, I missed most of the big air raids, but we had our share of gunfire and bombs in the smaller ones. At weekends we did daytime duty too. I arrived one Sunday morning to find Leadenhall Street blocked with debris from the bank which the previous day had stood on the corner of Lime Street. I joined in shovelling away the rubble, so that fire-engines could reach No. 27, which was burning vigorously. Chunks of cornice kept falling onto the front steps, as the firemen took the hoses inside. From the top of the Exchange, I could see some eighteen fires within easy distance.

The hours I spent at the M.R.A. headquarters were much more crowded, for among other functions it was a London home or port of call for numbers of service men from the

British and other forces. I once shared a double bunk with a Sikh major. Often another man and I would put 100 pounds of potatoes through the peeling machine and remove the defects in them, before breakfast. You never knew whom you would meet there. I met the Third Sea Lord once, and another time a group of miners who were considering a national strike. (They decided against it the next day.) And one day I spent a long time with a senior officer responsible for certain liaison work with the American forces. He said (without giving away secrets) that liaison was going very badly, but talked himself to a point where he could cure the trouble. The next day he did. I was just a listener, a catalyst if you like. But these and other experiences helped to build up the conviction that industrial and international conflicts could be healed, with the right approach. And also the conviction that I had been right to stay.

This is hardly an account of the City at war, but it gives a glimpse of one City man's life. Multiply it, and you have an idea of the whole. Sometimes we were without food when the restaurants were hit (though they usually improvised something). Posts and telephones were sometimes affected. Offices were destroyed. People just disappeared. We often forget those difficulties, just as we forget how brilliant the stars were on a clear night with the blackout enforced, the smell of rubble on a bombed site, the carpet of weeds and flowers and even small trees that after a few months would appear on the ruins, and the wild cats that hid amongst them. But through it all the business machine kept moving forward.

7

The Changing City

The City seems to me like some great animal or plant which has the power constantly to renew itself and adapt to changing circumstances.

It was a trading centre before the Romans came. The river, with a ford and very early in history a bridge, made it a natural centre of communications. It was burned in Boadicea's rebellion, and the inhabitants massacred, 1900 years ago. Probably it suffered the same fate a number of times. Norse sagas record the destruction of London Bridge in a battle between the Londoners, helped by Norwegian pirate-traders, and a turbulent settlement of Danes on the south bank of the Thames. Our children unknowingly commemorate this in the nursery song, "London Bridge is Falling Down". Most of the city was destroyed in the Great Fire of 1666.

Yet time and again the City has renewed itself. William, Duke of Normandy, was never conqueror of London. After some skirmishes and long negotiations, he was allowed to enter, upon promising that the ancient liberties would be maintained. To this day the Sovereign is met at the City boundaries by the Lord Mayor, who offers the hilt of the ceremonial sword in token of an invitation to enter.

After the Great Fire, Sir Christopher Wren — the architect to whom we owe St. Paul's Cathedral, many churches and much else besides — drew up for King Charles II a splendid plan to rebuild the huge devastated area, with avenues and open spaces to let air and light into the tangle of narrow, crooked streets. Most people who have seen the plan agree it would have been a vast improvement, but before it could even be approved by the proper authoritie, so much individual rebuilding had taken place that the plan was impossible to carry through.

In 1940 and 1941, and to some extent later in the war, the Luftwaffe, followed by the pilotless V-bombs and rockets, cleared large areas. The City Corporation has re-planned one of the larger areas in the Barbican, but elsewhere replacement and re-development has been piecemeal. A repetition of the 1666 rush of individuals to rebuild on the same land in the same alley was prevented by authority, but the fantastic value of the land after 1945 made it impossible for private interests to build on more than a small piece of it at a time. The City is now a hotchpotch of old and new, large and small, but then I suppose it always was. It is still an area of great interest and charm.

In the twenties there were few buildings of more than eight storeys. Regulations insisted that above a certain height, frontages had to be stepped back, and this made tall blocks uneconomic. Builders, too, had doubts about the stability of the London clay and gravel under heavy loads. Now, however, towers bristle against the skyline, some far higher than St. Paul's 360 feet, which has dominated the view for three hundred years. Round the base of the towers there is space to stroll, and sometimes grass, flowers and trees. Something has been lost, but something has been gained.

The offices of today are far more comfortable to work in than when I began. The solid stone-faced structures of that day let in far less light than the glass-faced steel skeletons of the modern tower blocks. Our old offices were mostly arranged round a large well, the base of which was the central dome of the Baltic Exchange. Only one wall therefore had windows and you could only see the sky from them by going close to them and looking up. The filing room where Victor Lofts and I worked, was, I suppose, 20 feet by 10 feet, and had one window in a corner, tall perhaps, but about 1½ feet wide. Some few years after I moved into it, Dawson Miller and Vos decided to remodel the offices. They came in, surveyed the scene, and Dawson observed to his partner, "You know, I wouldn't keep a dog in a place like this."

Part of the trouble was that window space was reduced by the massive chimneys, for in winter we had open fires as the only heating. In those large high rooms this usually meant you scorched by the fire, and froze away from it. Part of the juniors' duties was to keep all the fires going, a painful task when the luck of the game provided you with a scuttleful of coal that was mostly dust.

In those days, too, far more of the work was done by hand and, as far as delivery of letters was concerned, by feet. Labour was cheap, and even such mechanical aids as were

available were slow to win support from the more conservative employers. A few of our correspondents still relied on
hand-written letters in 1924. One was Waltons and Co. the
solicitors. Beautiful copperplate writing, with the signature
added in another hand at the bottom. The practice was for
the principal to dictate to a male shorthand writer, who then
wrote out the letter. Statements of account, and, I think,
occasional letters, came in longhand from Baring Bros. and
Co. the merchant bankers, who had provided certain facilities
for us for many years. They also impressed me by the simple
grandeur of their notepaper. Thick, cream, of beautiful
quality, it carried as the sole heading, die-stamped in square
black letters:

8 Bishopsgate Within
London E C.

Doubtless it reflected the conviction that the letter was a
private communication from one gentleman to another. It is
only in the last two or three years that Barings have felt it
better to put the name of the firm at the top, too, and I am
glad that this modernistic move does not seem to have
cheapened the old attitude towards the bank's customers.

The people who work in the City have changed as much as
the buildings, superficially at least. The biggest difference is
the girls. Girls, girls, girls are everywhere. I doubt if 5 per
cent of the office staffs were female in 1924. Now, it is over
50 per cent. And in their wake has come a mighty rash of
dress shops and lingerie shops. Half the stock of the chemists'
shops seems to be cosmetics. A man entering the corner
tobacconist for an ounce of pipe tobacco finds a huge array
of sweets as well, and packets of stockings and tights all over
the counter.

Basically, they are doubtless the same now as their
grandmothers were. Then and now they include the good girl,
the minx, the troublemaker, the dedicated career-girl, the
pin-money girl, and the girl who's saving hard for marriage
next year or the year after. But how different they do look.

In those far-off days we were accustomed to high heels and
short skirts, but what we regarded as a short skirt came below
the knee, necessarily. Any applicant for a job who dressed
provocatively or used more than discreet make-up was not
likely to get it. The ladies who gave answers to correspondents in the women's magazines advised 'the office girl' to
wear a dark coat and skirt, a black dress with white collar and
cuffs, or the like. Most of the women kept rather aloof from

the men, and I suppose one could say that many of the men shied away from the women. They were regarded somewhat as a regrettable necessity. They were usually addressed as Miss Brown, and addressed the men with equal formality, whereas now almost all our female staff, young and less young, are hailed by their Christian names, and I don't know the surnames of some.

At the risk of putting many cartoonists out of work, it may be worth recording that I have never yet dictated a letter to a secretary sitting on my knee, nor have I met or heard of a business man who has done so. I regard the procedure as quite impracticable. Sex must enter into a bi-sexual community, but it plays a smaller part than might be thought. However, it cannot be denied that the City is a brighter place, now that women are on a par with men in numbers and, in some respects, in status. A rainbow of colours brightens the pavements and passages. There is a quick click of heels everywhere, and half the voices are higher in pitch and lighter in tone. Moreover, since so many leave after a few years to start a family, their average age is far lower than that of the men. In every way, they rejuvenate the place.

There was a lot more formality and class-distinction then, and the women were in effect a separate class and not a high one. I was always addressed by my surname, without title, and was expected to say 'Sir' to the principals (which I did) and to the senior staff (which I rebelliously didn't).

The men's clothes to some extent reflected their standing in their firms, although the tendency of the ambitious was to dress above their position. Mr. Thorp as chief clerk always wore a square-tailed frock coat and a bowler hat, except when he represented the firm at a funeral, when it was a silk hat. The general wear was a dark suit, or a black jacket and waistcoat with striped trousers. Starched collars were almost universal, and bright ties or shirts unheard of. An exception was made for regimental or old boys' ties. Even if the stripes were vivid, these had respectable connotations. Spats were quite commonly worn over boots or shoes, and sometimes the tie was drawn through a gold ring, or a pearl stickpin used in it. A flower in the button hole was proper but optional. Most men wore a hat, bowler, homburg (the brim bound with narrow ribbon) or occasionally in summer the straw hat with a black band. If an umbrella was carried, it had to be rolled, unless the rain was more than a drizzle.

On the Baltic Exchange, rules of dress were rigidly

maintained, by public opinion more than by rule. When a man turned up in a tweed suit on a Saturday morning (we all worked every Saturday morning in those days) his fellow-members forcibly removed it. Yet formality did not affect the normal high spirits of youth. A conspicuous figure in St. Mary Axe at that time was a certain grain merchant, tall, portly and dignified. He invariably wore a black frock coat with a straight-sided flat-topped bowler of the kind Winston Churchill favoured. I was passing the Baltic one sunny lunch hour when I saw him descend the steps and proceed down the Axe with a magnificent peacock feather, tucked into the back of the hatband, waving gently above his head. A young man ran out after him and removed the feather with red-faced apologies. Apparently, it had not been intended that the joke extended outside the Exchange.

Another sweeping change over these years has been the introduction of more and more office machinery. This is supposed to save time and drudgery. Modern man sometimes thinks it does not, when computer-controlled insurance premiums take six weeks to pass from the assured in New York to the underwriter in London, or when a telex machine starts gabbling out what can only be a message from outer space. It also seems that the net result is not to save work, but to produce more paper to study, file and/or destroy. This, however, is surely the failure of those who instruct the machines, and not of the machines themselves. There is unpleasant truth in the tired old story of the factory which had to shut down production in order to cope with its splendidly complete records of production. When we first installed advanced accounting machines which with the help of a computer could give us better records of our insurances, it really was a stern battle to keep the enthusiasts within bounds. One of the problems of today is to ensure that machines serve men, rather than men serving machines.

But anyone who questions the value of machine aids should imagine, if he cannot remember, what office life was like without the computer, the telex, photo-copiers, adding machines, small and large, and with only crude telephones and typewriters in place of today's high-speed instruments. All accounting work was done by hand, and totals had to be checked and agreed between different books of account without the analyses which are spewed out by modern machines at the touch of a button. The mere totalling was a major task, although arithmetical skill seems to me almost entirely due to practice. If you have to do it a lot, you can do it fast and accurately. If you don't do it a lot, you lose the knack, if you ever had it. My father could add up columns of pounds, shillings and pence all at once, faster than a modern school-leaver can add a single column of digits.

Agreeing books of account by hand and eye was a wearisome business. So often the difference seemed to be ten shillings, and repeated checks would fail to unearth the missing figure, which could be maddening if you had to produce figures for a directors' meeting or annual general meeting. The banks in the City always closed on 31st December, to balance their books for the year, and their staffs kept at it till they did balance, if it took all night.

Photo-copying is taken for granted in a modern office. Without it, some tasks were arduous which have now disappeared. When a ship is fixed to load a particular cargo, the contract is made in a form called a charterparty. The name is said to come from a medieval habit of writing the terms of the bargain down twice on one sheet of parchment and tearing it into two complete texts. The raggedness of the tear helped to prevent forgery, for the two halves put together again had to match to establish their authenticity. Hence, "charte partie". The modern form varies from a single long printed sheet to four pages of print. Many alterations in the text are likely and often sheets of additional clauses as there is frequently hard bargaining on the terms of the contract, as well as the price. Back in the twenties, all the alterations were made in the original in ink, before signature by or on behalf of the parties. Then the suffering office staff had had to make around twelve copies. On each of the twelve, the clerk's pen had to make exactly the same additions, deletions, interlining of words, etc., without error. Then the copies went off to the ship's captain, her agents at the different ports, and so on. And the penalty for a small error could be a costly mistake or dispute.

Take a simpler thing, an internal office memorandum. It is so easy to photocopy enough replicas for all the principals and managers, but it used to be necessary to bang it out on a typewriter, original and copies. However hard the poor girl banged and however thin the paper, it would be marvellous if more than 10 copies could be made at one go.

You might think that modern facilities make for an easier business life, but I would say that the average City man now works harder and faster than his predecessor. At least, the senior men do, and this is so even though the City has come to work slightly shorter hours on five days of the week, and practically none on Saturday. The reason is, in the main, the increase in speed of communications, especially in long distance telephones and aircraft. Today it is very common for telephone conversations, sometimes very long ones, to take place with distant parts of the world at all hours of the day and night. With shipbrokers, they may be negotiating a charter for a voyage, or the sale of a ship, with an offer that must be accepted by close of business in some other city, and which turns out to be midnight or 3 a.m. in London.

With us, it is more likely to be unexpected legal proceedings, or a major casualty. For example, a London shipowner telephoned me at my home at 10.30 p.m. on Saturday evening. "I'm sorry to trouble you", said he. Like a proper P. and I. club manager, I forbore to comment. "One of our ships has gone ashore on the coast of Chile. She is on a year's time charter to a Chilean firm. The captain has radioed for instructions, and I don't even know where the place is." There was a suspicion of a wail in the last few words. I had to tell him that I didn't know either. The nearest port was a small one whose name I didn't recognise, but I knew no-one there, anyway. After a bit of a chat, it was so plain that we must in any event leave immediate decisions to the captain and others on the spot, that he decided to reply giving him complete authority. I went to bed and slept soundly, and I hope the shipowner did too.

Another late call was from Donald Kerr, our lawyer in Halifax, Nova Scotia. Some trouble had developed in a little port in the Maritimes, and I had suggested to Glenys Bevan, a woman barrister on our staff, that she sent Donald down to sort it out. He is quite a character in his unassuming way, and we got to know him well when he spent a year in our office as a student. A son of the manse (even though his father ended up as principal of Dalhousie University) he helped to finance his way through college, by such refined and studious occupations as deck hand on deep sea tankers, athletic coach, and professional boxing. From his soft voice and almost deprecating smile, you would never believe this, but it was so. He rang me up late that night to say that he'd had these instructions in a long telex message. Did he really have to go? It was 200 miles away and a perfectly foul journey. He was terribly busy (as I knew), and so on. I said I really felt he should go. If he did, he could end the trouble then and there.

If not, there might be years of litigation. So he agreed.

The trouble concerned a German ship owned by Reederei Richard Schröder of Hamburg which had been chartered to load a cargo of potatoes for Italy. The charterer had sold the potatoes under a contract which provided that the ship-owners should issue a 'clean bill of lading', a receipt saying that the cargo was in good condition when shipped. An Italian bank had advanced money on the strength of this contract, but when the cargo arrived for loading some of it was soft and sprouting. The captain insisted on stating this on the bill of lading. The charterer refused to agree. Deadlock.

There followed a fusillade of telexes, and not long afterwards, an eighteen-page report from Donald Kerr (obviously very pleased with himself) on the successful termination of the case in, I think, about forty-eight hours. At one point, when the charterer refused to yield, he sent for the sheriff of this little town and had the man arrested on a charge of attempting to obtain money under false pretences. A few hours in jail was enough to make the charterer cave in. He got his banker in Milan out of bed at four o'clock in the morning (there goes that telephone again) to alter the terms of the letter of credit. A last minute wavering produced another telephone call to the sheriff, and before that was completed, everything was agreed, signed and sealed, and the clean bills of lading accepted.

No wonder Schröders thought a lot of Donald Kerr and also of Glenys Bevan, who conducted this case and many others with a considerable flair.

The second factor which so complicates and speeds up life for the City man of today is the vast increase in business travelling. There has always been business travel from the City, at any rate since the merchants went out with the ships to buy wine from Gascony and Portugal, pepper from the spice islands, or furs from Muscovy. Buyers and salesmen of all kinds went out all over the world in the first quarter of this century. According to one story, one such salesman told another that business was a little slack. He hadn't sold a thing for three years. "What do you sell, then?" asked the other, aghast. "Bridges", was the reply.

However, for the very large section of the City which includes insurance, banking and finance, the situation was different. Travel there was, of course, to see the most important customers, but it was quite limited. Dawson Miller went to Germany, to New York, but the total was not great.

In general, the attitude was that we were here. If the world wanted our business, they were welcome to come and see us.

After 1945, this attitude was quickly modified. London might still be a mighty financial centre, but if this was going to continue, Londoners would have to meet their customers on their own ground. After the Second World War, there was a surge of nationalism far greater than that after the First World War, despite the effects of Woodrow Wilson's 1919 programme of self-determination for every ethnic group, and the new countries thus created. The very rapid decrease, almost the wiping out, of colonialism in a few years produced a rush of independent states, large and small. They all wanted to join the United Nations, not (it seemed) in order to produce unity so much as to assert their own freedom and independence. And in the business world many of them wanted their own national insurance company and their own national merchant marine.

One must remember, too, that Britain finished the war financially exhausted, and it sometimes seemed that measures to restore the wreckage of war gave precedence to former opponents over our own needs. Whether this was so or not, Britain found herself in a tough situation as regards industrial and commercial competition. Her business men had to go out to battle again, as it were, in a different sense from before.

This coincided with the sudden availability of air travel at a cost which made it sensible to spend the time and money involved, in order to get or keep business. The City took wing in a big way. Merchant bankers became familiar visitors in South America. Insurance brokers scoured Europe and the United States. Lawyers and accountants sped out to any place in the world where their services might be needed. On the day these lines were written I lunched with a solicitor who spoke casually of Japan and New Zealand, Hongkong, Pakistan and Bangladesh. Two days earlier I talked with another solicitor of Bombay, Beirut and Tangier. He was just off to Abu Dhabi, and asked if he could do anything for me while he was there.

For shipowners whose vessels go all over the world there is no longer a barrier of non-communication separating them from their ships. They can radio to them, sometimes speak by radio telephone, or send a man there in a day. Marine superintendents, engineers and management men often keep a packed travelling bag constantly in the office, and a passport in the pocket.

It is much the same with the P. and I. clubs. Two of my partners were recently in Japan (for one of them his third visit in the year). Initially, the occasion was an invitation to witness the launching of a huge tanker, but they took the opportunity to give a reception for the Japanese shipowners insured by the club, and for others who were considering joining. A younger man who went for the first time on one of these journeys said, half seriously, of the senior he accompanied, "I don't know how he does it. It's a series of visits and conferences, a dash back to the hotel for yet more Alka-Seltzer, and off for another series." My own last year before retiring from the firm turned out a quiet one, with only four journeys covering six countries in two continents.

Little wonder that one of my colleagues thinks that the airlines will soon stop teasing business travellers with elaborate meals and films in flight. Instead, they will put you to sleep after boarding with a shot from a hypodermic syringe, and wake you up at destination.

The City, then, goes out continually now, to get business, to keep it, to maintain friendly contact with its customers, and to deal with crises. At the same time, other countries are doing the same thing. From all the continents visitors come flooding in. The day I wrote this I had callers from France, Calcutta and Houston, Texas, as well as England, of course. Another day I had unexpected visitors from Burma, Turkey and the Philippines. Some camp on you for quite a while and use your telephone, your telex and even your secretary for odd jobs. But you may do the same to them next month or next year. Some stay half an hour, expect you to put everything aside to deal with them, and to know everything about the subjects on their minds without having to look up anything.

But of course we are delighted to see them. They are our business, and they may also be the people who entertained us so charmingly when we were out where they live.

The City is an enormous factor in the well-being of Britain. Take first the direct contribution to the country's balance of payments. It creates most of the 'invisible exports', payments from abroad for services rendered by British firms to other countries. Banks and insurance companies provide the bulk of these. It is an added advantage that to earn this type of export there is no need to import large quantities of iron ore or steel or any other kind of raw materials. The City's needs for paper and business machines are not enough to bulk large in the import figures.

However, this great concentration of banking, insurance and other financial expertise is not a disadvantage to other countries. Insurance is a good example. The essential for effective insurance is to spread the larger risks over as wide a field as possible. National insurance markets are healthier because they can farm out a large part of their risks to London. In some cases, they would not find it possible to operate without London's support. Norway, for example, is a small country in terms of population. But she has one of the largest merchant fleets in the world. Many of her ships are worth over two million pounds each. It would be folly for a moderate-sized Norwegian insurance company to take the whole risk of loss or damage to such a ship. On the other hand, London is glad to offer reinsurance lines to insurance markets all over the world, and thus to lay off part of its own business. Countries therefore help each other. The same is the case in banking and other fields.

Switzerland operates in much the same way as the City of London, but on a lesser scale. So do West Germany and U.S.A. The uninformed, and those who talk in a half-baked way about class war in relation to the finance men of the world, miss the main point. Financial power may sometimes be abused, like any other kind of power, but the functions of finance are still essential. What we call communist countries and they call socialist republics understand this very well. They co-operate effectively on the business plane with these markets.

As Rudyard Kipling wrote:

> . . . deep in the veins of Earth,
> And, fed by a thousand springs
> That comfort the market-place
> Or sap the power of Kings,
> The Fifth Great River had birth,
> Even as it was foretold —
> The Secret River of Gold!

Gold is only partly the basis of finance now, but those who understand that river are still worth consulting and employing.

The City is different now from days when the traders and their apprentices bawled their wares from the open-fronted shops, and the merchant adventurers picked their way on horseback or on foot over the cobblestones to their argosies loading at Billingsgate Hithe. What will it be a hundred or a thousand years from now?

Will the new Lord Mayor still show himself to the people each November, with brass bands and the Honourable Artillery Company's pikemen and arquebusiers, in the Lord Mayor's Show? Will there still be wardmotes to elect men to the Common Council, opened by the beadle in caped coat and cocked hat calling "Oyez, Oyez, Oyez"? Will the Lord Mayor still hold a banquet for the bankers and merchants of London? And will there still be turtle soup? How will it be different?

It is impossible to guess: but, come what may, it is hard to conceive that the City will not be carrying out some essential functions for the entire world.

8

The Changing Club

The City changes, and so do individual businesses. Many disappear. New ones start. Some move into London from outside. A few move out, and quite a number move out part of their staff to quieter and cheaper places, leaving only those in the centre who need to be there.

In my time Thos. R. Miller & Son's business increased twenty times in size, changed a good deal in character, and three new mutual insurance clubs were added to the first three. But it may be worth taking a longer perspective first.

In 1955 I was asked by the Insurance Institute of London to act as adviser to a small study group on the history and development of P. and I. clubs. It turned out to be a long and exacting task, but an interesting one.

Every year one or more groups of advanced students set out to prepare a report on some aspect of insurance. The group may be large or small, the subject wide or detailed. This was Advanced Study Group No.109, and consisted of three students only. For nearly three years we met fortnightly after work until the paper was finished, read and published.

I acted as chairman. I did no research, and regarded my task as mainly to direct the enthusiasm of the team into a few well-defined channels, and to ban entry into the very numerous side turnings which seemed enticing. The paper was indeed a slim volume, but it has a well-defined place in the archives of the institute, and most of its facts do not seem ever to have been published before.

One thing that strikes me now is that the P. and I. clubs of 1924 (and the others were not very different from the United Kingdom Club) were still near to what they were when they were found sixty or seventy years before, both in principles and practice. But how they have changed in the shorter period since!

The first two P. and I. clubs started business in 1856, one

(now the Britannia) in London, one at Topsham in Devon, called the West of England Club. The first was managed by Peter Tindall, an insurance broker who also managed mutual hill insurance clubs, and his brother-in-law, John Riley, who gave up farming to assist. The other was managed by John Holman, a shipowner, and its original office was on his estate near Exeter. Each originally consisted of a group of small shipowners who probably all knew each other.

The study group established that these and other P. and I. Clubs all drew their inspiration and many of their practices from mutual hill clubs. At one time ships could by law only be insured in England by Lloyd's underwriters and two particular companies, The London Assurance and the Royal Exchange Assurance. This near-monopoly was so unsatisfactory and made the cost of insurance so high that many shipowners got together in groups to pool their losses, as a kind of collective self-insurance. Often they were a group of similar ships, the transports which accompanied the Navy during the war with France, colliers, coasters, or ships in the eastern trade. A government enquiry into marine insurance in 1810 reported that these 'clubs' were illegal, but they were doing such a useful job that their activities should be made legal.

There were quite a number of them on the north-east coast of England, and the nickname 'club' was very expressive of the atmosphere prevailing in them. One at least had a luncheon for the members after their annual general meeting. If the discussions were lengthy, the chairman passed out a message for the waiters to carry the smoking joints of meat through the meeting room to the dining room. This soon put a period to oratory. Stanley Mitcalfe, the Newcastle solicitor and antiquary, told the study group of this. His father had been underwriter and manager of a hull club. One day at breakfast news was brought that a ship he insured had gone on the rocks not many miles away. He called for his horse and rode off across country to the spot, where he took charge of the salvage operations himself.

We found out the reason why the clubs start their financial year on 20th February. It was a carry-over from the hull clubs. For many of them, the most important trade was to and from the ports round the Baltic Sea. Those ports were ice-bound in winter. The ice began to break up about 20th February, so that the insurance policies attached from that date. On a visit to Karachi, I was in the office of the National

Shipping Corporation when I was asked, "Why 20th February?" I said that was when the ice melted in the Baltic. The joke had to be explained, but the Pakistanis enjoyed it mightily.

The clubs were cosy family affairs even when I joined them. They still are to a great extent, but the changes have been great. Every change in the shipping industry has brought changes in the clubs. The greatest is in the direction of internationalization. After the Napoleonic wars the British flag flew over most of the world's shipping. Enemies had mostly been destroyed or captured. Neutrals had been so harried in the course of the naval war that they almost gave up. In the 1920s, Britain still had some 40 per cent of the world's shipping, today some 20 per cent. There is still a powerful British merchant fleet, but nationalism and the astonishing enterprise of Greeks, Norwegians and others have carried other countries ahead proportionately far faster than the British.

Even before the 1939-45 war Dawson Miller expanded the club greatly into a number of national merchant fleets. The friends he made usually stayed friends for life, and if they had been enemies in war they were back as friends soon after. But after 1945 a period of rapid expansion began. The key to this was in countries like Germany and France, where shipowners had often done without P. and I. insurance, and countries like Sweden and later Japan, where shipowners were dissatisfied with the insurance they could get locally.

As the club grew, the staff had to be increased, and more partners had to be made (of which I was the first). Moreover, it was considered an anachronism to have a wholly British group of shipowners to act as directors for an international association. The first sign of a new regime was the arrival of a French director, from the great Compagnie des Messageries Maritimes. He was followed by a German from the Hamburg America Line. The process thus started has slowly developed until the board now covers ten nationalities from three continents, and the British are in the minority.

The biggest developments of the business in recent years have been with the shipowning interests of Japan and Russia. Neither came easily. There were four years of visits to Japan before the club got its first Japanese member, but it was well worth the trouble involved as some 10 per cent of the total business now comes from Japan.

Russia took even longer. We were approached by several

different agencies, over a period of years, before anything crystallized. I suppose that, while we were collecting information on them, they were collecting information on us. Some of us in the office were very suspicious. After all, the true Marxist-Lenninist doctrine lays down that anything that advances communism is right, and it was felt that, if this was their objective, it was not the wish of the members generally that the club should support such an objective. However, we gradually became convinced that the Russians were interested for business reasons. In particular, now that their ships were trading internationally, they found some difficulty in dealing with claimants against them in capitalist countries. Their knowledge of the law in other countries was not complete, and many of the people they were forced to deal with were prejudiced against them. They needed some protection and were ready to pay proper premiums for it.

Negotiations were lengthy. Bargaining was hard. Both moved forward better after Russia decided to decentralise its great merchant fleet, as Yugoslavia had done earlier, into a number of units. When once terms were agreed, we found, as I believe all others have done, that the Russians are completely honourable in acting on their undertakings, and prompt in their payments. The agreements we have with them in several fields represent a lot of business. They also represent a lot of hard work, with lengthy meetings in Moscow, Leningrad and Murmansk, in Odessa and Nakhodka.

It is the members who make up the club — the enormous fleets of tankers owned by BP and Shell; the constantly growing Greek Merchant Navy, embodying all kinds of owners from the family which owns one or two ships to groups which count their tonnage in millions; the liner owners, British, French, German, Italian, American, their fleets now often coagulating into a smaller number of large container ships; little ships in Iceland, in Finland, and on the South American rivers; coastal tankers in Thailand; government-owned fleets in Pakistan and Singapore, Argentina and the German Democratic Republic; fruit-carriers owned in Sweden and in Jamaica; ore carriers and grain ships on the Great Lakes of America — the total is many times what it was when I began work in 1924.

With this diversification of flags and types of ships has also come a great diversification of risk. Some liabilities have been invented, as it were, during these years — wages for seamen unemployed after shipwreck; payment for their clothes destroyed in an accident; new liabilities for oil pollution of the sea or for smoke pollution of the air. The internationalising of shipping has complicated the work of a P. and I. man far more. He must know what liabilities a shipowner has to his crew in Hong Kong or Chile, or to stevedores in Australia or U.S.A. He must know the customs regulations of Brazil, the Turkish law on limitation of liability, and how blame for a collision is dealt with in Venezuela. The rates for foreign exchange of currency concern him deeply; so do questions of investment, for the sums he handles are so much greater than in the past.

It is, I think, impossible to pick up a copy of the London *Times* or a similar paper without reading some item of news which affects P. and I. clubs. It may be a marine casualty, a change in the law somewhere, or a new development in overseas trade. There is always something. But fortunately we have not yet had to consider the problems of outer space.

Between 1960 and 1968 we formed (or helped to form) three entirely new clubs. The first was the Hellenic War Risks Association. We were formally approached by a delegation of the Greek Shipowners Cooperation Committee in London with the offer to manage a new association. Its task was to provide insurance against war risks on a collective, non-profit-making basis, for Greek flag and Greek-owned ships. It was thought that this would reduce the cost somewhat, but in the minds of the chairman, John Kulukundis, and others, it was much more to be a demonstration of unity by the Greek shipowners.

It was a compliment to us to be asked to take on the task, as the Greeks used other P. and I. clubs as well. Technically it was a great challenge. In several ways it would have to be different from anything done before. The drafting of the basic documents, including the policy, was one of the hardest tasks I have ever shared in. Anyone who doubts that should sit down and compose an insurance policy. A sonnet is much easier; a symphony may not be much harder.

Despite the enthusiastic support of the Greek Committee, there was also a lot of explanation and promotion to be done. Two of us drew up lists of some sixty firms which had not agreed to join and worked right through them with long telephone conversations. Every one of them had different queries, doubts, points of view to discuss, but nearly all decided to join.

An interesting point arose on a side-issue of the

operation — that of our management fee. Nothing has been said about this by anyone. We found ourselves pulled two ways. On the one hand we felt we should have a reasonable remuneration. It would not be fair to the British members of the United Kingdom War Risks Association if the Greeks paid us less for managing their club than the British did. On the other hand, there was an urgent need in such an operation to get some money in the bank to cover expenses and claims, and to build up a reserve against big claims in the future.

For some time we could not see a way out. Then, in that early morning time of quiet, I worked out a formula. It started by saying that the management fee would be at the same rate as in the British clubs, and went on to say that the managers (Thos. R. Miller & Son) would waive the fee in the first year, and draw only 50 per cent for the next four years. This was, of course, a sacrifice, involving a good many thousand pounds. The first year we would ourselves be losing money, while the club gained. For four years it would be very tight; then it would be comfortable.

When I got to the office I wrote out the formula and took it in to Dawson Miller. After one look he said, "The very thing." At the Directors' Meeting an hour later he read it out, and they approved it out of hand. One of them said to me afterwards, "It was generous and dignified." Its effect was that (since the Club was at first running on a narrow margin) reserves were built up much quicker than had been expected, and the whole operation has been a great success.

In the other new clubs launched in 1967 and 1968, Millers have waived any remuneration in the first year of both of them.

One was directed at insuring shipowners against delays by strikes. This may seem an odd sort of insurance, but there were already two such insurance associations operating, one in Oslo, one in London, when we decided to start one for some of our P. and I. members. The fact is that most of the strikes which delay ships arise from disputes between port workers and their employers ashore. The shipowners are not involved, but they suffer heavily. The club's purpose was to spread the risk, for, of two ships loading at a port, one might sail the day before a strike and suffer no loss, the other be ready to sail the next day and be delayed for three months at a cost in running expenses alone of a thousand pounds a day. This club has attracted a number of shipowners, from Finland to Chile to Japan. It has, however, been difficult to manage. One reason is the limited information available on the risks to be covered. Another is the unprecedently high incidence of port strikes in the early 1970s, especially in the United States.

The other new club is even more unusual. There is no other like it. It covers some risks which had only just begun to appear, and even some which were unknown but which we foresaw when we were planning it. Its membership is more varied than any other mutual club that I know of, and it has a unique system of management. I had the privilege of sharing in the planning from the start and of being the person primarily in charge of running it for the first four years.

It is called the Through Transit Marine Mutual Assurance Association, and it is jointly managed by three separate firms.

Its origin was in containers, those big boxes 20 feet by 8 by 8, or larger, which one sees everywhere on road, rail and quayside. Their chief advantage is that packing goods in them reduces the number of handlings of the goods, and ships are less time in port. Cargo still has to be lifted into most ships, and lifted out. It is far quicker to lift fifteen or more tons at a time in a quickly attached container than a ton or so at a time in a sling, which itself has to be packed and unpacked. In some of the general cargo trades ships spend up to 40 per cent of each year in port. Little wonder that container ships have taken over, in a few years, a large proportion of the general cargo carriage of the world. They are not, as some journalists suggest, the answer to everything, for, to operate them economically, specially equipped ports are needed, and good rail and road connections to support them. Moreover, in some trades, especially those with short sea passages, roll-on, roll-off equipment is more useful, and most bulk cargoes are quite unsuitable for container carriage anyway.

Together with the spread of containers came a great surge in the concept of through transit, also called combined transport or intermodal transport. A single carrier undertook the whole carriage from, say, Salt Lake City to Geneva, even though the carriage might be done in stages by a truck, a ship, a railway car, a barge or an aeroplane, under a string of sub-contracts. At one conference a speaker thought that another possibility might be the sending of containers by a pneumatic tube.

The carriage might also traverse a number of countries, and different laws or conditions might apply to the different stages of the journey. The goods might arrive damaged, and there might be no way of telling at what part of the journey the damage occurred, since there was no intermediate inspection of a closed container. Most shipowners, including those who were directors of P. and I. associations, approached these problems very circumspectly, and for a number of years the clubs would not cover the risk on cargo carried in containers, except for the ocean voyage. Someone therefore had to insure the risk for the rest of the carriage.

There was also the question of the containers themselves. Suppose a twenty-foot box cost £600, a large container ship carries two thousand boxes, and the shipowner owns or hires three 'suits' of containers, since some are ashore at each end while some are afloat. He has £3,600,000 worth of containers for every ship in service, a massive pool of property at risk.

One day in 1967 a Swedish shipowner came into the office. He represented a group of owners who were pooling their resources to build container ships. The group was concerned about liabilities to cargo under a through transit type of carriage, for it was proposed to carry goods house to house for those who wanted it, against the old style port to port. Could we form a club to insure such liabilities?

"Certainly", we said, for we had been developing plans for such a facility for the past year. Could we also insure them for loss or damage to the containers? "Of course", we said, and added that there were certain other risks which he might not have thought of. We rattled off a few. How soon could we start business? As soon as he liked, we said. He promised that colleagues of his would come back to discuss details.

We got down to completing our preparations. Before this could be done we were approached by our friendly rivals, the managers of the West of England P. and I. Association, the same outfit that had started at Topsham in Devon a hundred years before. They were working on a similar scheme. The field was not a very large one. Would it not be better to work together? We were disposed to agree, but we knew there was a third new club of this type being prepared, and we made our agreement conditional on their coming in too.

Charles Taylor & Co., managers of the Standard P. and I. Club, had done a great deal of preparatory work. Their approach was rather different from ours. They felt that they were well equipped to deal with the problem, through their very good contacts with the British liner companies. In fact they very much wanted to go it alone. However, business considerations and the sheer logic of the situation prevailed.

There was to be one club, with three joint managers.

In the summer of 1968 we started business with four members, but many more joined before the year ended. Some were old shipowner friends of ours, others were what we have begun to call NVO's (non-vessel-owning carriers who use other people's ships for the sea carriage). They may be basically road hauliers, or forwarding agents, or new entrants into container business.

In four years the business grew to the point where it was insuring (as far as could be checked) half the containers in the world. In addition at least a dozen carriers were operating under contracts of carriage which we had drafted to fit their individual needs, and representatives of the joint managers had been asked to lecture on container insurance at conferences in Russia, Italy, Norway and the United States.

Including the part interest in the Through Transit Club, Thos. R. Miller & Son now had six mutual insurance associations under their management.

Among many changes over recent years, financial changes have been the most important.

In the autumn of 1967 the pound sterling was devalued by about 14 per cent against the U.S. dollar. It was a severe blow to the P. and I. clubs, as well as to countless other people, a blow the severity of which did not become clear for some time. Because the clubs have power to call up from their members whatever funds they need to meet claims, they do not maintain the same volume of reserves as are carried by conventional insurance companies. However, it is wise to have money in hand to cover most of the expected claims at any one time.

By this time only one sixth of the shipping insured by the United Kingdom P. and I. Association was British. The club was registered under English law as a company limited by guarantee. It was bound by English law generally, including tax laws and exchange control. As an entirely mutual operation which did not make profits, it naturally did not pay corporation tax on profits; but it had been conceded years before that tax had to be paid on income from the investment of such premiums as were not immediately required for claims and expenses. Tax also had to be paid on capital gains on these investments. These matters involved large sums of money.

An even stronger influence on our operations was the ruling of the exchange control that most of these funds must be kept exclusively in sterling. We had to pay a very large proportion of the claims in currencies other than sterling, and particularly in U.S. dollars, deutschmarks and so on, for every six we had expected to pay. The total of our losses ran into millions of pounds and put all our forecasts for running the finances of the business out of gear for several years.

Many discussions took place with the authorities, the Treasury and the Bank of England, to see if there was any way in which similar trouble could be avoided in the future. They were sympathetic and helpful; and, later, some adjustments were made in the regulations. On the main issues they were unable to help. It was impracticable to make exceptions to the rules for English companies in the few cases where most of the funds were in effect owned in other countries. They agreed that it was illogical that the non-British members of the club were hampered by paying British taxes and bound by British exchange control. So some other solution would have to be found outside the British framework.

The directors decided that the business of the P. and I. club should be allowed to run right down and be replaced by a similar business in Bermuda. Exchange control was more important than tax immunity. Under the Bermudian regulations we could keep the association's money in any currency or currencies, and thus avoid loss from a sudden depreciation.

A new partnership was formed in Bermuda to manage the new club. Naturally the Bermudian partnership engaged the old partnership to act as its London agents and to provide the fullest possible service in London. However, the Bermuda office is not just a brass plate. It is a bustling business on Front Street in Hamilton, Bermuda. There all the contracts of insurance are made with the individual shipowners. Meetings are called for there, and from there all the bank accounts and investments are controlled.

There was irony in the fact that in 1969 we celebrated the centenary of the United Kingdom Mutual Steam Ship Assurance Association Limited. Simultaneously the new association, with a similar name, started business in Bermuda, and most of the members moved across.

In the ensuing months three more of the clubs operated from the Miller office were duplicated in Bermuda. The other two, one of which has a wholly British membership, were unaffected.

Not long after the Bermuda arrangements were completed Britain became a member of the European Economic

Community, and the whole situation had to be re-thought. The 'Six' were already debating statutes to govern insurance in the Community. They would apply to all companies insuring anyone living within the Community area. Again we became immersed in study and negotiations, to find out the best way of protecting the insured shipowners in the context of political and legal issues.

It seems that nowadays insurance does not need people who are merely expert on premiums or claims. They must also be lawyers, tax experts and financiers to do the job required of them.

9

City Men and Institutions

The City, then, is constantly changing, but what really goes on there? To some, it's an arcane business, like an English version of the 'gnomes of Zurich', and more so. Some imagine mysterious figures using financial wizardry to make and unmake governments across the world, foment wars, and keep whole countries in economic slavery. This is why some left-wing theorists dream of nationalising banking and finance. They want the money and the power. But, if they ever were in a position to do this, they would find the true situation very different, and what money and authority they did try to take over would to a large extent trickle through their grasping fingers. Much of what the City does could never be done by a public authority. It depends on personal relationships, where a man uses another to do something he cannot do for himself (or would do less well) and is prepared to pay for that service.

Two incidents which came to my notice give a little insight into the true situation. In Zagreb I once discussed the workings of capitalism with Yugoslav communist officials. I told them that British financial institutions felt themselves bound to support British government policies, whether or not they agreed with them. The government ideas might, for example, be much more socialistic than those round the table in City boardrooms; but banks, insurance companies, and so on, would still follow loyally the line given from Whitehall on matters of currency and investment. You could call it patriotism if you liked. It was a feeling that our great financial institutions were part of the country, and they went the way the country went. That was the broad picture, anyway. The communists were staggered, though I am not sure they believed me.

Some years later a City solicitor I knew was playing week-end golf with one of the top bankers in the country, and told me a day or two later the gist of their conversation.

It was at the time of one of our major currency crises, when the newspaper headlines screamed of the danger to the pound, and the banker had been one of half a dozen moulders of City policy invited to Downing Street to meet the then Prime Minister and Chancellor of the Exchequer. It was terrible, he said. The ministers gave the impression of being exhausted men, at their wits' end. The City men asked in what way they could help, but the politicians had no suggestions whatever. The crisis was ultimately overcome, as crises always seem to be, but the interesting point to me was the attitude of the men from the City. They had gone with open hands and open minds, not to put across a point of view, but to find a basis for co-operation. And they expected initiative from the government, although doubtless they would have been ready to offer constructive criticism if the policy seemed unwise.

Parts of the structure of the community we call 'the City' I know well. Other parts I know superficially or not at all. Probably any City man would have to say the same. Its distinctive function, if it can be described in a sentence, is to help in making money available when and where it is needed. Many things also go on in 'the square mile' which do not seem to relate to that, but if there is a pattern, that is the pattern.

Any community is made up by its people and institutions. If I refer to the first of these two factors as 'men', the ladies will realise that is only because few of them have so far reached positions of influence in City institutions.

First of the institutions is, of course, the City itself, still governed in much the same manner as in medieval times, and indeed not so differently from when William the Conqueror treated with "William the bishop, Geoffrey the portreeve and all the citizens within London" in 1066. The Lord Mayor is still elected by acclamation at a meeting in Guildhall, and the City's affairs are still ruled by the Court of Common Council and the Court of Aldermen. They meet with considerable pomp, and at state banquets entertain visiting monarchs and heads of state. There is also annually a banquet for Her Majesty's Government, given by the Lord Mayor, with "bankers and merchants of the City of London". This is often a good occasion for the public airing of government policies and the City's response to them.

The square mile is still divided into wards, a word which doubtless derives from the organisation for defence, as well as from the need to 'keep the peace' in a more social context. One of my partners was a 'pikeman' serving in the ranks of the Honourable Artillery Company, a City-based unit of part-time soldiers, now equipped with modern artillery as well as the pikes and arquebuses they carry on ceremonial occasions. When he was summoned for jury duty at the Old Bailey he pleaded that he was exempt, since, as a member of the 'trained bands', he had to be available at a moment's notice to man the walls in case of war. This resulted in a delightful academic dispute until the correspondence revealed that he was exempt on other grounds as well as those alleged historically.

Elections to Common Council are almost entirely on a non-political basis. In addition to governing the affairs of the square mile, its duties include running a separate police force for the City, supervising health and hygiene on all ships entering the Port of London, and the upkeep of various open spaces the City has acquired for the benefit of London as a whole, of which the best known are Epping Forest and Burnham Beeches.

I must admit that I enjoyed attending wardmotes, summoned by the Alderman of the Aldgate Ward, and participating in the ancient ritual of elections. I did not, however, much enjoy the duty which also fell on me as a City voter — to act as a juryman at the Old Bailey for a week. The crude details of robbery with violence and unlawful carnal knowledge are far from amusing.

I have not been deeply engaged in civic affairs, so I suppose I am fortunate in having met some of the Lord Mayors of my time. Sir Frederick Rowland, a chartered accountant, was a chubby little man, something between Mr. Pickwick and a London sparrow. He was a warm and human personality, and was, I think, the first Lord Mayor to entertain a group of distinguished Japanese, notwithstanding the bitter feelings which many felt after the 1939-45 war. The Lord Mayor I have known best, however, is Sir Charles Trinder, not so much because of his being alderman of our ward, but through the half-century or more of business touch between our firm and the Tinder firm of shipowners and ship managers. He is a big man, who strides about the streets, bowler hat pulled squarely down over his ears, at a rate which makes one puff to keep up. He is intensely serious about the civic side of his life, to which he gives a vast amount of time. Off duty, as it were, he produces streams of quips, and has a freak memory which makes it possible to recite long poems and prose passages without hesitation.

Civic affairs, however, are not the real business of the community. This is immensely complex and varied, and only an encyclopaedia could describe it all.

Three major bastions are the three great exchanges — the Stock Exchange, Lloyd's and the Baltic. There are a number of others, the Corn Exchange, Metal Exchange and so on, but they are dwarfed by the big three.

The Stock Exchange is a place I have never entered, but one stockbroker — my own — was a good friend. James Hurst died suddenly a few months ago of the coronary which often attacks men who work too hard. He looked like a farmer, with a burly figure and a round red face, and rowed regularly for exercise until he was sixty or more. His knowledge of investment was immense, and he would pour out information in a flood of quick words. However, he was equally frank to say when he did not know a material fact, or to deny any means of forecasting a trend. The thing I remember most about him is his almost tender care for the needs of individuals. An elderly retired doctor sang his praises because he rearranged her modest investments to increase her income to almost double the figure. To another client he recommended, in the particular circumstances, a course which would mean no commission to the broker — the purchase of a government annuity. I consulted him about my own mother's small capital, and as to whether it could be reinvested profitably. His reaction was, "Why worry to do that? She seems to have enough for her needs and to last out her time with a margin to spare. Why bother the old lady? At her age any sort of unnecessary change may disturb or even frighten her. Leave it as it is." Again, no commission!

The picture is not like the common misconception of the Stock Exchange, which is of a gambling place, parasitical on the body of society. There is certainly an element of speculation, but basically it is just what its practitioners often call it — 'the market', a place where investments are bought and sold. Its most important function is to help the public to provide funds for the government and public bodies, and for industrial and commercial developments. If you need a million pounds to build a new factory, the way to get it may well be a new issue, an invitation to all and sundry to subscribe for additional shares in your company. But if someone wants to buy £1,000 or £20,000 of the new shares, he needs to know that he can re-sell them easily if he needs the money again. The Stock Exchange provides this facility, and to protect investors the Exchange must approve the details of any new issue before it can be quoted for re-sale on the Exchange. The fluctuations which fill the City pages of the newspapers are the cream on the cake, not the cake itself.

Lloyd's is another sort of market, a centre for insurance that is unique. The underwriting room handles more business each year than any other single room in the world. I forget how many hundreds of million pounds it runs at now. Its basis of operation is well known, with its syndicates of underwriters, each making a separate contract to insure part of a risk. Most people have seen photographs of the 'boxes' where the underwriters sit at enclosed tables like those in some old-fashioned restaurants, and the brokers (for business can only be introduced by the Lloyd's brokers) queue for a few minutes' interview.

A Lloyd's underwriter told me once that the chief qualification for his job was an acute sense of smell. So many risks were put before him in a day that he often had to say yes or no almost by instinct. Doubtless experience, or knowledge of the broker presenting the risk, plays a big part too. Certainly the data typed out on the 'slip', a smallish piece of thin card, gives only an outline. There may be footnotes headed, "Information, not warranty", and the underwriter is free to ask any questions, but time is often short, and lightning decisions have to be made.

A story is told of Aristotle Onassis deciding to send a whaling factory ship and a fleet of catchers to fish off the coast of Peru. That country had just announced (unilaterally) an extension of its fishing limits to 200 miles from the coast, and written warning had been given that unlicensed fishing would result in seizure of the ships concerned. Would they act on the threat? Onassis decided to insure against it. "Rubbish. They will never do it", was the attitude of many at Lloyd's. "The premium will be money for jam." A cover was completed, so I was told, for four million pounds, at a premium of 3½ per cent. The ships arrived, and the Peruvians seized the lot.

This may be an unkind example. There must be many where a mere whisper of information, or merely the twitch of a sensitive nostril for a trace of bad smell, has meant that a bad risk has been written at a high rate, or refused entirely. It is said that one Lloyd's syndicate made consistently good profits on motor insurance – and that is in the miracle class – by a policy of "No Jaguars, no sports cars, no Minis, and no drivers under twenty-five years old".

The tight nature of the Lloyd's community, with its few hundred working underwriters (representing several thousand 'names' in the syndicates) is also a force working towards high standards. Any departure from 'utmost good faith' and even any blunder tends to get quickly known.

A good many years ago an employee of an insurance company landed in prison for a series of ingenious frauds. His system was to insure various non-existent houses at Lloyd's, spreading the business round many brokers. After a few months an 'accident' or a 'fire' would be reported, producing a claim which was too small to call for a surveyor or assessor to be sent to inspect the damage, and the underwriters would pay. The scheme was skilfully organised, with a chain of accommodation addresses and a printing press in the man's garage to prepare builders' estimates and letter headings. Several thousands a year were collected successfully, until one day a bright young broker was waiting in line at an underwriting box at Lloyd's with a claim to be initialled for payment. He idly glanced over the shoulder of the man in front of him and noted that he was holding a letter about another claim, by a different person, but one whose writing was identical with that on the documents in his hand. The two compared notes. The whole system of frauds was uncovered. One nicety of the scheme amused me. A broker, when offered business, might ask to what did he owe the pleasure of the introduction. The swindler would always write, "I was recommended to approach you by Mr. Dash of the Blank Insurance Company" (his real name), and so establish a natural background.

The underwriting room at Lloyd's is huge, and teems with people. It is brightly lit, and on a good day the sun streams in through the tall double-glazed windows. It has an air of tremendous bustle. The Lloyd's man mostly moves at a brisk pace. He is well-dressed, too. The older men mostly favour a sober suit and a 'short back and sides', but vivid shirts and ties are not unknown. Some of the younger men favour more luxurient hair styles, akin to their nineteenth or eighteenth-century counterparts; but they, too, are well turned out. They are conscious that they need to make a good impression to do a good job.

My mental picture of a Lloyd's broker on the street is of a

man moving at full stride, four miles an hour at least. It may be an icy cold day, but he has no coat or hat. He carries an umbrella, but if there is wind about it is closed in anything short of a cloudburst. The only other thing he carries is a small flat document case of black leather, perhaps ten inches by four. This holds his "slips". Letters are stuffed in an inside pocket. He speaks quickly, lucidly, and very persuasively, but he has long since learnt, too, the old saying, "When the underwriter picks up his pencil, stop talking". So he knows when to wait.

Many Lloyd's men have the polish of public school and university, but it is not essential to success there. Some are quite rough-hewn. In fact, they come in all types. If one arrives at work in a Rolls, more walk from the Tube. But they are a very close-knit community. Christian names are often used, or obvious nicknames. 'Vic' Oliver, a prominent cargo underwriter, was not christened Victor, and the name was presumably borrowed because he is so unlike the comedian of past days. Sir Henry Mance, a recent chairman, is always called Jackie. Incidentally, it is generally said that, although undistinguished as an underwriter, he was an outstandingly good chairman and a great ambassador for Lloyd's in Australia and the United States. 'Dick' Turpin, a broker I knew well until his retirement, had an unusual hobby. A prominent member of the Magic Circle, he specialised in pocket tricks, and was said to produce one to ease the way if a business talk proved sticky. The last time I saw him he pulled out a lady's silk square and two large safety pins. He folded the scarf over and over, stuck the pins through the lot and clipped them shut. Then he pulled out two corners, gave a tug, the scarf unfolded completely and the pins, still closed, tinkled on to the table.

The achievements of Lloyd's are inexplicable to many. How do they find four million pounds for Mr. Onassis' whalers, or ten million for a hi-jacked jumbo jet? The answer is of course in spreading the risk. Few underwriting syndicates would take more than £50,000 on such a risk. Some of that may well be reinsured in Switzerland, Germany or the United States. And that is not so grave a claim when one considers the continual inflow of premiums.

Lloyd's has bad years. Recently there were three in a row. But all things pass and in the long run it is still a good investment to be a 'name' in a syndicate. To be this, you must be acceptable to the working underwriter who runs the syndicate, and sustain an interview with the committee, or some of them. You must, too, pledge many thousands of pounds in securities with the Committee, to cover your obligations for claims, and personally back these obligations with every penny you possess.

Lloyd's insures almost anything. The very name has become a synonym for reliability. People who have been around for as many years as I have (though my work has been alongside rather than in the market) tend to say that Lloyd's is not what it was. With such a tight community, it is easy for conformity to replace adventure in business, and for a grey, dull mentality to become the norm. However, the market keeps throwing up characters who break the pattern, to the advantage of all. A generation ago, the late 'Toby' Green was known to all as a daring underwriter who refused to conform to standard patterns. He did things no one else would do, and both made and lost large sums. His son Peter has ploughed a different furrow. More conventional than his sometimes outrageous father, he is still bold, quick, and always willing to say 'yes' or 'no' to any risk when others hesitate or confer or hedge. Comparisons are odorous, as Dogberry said (not Mrs. Malaprop), but the son may be an even greater force in the market than the father. Certainly, if you want your broker to place a very large or very difficult marine risk, it is quite likely that he will first approach that syndicate.

Hundreds of good stories come out of Lloyd's. So much goes on there that a new one is spawned every week. And they are all true! Here is one example.

The saga of the *Girl Pat* produced headlines in the daily papers for weeks during the thirties. It also produced a fascinating legal and insurance problem. The *Girl Pat* was a trawler, large for those days, owned by the Marstrand Fishing Company of Hull. She set off on a routine fishing trip, and completely disappeared. No radio messages came. No-one sighted her. Rumours began, grew, and multiplied. After some weeks, she suddenly appeared, and again vanished. Lloyd's agents in Dakar, in French West Africa, reported that she had called briefly for stores. She was thousands of miles away from her fishing grounds, and she might have gone on again to almost any part of the hemisphere. All sorts of guesses were made as to the motives and objectives of Skipper Orsborne and his crew. Or had the ship been seized by pirates, or some other extraordinary group?

After a further long gap, the craft was found in the West Indies, badly damaged, and it transpired that skipper and crew had gone off on a wholly unsuccessful search for buried treasure. Were they heroic adventurers, rather ineffective crooks, or what? Different newspapers took different views.

Meanwhile, after the second disappearance on leaving Dakar, and before the solution to the mystery, the marine insurance world had suffered a minor convulsion. The vessel was a large trawler for those days, insured for £18,000, which again were rather larger pounds than those of today. She was insured with Lloyd's underwriters and insurance companies in the usual way, and her owners made a claim for total loss by barratry — the wrongful act of the captain or crew. Such a claim is virtually unknown nowadays, but historically this was not so, and the principles relating to such a claim were well recognised. If the ship was taken away by the crew, against the owners' orders and interests, and there was no reasonable chance of her being returned, a claim for total loss would succeed. With the ship's whereabouts unknown, and the crew's aims equally mysterious, was there a reasonable chance or not?

As most people know, underwriters are people who write their names (or initials) under each other to confirm that they take an indicated share of an insurance risk. Each makes a separate contract. It is usual but not obligatory for all to follow the settlements by the underwriter at the head of the list. The leading underwriter in this case was the Neville Dixey syndicate at Lloyd's. Mr. Dixey was then Chairman of Lloyd's, virtually a full-time job during his period of office. His deputy in charge of the underwriting box was W.F. Halford, a good friend of mine.

Willy Halford was on the old-fashioned side, soberly dressed, serious and exact in speech. He was an evangelical Christian, a man with a real faith which affected all he did in business as well as elsewhere. I respected him greatly, although I liked to tease him a little. He told me that, faced with this problem, he consulted several of the other underwriters, both Lloyd's and companies, and they all agreed that despite the doubt the claim should be paid. Their example was followed by all the insurers involved, except for three companies at the very bottom of the list, covering a total of only £450 out of the £18,000. They refused.

The trawler owners felt bound, in fairness to those who had paid, to bring an action in the courts against those who had not, even though the costs might exceed the sum outstanding. And the action failed! It would be easy to think that the judge's view was affected by the ship having been found before the action was heard before him, but I do not think this was so.

The day after judgement was given I chanced to meet Mr. Halford in Lime Street outside Lloyd's. I could not resist the temptation to ask, "Well, Willy, what about your settlement now?" He sniffed and looked embarrassed, for a City man dislikes enunciating points of principle. But he replied, firmly, "My settlement was in accordance with the traditions of Lloyd's."

A somewhat similar issue arose in the 1960s as a result of the Israeli-Arab war in 1967. Sunken ships blocked both ends of the Suez Canal, and a dozen or more merchant ships, Russian, Polish, British, German, Swedish, were trapped in the middle. They are still there as I write. Their bored crews, reduced in number, polished brass and competed in rowing races, until an informal arrangement was made that a few Poles should look after them all.

It was clear that the shipowners had lost the effective control of their ships by a warlike operation, although the belligerents made no attempt to seize them. There would have been no profit in it if they had. War risks on ships are insured separately from marine risks. Various insurers were involved, including Lloyd's and insurance companies, and British and Swedish mutual insurance associations, like the one managed by Millers.

Lawyers said that there had never been a case like this, but a total loss claim was payable if there was no reasonable chance of the ships being released — a similar point to that in the *Girl Pat*. And, they added, in their view there was a reasonable chance they would be. The insurers, cautious men, declined to pay. Months went by, then years. At intervals, the lawyers were asked, and still replied that the canal might be opened at any time. In the end, of course, the claims had to be paid. As a mutual man myself, I was a bit mortified to hear that German and Swedish insurers made up their minds to pay before the British war risk clubs did. I thought a point might have been stretched in the shipowners' favour a good deal earlier.

The ships thus paid for now belong to the insurers concerned. They would, I am sure, consider a reasonable offer. Would anyone care to buy a good ship at a safe mooring in the Great Bitter Lake? I would be glad to act as broker.

Will the Suez Canal open again? I imagine so, some time and in some degree. Hostility is not immutable. Geography makes the canal of some value, even though much of the oil which produced traffic through the canal now goes round Africa in tankers far too large for any canal. The passenger traffic, too, all goes by air. Russia, Yogoslavia, Italy and other Mediterranean powers suffer by the barrier to seaborne communication. Others may not care and, for military reasons, may even welcome it. But one day ships will again sail through the desert.

A British shipowner told me that he made a bet with the Russian commissar for the mercantile marine, who prophesied that the canal would be reopened by a date some two years after it was blocked. In due course there arrived a charming letter from Moscow, enclosing a silver rouble. The letter said that it was illegal to export coinage from Russia, but the writer considered a debt of honour even more important than obeying the law!

The Baltic, third of the great exchanges, is closest to my heart. Lloyd's is my neighbour, but the Baltic is, in a sense, my home. I feel honoured that I have been elected a life member.

Two Stock Exchange men will arrange to meet at 'the House'. Two Lloyd's men meet in 'the Room'. Baltic men meet 'on the Floor'. And that means a spreading hall, its ceiling some thirty feet high, and a central dome and side domes above that. The walls and pillars are marble, the windows stained glass — a rich piece of Edwardiana. Go there at one o'clock, or four on a working day, and the floor is thronged with brokers and principals. Go there at ten thirty or two, and it is deserted. Many small conferences of two, three or four are going on downstairs in the coffee-room, bars, and dining rooms throughout the day, but if you want to feel out the market, you go before lunch or before the exchange closes at four thirty.

These two brief periods of busy trading each day puzzle outsiders, but the practice is logical enough. The first part of the morning is spent in considering incoming mail and in telephone conferences on what should be done that day. After lunch people go back to their offices, particularly for the American link. At that time the New York offices have opened, and their orders and comments come in by cable, telephone and, especially nowadays, by telex. And a busy broker may still be dealing with this side of the business up to eleven at night at his home.

They say that a broker can tell the state of the market by just walking on to the floor. A stroll across or round the room will give him the latest rates. He will know, too, the exact spot on the floor (for everyone stands about and there are only a few benches against the walls) where he will find the time charter market, or the oil companies' men, or the South American or Far Eastern charterers. The chartering of ships is, of course, the main business of the exchange, but you will find the air chartering brokers in the south-west corner, and in the opposite corner you can buy or sell grain cargoes. These things have grown by habit.

Some firms supply their junior brokers with stencilled lists of the business they are offering, and you can pick a pink, green or yellow list from various hands as you stroll along. But the bulk of the work is done by word of mouth, with brief jottings in a notebook. The proud motto of the Baltic is "Our Word, Our Bond"; and this is taken very seriously.

One good friend of mine, a member of the Greek community, has been described to me by different people as "a real Baltic man". He is a Cypriot, unusually square in the shoulders, broad in the chest, and round in the lower chest. A very big head is covered with bristly hair. There are twinkling eyes, and a smile about six inches wide. One man told me he could stop him on the floor and ask if he would do a cargo of so many tons of such a cargo on such a voyage, November loading, at, say, £1.70. He would think for a moment and reply, "No. But I will at £1.85." And if a firm order came from the charterer, on normal conditions, he would know he had a binding contract without a quibble of any kind.

In that moment of consideration he would first check if he had a suitable ship for such a cargo in the right part of the world at the right time. Then he had to do a mental calculation of the freight offered, and compare it with other business offering at the time. He would also probe his mind as to whether there were any snags. Was it the hurricane season? What was the current price of bunker oil in that part of the world? Would any special insurances be needed? Were there reports of labour troubles in that area? Were the ports likely to be congested in November? These are some of the things which go into the art of chartering.

A dispute I had to deal with early in my business life

involved some expenses under a time charter and the meaning of three words typed in on the contract. It was a question of special fittings for carrying bulk grain. The shipowner in London and the charter in New York disagreed. A fair sum was involved. What should be done? A lawsuit? An arbitration? The two principals decided that their respective brokers should meet and see if they could agree what they meant exactly when they put in the three words during their negotiations on the Baltic. They met, and agreed, and the charterers got their money.

Baltic men, like Lloyd's men, come in all shapes and sizes. The young, who are numerous, for firms can appoint chartering clerks from twenty-one years old upwards, show much of the flourish of modern youth — loud shirts, natty tailoring, and a violent addiction to motor rallies, dinghy racing, and the like. My own friends are mostly among the older men, whose variety and richness of character have been a joy.

I think of one man who works entirely as a sale and purchase broker, buying and selling ships, his income arising from the small commissions on the large sums involved. In such a hazardous business he seems paradoxical, for he poses as an arch-conservative. His political views (I still wonder if they are in part a pose) make Enoch Powell look a richly pink socialist. A small, somewhat gnome-like figure, he delivers his violent opinions with the twinkling gaiety of a favourite uncle. In business he is sound, methodical, exact, and his hobbies are pursued in the same manner — military history and fell walking.

Another in the same section of the market is as big as the first man is small — tall, dark and handsome. He speaks quietly and seldom, in a low voice, and with a trace of the accent of his mother tongue, which is French. Behind his exquisite manners, his pleasure in food and wine, and his business expertise, there is something equally surprising. Of dual nationality, he elected in 1939 to join the British Army and was dropped into Provence, where he headed a large resistance group, and had an extremely cloak-and-dagger war. He goes back annually for reunions with other survivors. As for his expertise, I once asked him if he could buy me a secondhand lightship. A ship had sunk a lightship, and I was thinking of offering to provide a replacement. The market for such vessels must be non-existent, except as scrap material, but he quickly came up with an offer. Unfortunately the

Australian lights authority insisted on cash.

A unique personality, who nevertheless is in some ways a typical Baltic man, is Captain 'Jack' Pezelj, the Yugoslav who for twenty-five years represented on the exchange all the shipowning and chartering interests of his country. He came to Britain in 1943 when his ship was torpedoed, married an Englishwoman, and stayed. The broad face, the springing hair, and occasionally a touch of colour in hat or tie, still show the Slav. In fact he is very proudly a Yugoslav, and spends time every year in his homeland. To me he reflects the best traditions and standards of the City. Perhaps it is partly assimilation, but it is surely also a deep response in the man to values of honesty and consideration for others which are universal. His London friends regard him as a worthy representative of his country, his Yugoslav friends (of whom I know many) as a worthy representative of the City of London.

It is strange how often in a business community the needle of attention swings back to honesty, especially when we English find moral questions such an embarrassing subject. I was once asked what was the relevance of honesty to business. When I tried to think it out, it surprised me and others. Firstly, it would be impossible to do business as we do if there were not a high level of honesty in most people. To give one example only, I once gave a guarantee for over a million pounds on the basis of a single telephone call. To a City man that is not remarkable — provided the man who telephoned can be trusted. And for a number of years I worked to build up a network of people across the world to whom I offered and from whom I expected absolute honesty, or as near to that as is humanly possible. Imagine the value, in the complicated world of today, of knowing that your cable to Hongkong or telephone call to New York will get the real facts, palatable or not, or a really honest opinion.

On the Baltic — "Our Word Our Bond" — honesty is taken for granted in most cases, which makes more glaring the occasional departure from it. In such cases members may be asked by the secretary to give an explanation and even be summoned to appear before the directors, a rare and, I imagine, unnerving experience. Delinquent firms represented on the exchange, even by agents, may be 'posted', a notice of the event being thus published to all members. This is reserved for very serious matters. Those less serious may warrant a notice which simply says, "Members contemplating doing business with Blank and Co. are invited to communicate with the Secretary".

The story goes that one remarkable Baltic character — head of a broking firm and a member for sixty years — was summoned befoe the directors and asked if it were true that he had accepted an offer of a contract without the authority of his overseas principal. He replied, "Of course I did. And I still can't understand why the damned fool didn't confirm what I did. It was jolly good business." I imagine the reprimand by the directors was something in the spirit of one beating I was given at school, when my housemaster was chuckling so much that I hardly felt the cane.

A more serious case arose when a very large broking firm, the control of which had passed to a finance house shortly before, was charged with blatantly and dishonestly poaching business from a much smaller member firm. The complaint was upheld and the big firm was banned from the exchange for six months. Strong feelings were expressed by members, one of them telling a director that if they didn't take severe measures they might as well close the exchange as such and only keep open the lavatories! I happened to lunch with the complainant on the day the decision was 'posted', and many members came up to him in the coffee room with congratulations. A director of a rival financial firm to that controlling the big brokers commented to a friend of mine, "They ought to know that the methods they are notorious for in other fields don't go on the Baltic."

The Baltic is one of many City groupings which, one feels, would almost have to be invented again if they were suddenly abolished. On the Antwerp Bourse I was interested to find a small market for chartering ships, only to be told that it was almost all business repeated from the Baltic. The same is the case in other countries. A little business is carried through in Scandinavia, Rotterdam or Piraeus, and a larger amount in New York, done by a laborious round of telephoning. The great bulk is done in London. If a very big contract is made, it may be done direct in the offices of the oil company or steel producer. This is in fact a growing practice, but a mass of business for the thousands of deep sea ships which have to match themselves with cargoes is fixed on the Baltic.

To some, every business man is a hard-faced and ruthless exploiter. It would be folly to pretend that such men do not exist. They do. I have met some of them. But in my experience there are more men in the City who simply do a job, and in doing it apply decent standards of conduct and make a practice of being understanding and helpful to others.

Nature draws a distinction between parasites and symbiotes. A parasite preys on its host, and draws strength from it. In a symbiotic relationship the two live together and help each other, in some cases to the extent that neither can live without its partner.

I doubt if society is imperilled by the occasional crook in the world of money. Similarly, the selfish money-making of some is hedged around by legal safeguards. It may weaken but cannot destroy a good system. The larger number (still a small minority, I think) who exploit expense accounts or sail close to the wind on taxation questions are perhaps more dangerous, as sapping the moral standards of the community as a whole.

The real danger, it seems to me, is of the financial community being subtly taken over entirely by materialism. Good men living in surroundings deeply impregnated with monetary considerations, and divorced by distance and acres of paper from the real issues of living, can lose their human qualities, and put things before people, expediency before principle.

This is not a question of right or left wing politics, or of economic doctrines. In fact, some of our most materialistic theorists put forward their bloodless and unfeeling ideas in the name of social progress. It is a question of what rules in a man's heart.

What is the right approach to life of a man who works in a place where money pervades most of his activities? Is it possible — and right? — to work in such surroundings with something of the simplicity and purity of a barefoot friar, and each day to set a clear standard of what is really important?

Such questions have often challenged my own business life, especially in those morning times of quiet. I must hope that (as Peter Howard said in his biography of Beaverbrook), when the time comes, I too will be judged with charity.

10

Negotiation

The 'club' atmosphere in our type of business is reflected in a number of ways. One is the manner in which claims against the insured shipowners are handled. Frequently the managers (or their London agents in the case of a Bermuda club) take over the entire conduct of the claim from the start. London is still such an important centre that a large proportion of the claims need to be handled there. For those which must be handled elsewhere, the club has a network of lawyers, surveyors, shipping and insurance firms, who can be called on as required. They also report to London for instructions.

Our firm starts about twenty-five thousand new claims files every year in London, and the vast majority of these are dealt with by negotiation. Perhaps one per cent produce litigation. The art of negotiation is therefore one which a P. and I. man has to practise daily. It is an art you go on learning all through life. Technique and knowledge play their part, but the basic lies in human relationships.

R.A. Clyde, the wise and witty solicitor-turned-arbitrator so well-known in the City, once told me, as we were settling a case in which we were on opposite sides, that his father used to say, "A bad settlement is better than a good lawsuit." Certainly, one's own pigheadedness is the biggest enemy in negotiations, far more dangerous than the most skilled and devious opponent. A number of times I have stuck at some point, only to finish by paying more than was then being asked. Even the steadily accruing interest and legal costs, as delay continues can produce this effect. And a small settlement may cost less than it would require to fight a case and win it.

Perhaps, therefore, I can start by quoting the most outstanding piece of negotiation I remember. I had no part in it myself. It was handled by a younger partner, David Martin Clark, by an executive specialising in life and injury claims, John Tilley, and by Yves Denniel, a lawyer employed by the eminent French shipowners, Nouvelle Compagnie Havraise Peninsulaire. One of their ships had a disastrous collision in the Mediterranean with the *Sirius*, a Norwegian tanker, which broke in two. One half sank; the other was destroyed by the French navy as a menace to navigation. Twenty-one Norwegian lives were lost.

We always feel a special urgency about cases in which there is loss of life. It is impossible to forget the bereaved families. Yet when very large sums of money and difficult legal questions are involved it is hard to avoid years of litigation. A quick but thorough investigation in this case produced an unusual fact. Both ships seemed to have been in some degree to blame for the collision, but whichever way the legal question on this worked out, the French ship would certainly have to pay her maximum liability under statute. As far as insurance was concerned, this would be divided between French insurance companies and the club. Our share was some hundreds of thousands of dollars. There was a certain margin on the amount of liability, a certain area for argument. The three men named set off for Norway with full authority to negotiate. For days they discussed the details with a panel of a dozen Norwegians. Over dinner one evening the last obstacle was overcome. The best reasonable settlement was agreed. The money was obtained from Paris and Bermuda and was paid over only one month and two days after the collision.

Two unusual details may be mentioned. The compensation for the twenty one families, each of whom had lost a breadwinner, was paid in one sum to the Norwegian maritime trades unions, who undertook to make a fair and equitable distribution, a remarkable tribute to trade union integrity. And the English and French negotiators were invited to the centenary dinner of the insurance company which led the team opposing them, and presented publicly to the one hundred and thirty shipowners present, with a tribute to their attitude throughout the case.

Negotiation can indeed be better than litigation. Not long after I started in the City, the clubs experienced what was then their biggest claim ever. It concerned the liner *Poleric*, insured with the Standard Association, but the claim was so big that a number of other clubs shared in it by reinsurance. A fire in the engine-room had caused much damage to the cargo of the *Poleric* and legal proceedings were started in America. Normally, a shipowner is not responsible for cargo damage by fire, which can so easily and terribly get out of control at sea. In this case, allegations were made which reopened this issue. A stern legal battle went on for ten years, ending in 1930 with the shock of a decision by the Supreme Court of the United States against the shipowners for some three million dollars. The only hope was a motion for a new trial, to review certain of the facts. While this was pending, two men, William Clifton the solicitor and William Richards the average adjuster (if my memory is true), went out to New York and compromised the claim for one million dollars. I never heard how they managed it, but that was something like negotiation!

One of the biggest cases I handled arose out of the collision of three ships, all of which were insured with us. This of course did not mean that we carried the whole risk. The hull underwriters were concerned with damage received by the ships, and part liability for damage to other ships. We covered the balance of the collision liability to other ships, plus loss of life, personal injury and other crew claims.

The primary collision was between two large tankers, the *World Harmony* owned by one of the Niarchos companies and the *Petar Zoranic*, the largest vessel in the Yugoslav merchant fleet. One was in ballast, but not gas-freed; the other carried a full cargo of crude oil. An explosion and fire enveloped them both. One of them drifted down on the Turkish passenger ship *Tarsus*. She also caught fire, and all three ships were totally destroyed. Fifty one lives were lost, and the *Petar Zoranic* burned for a solid month on the beach in the Bosphorus.

There were several difficulties about handling the case. One was the large sum involved — the three ships were insured for a total of 3¼ million pounds, quite apart from the life claims and various subsidiary matters. Another was that Greeks, Yugoslavs and Turks have not always been known to agree on everything, and the same could be said of the insurers involved, who were British, French, Yugoslav and Italian. A third was that when the flames swept the decks and bridges of the two tankers, every witness of the collision had been killed, probably with a merciful quickness. But how could lawyers determine the blame for the collision?

It was not I but a Yugoslav insurance man, Dr. Milorad Maksimovic, who first realised that the third difficulty was, in an insurance sense, an advantage. The unusual circumstances, he suggested, pointed to a 'drop-hands' settlement, whereby the two ships originally in collision dropped their claims against each other. But it was I, in partnership with Hugh Mitchell and Dick Rutherford of Lloyd's clams office, who got all the principal parties together into our boardroom in St. Mary Axe less than a year after the collision. The negotiations were not too difficult. One party tried to back down, after agreeing, and had to be persuaded with some firmness to honour the half-promise he had made earlier. And the agreement was signed.

To us fell the obligation to settle all the life claims, in Greece, Turkey and Yugoslavia. The only solace in this painful occupation was that if we had gone to the courts, it would probably have been three years or more before the families got any compensation. Some ten years afterwards, Dick Rutherford recalled this case and said to me, "Every time I think of it, I am more certain that we did the right thing." Technically, the settlement was highly unorthodox. But I agree also that it was right.

Is it possible to negotiate a settlement that is entirely right? One could as well ask if the law courts produce absolute justice. The best one can do is to aim at it sincerely and constantly. When I decided always to negotiate on a basis of absolute honesty, it meant a firm resolution never to make a false statement, or one that was misleadingly half-true. Absolute unselfishness meant aiming at a settlement that was also right for one's adversary. It does a bully no good if you allow yourself to be cowed, and a crook no good if you allow yourself to be deceived.

Shipowners had many disputes with the big international grain firms. Occasionally friction resulted. I found that they respected someone who fought hard and straight for what he felt was right. As merchants, they were mostly quite tough characters themselves, and we got to the point with most of them where each of us could trust the other's word on anything. This was an agreeable basis on which to thrash out a dispute.

With some of the average agents (not to be confused with average adjusters) it was advisable to give them no information whatever. These are the firms who pursue claims for insurers against shipowners and others, and are mostly paid a percentage of their recoveries. Their tactics may be to press for information on a matter, which they then use against you. It is quite legitimate if you are fool enough to fall for it.

But when you get to know them well enough, you can deal

with them with complete openness on both sides. It helps a lot if, as I learnt to do, justified claims are admitted and paid out of hand.

Lloyd's runs a Recoveries Department to deal with matters of this kind for Lloyd's underwriters. A former senior official of this department once put forward a claim for some seventy thousand dollars for short deliveries of dates on several ships in the same trade over a period of two or three months. I did a very thorough investigation at both ends of the voyage, and then asked the man round to discuss it. Knowing him as I did, I told him the whole facts. There was no evidence of any kind to explain why the cargo was missing. The tally sheets seemed to prove that all of it was loaded in Iraq, but equally it was not discharged at New York. At Busra, the ship had loaded from barges at an anchorage in the river, working day and night. One theory was that a swindle could have been worked between the tally clerks on the ship (they were of course local people) and the men on the barges. Some of the cases could have been left in the barges covered by tarpaulins, although the papers drawn up on the ship showed that the full quantity was loaded. Then, in the darkness, the barges could have dropped down river into Iranian waters, and the dates been sold to merchants ashore. But there was no evidence of this at all.

I told my opponent frankly that if he pressed the claim to court, he would recover in full. I was convinced that the shipowners had not misdelivered the goods, but all the evidence was against them. It was a bit hard. He said he would think it over. A week later, he telephoned to say that the underwriters pressing the claim were prepared to accept fifty thousand dollars. Did I agree? I did.

Dick Clyde, when he was senior partner in the firm of solicitors he founded, always liked to come round to the Axe to argue cases. I have always appreciated those lawyers who get enjoyment and even fun out of the law, and would rank Dickie at the top of this class. He once put forward a claim for several thousand pounds for short delivery of old motor tyres at Baghdad. In the difficult days after the war, the Arabs cut them up to make into shoes. At our confrontation, I went farther than I did over the dates. I admitted that the shipments had got into great confusion, and that many of the tyres had never been delivered. He said he assumed I would pay, but I replied that I would not pay a penny. We had evidence from Iraq that when the cargo arrived (or should have arrived), the market for the goods had collapsed. No-one was buying old motor tyres at any price, and shortly afterwards the customs burnt great stacks of them as worthless. The shipowners admitted the breach of contract, but the damages were nil.

Clyde was delighted. He said he could not remember such an interesting defence to a claim. "But I reject your evidence", he said theatrically. "Wait until you hear my evidence. I have not asked my clients in Iraq about it, but I am sure they will swear that their old motor tyres were beyond price. I will bring them all here to give evidence at the trial. The Law Courts and the Strand will be thronged with my witnesses, all in picturesque native costume." We compromised at five hundred pounds.

The Irish have their own ways with negotiation, as with other things. I am half Irish myself. When I went to Dublin to argue over some claims, I was warned that an agreement was not considered binding unless it had been moistened in the nearest bar. I said that I was off alcohol, but apparently that didn't matter. One had to drink something. Even water would do. We dealt with someone from a soap factory in Cork. It was something about some damaged tallow. Sure enough, when we had agreed on a figure, the man from Cork spat on his palms, smacked his hands together and said, "Where do we drink?" Out we went, as predicted.

By and large, negotiation is best done face to face. It is so easy to get a wrong impression of a man from letters, telex or telephone. And if you do not assess him properly, you may not assess his arguments or his offers correctly. A New York lawyer once called on me. We had corresponded but not met before. The conversation seemed rather pointless, but as he left he said, "I wanted to meet you because it did not seem to me possible that you could be such an icily correct person as you seemed to be from your letters."

To get to grips with difficult cases, my partners and I have often travelled thousands of miles to negotiate face to face in Hong Kong, New Zealand or Florida. In connection with one dispute between a Greek shipowner and a Dutch shipbuilder, I travelled to Holland five times in one year. It is sometimes an advantage to be on your opponent's ground. He feels more at home, and less defensive. In this case, we recovered more than was legally due to the shipowner, though not, in my view, the full amount that was morally due.

A case I look back on with some pleasure concerned a

Yugoslav ship, an oldish ship, one of the Liberty type built during the 1939-45 war, which foundered off Hudson Bay. Ice conditions were bad that year, and all the evidence I ever saw showed that ice damage to the hull was the cause of the accident. A great expert on polar navigation told me that in freezing conditions a wind is considered to have the effect of a one-degree drop of temperature for every mile an hour velocity. Moreover, the floes which break away from the Greenland glaciers travel long distances with chunks of rock embodied in them, an even worse danger to a ship's plates than the ice itself.

Unfortunately, when the crew were brought back to Churchill, their story as reported in the Canadian newspapers was not convincing. As far as I know, it was on the basis of this and of unfounded rumours that the insurers of the cargo brought an action against the shipowners in the English courts, claiming some three hundred thousand pounds for the loss of the wheat. An exceedingly careful investigation followed. In theory, it was the responsibility of the ship-owners to show that the loss was due to a peril of the sea. In practice, both parties set up rival theories in a case like this, and the cargo interests would obviously try to show that the ship was unseaworthy.

Lawyers made two lengthy visits to Yugoslavia to take statements from the crew. Other evidence was obtained in Canada. The claimants showed great confidence. I came into the affair at a rather late stage, at the request of a young man who was handling it in our office, and I went with him to a major conference with eminent counsel, when the situation was reviewed. The emphasis was very much on the need for us to present a case which would be completely watertight, if that expression is permissible in the context. Fourteen witnesses would need to be called, nine from Yugoslavia (and translation would lengthen the trial), three from Canada. The trial might take five or six weeks. The technical evidence was doubtful, said eminent counsel. We could not wholly establish how so much water could have got in, ton by ton, to sink the ship in the time. If a chance came up to settle the case for 50 per cent or more, it should be taken.

I had an advantage over the others present, because I had done none of the detailed work on the evidence. Since I was farther from the trees, I could see the shape of the wood. The incursion of seawater was itself a peril of the sea. There was no direct evidence of any defect in the ship at all. I took a more cheerful view, but was in a minority of one.

I said, "Why don't we make a demonstration of strength, and tell the plaintiffs that if they withdraw their claim we will not ask for costs against them?" Eminent counsel smiled, rather pityingly, I thought. It could do no harm, he said. We went back from the Temple to the City. The solicitors wrote the letter I suggested. The offer was contemptuously refused. So we went on preparing for trial, which was set to start on a Monday.

On the Friday morning, I had a telephone call. Our solicitors had heard from the plaintiffs' solicitors, who said that their clients were worried about the costs being incurred (I reckoned that we had incurred ten thousand pounds of costs). Would the shipowners agree to settle by paying 25 per cent of the claim? I asked if counsel had given his opinion on the offer. No, said our solicitor, but we know what counsel would say — "take it". In that case, I said, don't ask him, but tell the opposing solicitor that the most we would do was to repeat that if they would withdraw their claim, we would not ask for costs against them. Half an hour later, he rang back to say that they had agreed.

I had a charming letter from eminent counsel (now a judge) thanking me for giving him a weekend with his family, instead of spending it studying the papers for the trial. He asked how we had managed it? I am afraid I could not resist the temptation to reply that the secret was to know when not to ask the advice of counsel.

11

Litigation

Even if less than one per cent of the club's claim files results in litigation, this represents a lot of litigation. It may be necessary to fight a case because the claim seems quite unjustified, or the damages claimed far too high, or in a few cases to establish a point of principle.

Litigation has brought me into close touch with many ripe characters in the legal community. Lawyers are a vital element in civilisation, and have enriched and brightened my business life.

Some of the men with whom I have spent hours in conference in the Temple are now judges — Mocatta, Roskill, Megaw, Donaldson, Brandon and Kerr. I must be careful what I say about them. Others, both solicitors and barristers, are retired, and some are dead. They will not mind a few stories about them, nor, I hope, will those who still serve their clients and their blindfold mistress with the sword and scales.

Legally speaking, the most historic lawsuit I was ever involved in was that of the *Wagon Mound.* The B.B.C. Third Programme ran two lectures and a debate on the legal issues involved, and it figures in the studies of every law student in Britain and, for all I know, throughout the Anglo-Saxon world. It began in Australia, but I have discussed it with barristers in Belfast and Bermuda and other places, too.

It is not strictly right to say that the *Wagon Mound* decision (or decisions, as I shall explain) changed the law of negligence. In English common law, so I am told, the law is the law, and in theory is immutable. If a competent court pronounces that a certain colour is blue, then it is blue and it has always been blue. Should it happen later on that a superior court overrules that decision and makes a finding that the colour in question is brown, then brown it is and it has always been brown. The law does not change. The courts' function is to help us all to understand what the law is. So the "Wagon Mound" case clarified certain aspects of the law of negligence.

It all began in Australia, when the tanker *Wagon Mound* was taking on bunker oil at a berth in Sydney harbour. Through carelessness of the crew, some of the fuel oil was spilled into the harbour. The captain asked the people at the oil berth if there was danger of fire, but they said not. Two days later, a fire occurred at Mort's Dock shipyard, a short distance away, and about two hundred thousand pounds worth of damage was done to the shipyard and to two ships repairing there.

It seemed to us unlucky that anyone should blame the tanker. Neither the captain nor the oil company thought it possible to ignite a film of oil floating on seawater. But when we consulted local solicitors, we knew we were in collision with the law as it was then understood to be. English law takes a lot of notice of precedents, decisions in similar cases. This attitude must go back to the folk gatherings of Saxon times, when ancient men recalled how some dispute was decided in their great grandfathers' time. A number of precedents bore on the point involved this time, but the one which was most clearly against us was a decision by the Court of Appeal in England in a case referred to by lawyers as 'In re Polemis'. This included a strong statement that if someone committed the tort or actionable wrong of negligence, and some damage might be expected to be caused to somebody else, the wrongdoer was liable for all the damage caused by anybody. He only escaped if no damage was reasonably foreseeable. The captain of the *Wagon Mound* could foresee that his spilt oil would dirty the yachts at the mornings across the inlet. It looked as if his ship would therefore be responsible also for the fire.

A precedent set by a lower court can be upset only by a higher court. The only court in England above the Court of Appeal was the House of Lords, so this was the only court which could reverse 'In re Polemis'. Technically, the courts in Australia are not bound by precedents set in England. They are merely regarded as persuasive. But in those days there was a right of appeal from Australian courts to the Judicial Committee of the Privy Council in London which was of equal authority with the House of Lords, and largely consisted of the same judges. If we were going to fight the *Wagon Mound* claims, it would mean a series of trials through the courts right up to the Privy Council.

Our decision to do this was not based on the two hundred thousand pounds, but on the fact that this was a good chance to challenge 'Polemis'. We felt it would be much more satisfactory if the tortfeasor was responsible only for such losses as could reasonably be foreseen. So we said no to the claimants, who duly started actions in New South Wales.

The actions seemed to us to proceed very slowly, and so did the collection of evidence. We wanted to be sure of doing the job thoroughly, so I cleared it with my partners that I would go to Australia to confer with the lawyers there, and help with the collection of evidence. One difficulty was that there was no direct information on what started the fire, although there was little doubt that the oil which fed it came from the *Wagon Mound*. On arrival at Sydney, I inspected 'the scene of the crime', and then spent an afternoon at Sydney University discussing with Professor Hunter of the Department of Chemical Engineering how to deal with the technical questions involved. Later, he was highly complimented by the judge on the series of two hundred experiments which we planned that day and which he carried through. These showed that fuel oil on water can only ignite if the thickness of the layer is between quite narrow limits, if there is a steady wind, strong enough but not too strong, if there is an igniting agent and if there is also something present to act as a wick, to conduct the vaporised oil upwards into the air so that it will burn.

Years afterwards, a man walked into the office of the club's solicitors in Sydney. He had been a welder working at Mort's Dock when the fire occurred and had seen the whole thing. Out of loyalty to his employers, he had kept silent, but now the company was in liquidation and he felt free to talk. He described the exact situation which Professor Hunter had synthesised by experiment, the thin film of oil, the steady breeze, a piece of burning tow dropped by a fellow welder which fell onto some driftwood floating in the oil. And the smouldering of the tow developing quickly into a rush of flame.

As foretold by the lawyers, the Australian courts felt themselves persuaded to follow 'Polemis'. Fortunately, the evidence to indicate that the fire was not reasonably foreseeable came out clearly, and the judge of first instance made a finding that that was so. The shipowners' case was argued before the Privy Council by Ashton Roskill, Q.C. (now the chairman of the Monopolies Commission), supported by Leycester Meares, Q.C., from Australia, later a judge. I went up one day to listen, and found the proceedings much more informal than in the Queen's Bench Division. Five judges in business suits sitting at ease, with learned counsel in wig and gown standing at a wooden lectern in front of them. For this court, the parties' arguments had to be outlined in a printed 'case', book size, supplied to their Lordships before the hearing, but counsel had to expound on it for days at a time, and face a barrage of questions and comments. It took a very disciplined mind.

We were delighted when the Judicial Committee's decision was published. 'In re Polemis' was 'blown upon', as they say, and a clear statement made that foreseeability should be the test. If you did something stupidly and actionably wrong, you were legally responsible only for the damage a reasonable person would think might result. Parenthetically, this principle has been qualified by later decisions, but it was a real landmark all the same.

One minor point caused us little concern. The judgment pointed out that originally the formal claim had included allegations that the oil spill could be regarded as either of two different torts, negligence or nuisance. In Australia, the question of nuisance had never been argued in court. The Privy Council said that in view of that they must refer the case back to the court of first instance, in case this alternative claim should be pursued. And they added that the judgment should not be taken to mean that the same rules applied to nuisance as to negligence. All this seemed very fair, but of no significance.

By this time, Mort's Dock was in liquidation, and the liquidator decided it was not his duty to start all over again in the hope that a nuisance claim would succeed. So that was that.

Then came the surprise. We knew there was a second claim, a separate action by the owners of the fire-damaged ships, waiting for the decision in the Mort's Dock case. To everyone's astonishment, they decided to press on with their action, claiming in nuisance and also in negligence. On and on the case went, entitled 'The *Wagon Mound* (No. 2)', until it reached the Privy Council again. A different panel of judges sat this time.

Ashton Roskill prepared the 'case', but before the hearing he was appointed to the Monopolies Commission and had to withdraw. Mark Littman, Q.C., had the very difficult task of arguing on the basis of a case prepared by someone else.

In 'The *Wagon Mound* (No. 1)' we had seen close argument and logical reasoning, the legal mind at its best. With the utmost respect to the eminent gentlemen involved, I find it hard not to consider the judgment in 'The *Wagon Mound* (No. 2)' as showing the legal mind at its worst. It started by stating, with strong supporting arguments, that the same rules as to foreseeability should apply to the tort of nuisance as to the tort of negligence, and that on that basis the claim based on nuisance failed. It then considered the claim based on negligence, pointed out a slight difference in the description of the facts by the Australian judges in the two actions (the same facts, remember), concluded that the fire was foreseeable, and that the claim succeeded. I have yet to find the layman or lawyer who can see logic in that. Perhaps one of the judges wrote one part, and another the other part, but the five issued this contradiction as their joint opinion. It cost the club eighty thousand pounds, plus the legal expenses of both sides in 'The *Wagon Mound* (No. 2)'. Fortunately the part about the same rule applying seems to be clear enough.

Although I cannot understand why I had to lose 'The *Wagon Mound* (No. 2)', here is the story of a case I deserved to lose.

The *Sheaf Water*, a British cargo vessel, was outward bound in the Thames when she collided with an inward bound ship and then ran into a jetty. The evidence of the witnesses from the *Sheaf Water*, the ship with which we were concerned, suggested that her navigation was hampered by a third vessel which overtook her just before the collision. The result was a three-cornered action in the Admiralty Court, where Mr. Justice Langton brought in a judgment which put most of the blame on the *Sheaf Water*, the rest on the other colliding vessel, and none on the overtaking vessel.

I violently disagreed with this, and urged an appeal. Solicitors and counsel advised against it. The shipowners were reluctant. The ship's hull underwriters, who shared the insurance risk with the club, said that they would not contribute to the further legal costs if an appeal was taken. I was determined, and the lawyers were instructed to go ahead at the club's sole expense. We even brought in another leading counsel, Mr. Frederick Sellers, as well as Mr. R.F. Hayward. Counsel made a mighty effort, including explanations to the Court of Appeal of the effects of the varying areas of pressure in the water between two ships passing close to each other. When our case was completed, opposing counsel rose to reply. I saw Lord Wright, who was sitting in the Court of Appeal with two more junior judges, exchange a few words with them. He then said to our opponent, "We need not trouble you", and proceeded to deliver judgment against us. Our attack was considered so weak that we were defeated without the other side striking a blow. My hurt pride was hardly assuaged when we got the bill for the costs of both sides in the Court of Appeal.

Sir George Langton, when he was appointed to the Probate, Divorce and Admiralty Division of the Law Courts is reported to have said, "It seems to be my fate to stand in future with one foot in the sea and one in the sewer." But he carried a considerable reputation as a judge in Admiralty.

His acuteness was exhibited in another case concerning a ship we insured which collided with a trawler in the Humber. The hull pilot gave evidence, describing the weather at the time as 'moozy', a word which delighted the judge. Then our captain took the witness box, to describe the manoeuvres, the orders to the engines, and so on. He was examined and cross-examined, and there was a suspicion — no more — that the vital order 'full astern' had been given by the master, and not the pilot. This, however, was passed over, until the judge, leaning from the bench said, "Captain, didn't you think that your pilot was leaving it a little late?" There was silence for a moment, then the captain said, "Yes", and our carefully constructed case collapsed like a house of cards.

What makes a good judge? I do not believe it is possible to say. Some barristers who were an immense success at the bar have made very poor judges. Others, less distinguished, have made excellent judges. I recall acid comments in legal circles when one of today's judges was appointed. He was alleged to have been a political appointment by the government of the day. Within a few months he established a reputation for sound and unbiased judgment which has grown ever since.

Every now and then a particular judge seems to have his decisions reversed by higher courts far more often than is usual. I dare not point the finger at any judge now living, but forty years or so ago, Mr. Justice Atkinson had this reputation, deservedly or not. It was said that on one occasion counsel opened his speech to the Court of Appeal with the words: "My Lords, this is an appeal from a judgment by Mr. Justice Atkinson", and one of the judges intervened with the question, "Are there any other grounds for appeal?" I suspect, however, this is one of those hoary old stories which are trotted out every generation, and attached to any judge who seems appropriate.

I know some of today's judges, it is true. Others I have observed only from the public seats at the back of the court, or an unobtrusive client's seat at the solicitors' table. The same applies to the judges of yesterday.

When I took a Swiss lawyer to get a glimpse of an English court at work, we chanced to hear a plantiff examined before Lord Justice Lawrence, who became internationally known for his work on the Allied tribunal at Nuremberg which tried Goering, Hess and others for war crimes. The claimant was a former Czech national, a refugee from Nazism, and he was claiming damages for wrongful dismissal. He had been a commercial traveller selling paperback books, and claimed to have been making a very good income. When he was questioned about it, he got defensive, and said belligerently that he had to work very hard, and he was not damaging anyone in England by working harder than some people did. Lord Justice Lawrence explained with great kindness that no-one was suggesting this was so. "I am very glad", he said, "that you can come to this country when you are in trouble, and that by working hard in your new surroundings you can make a good living. I congratulate you." The back of the little man in the witness box straightened, and he went pink with pleasure. And my Swiss friend was much impressed.

Lord Denning must surely be one of the outstanding judges of recent years, whether he is regarded (as by some) as a constructive reformer or (as by others) as dangerously radical in his view of the law. The only time I saw him in court was when he was senior of the three judges in the Court of Appeal considering a dispute under a charter-party for the steamer *Ann Stathatos*. All three came firmly down against the shipowner, whose counsel, Ashton Roskill, rose and applied the usual form for leave to appeal to the House of Lords. As it happened, that very morning it had been announced that Lord Denning had been promoted (if that is the word) to sit as a judge in the House of Lords. He consulted his two colleagues, and replied to Roskill with a smile, "Yes. You may go. But, if you go, go quickly."

I assisted Mr. Michael Xylas, the owner of the *Alma*, with another charter-party dispute, which was so complicated compared to the moderate amount of money involved that the parties agreed on a simple procedure. No witnesses would be called, a statement of the facts agreed to by both parties would be put before the court, and only junior counsel would be employed. The case was heard by Mr. Justice Devlin, as he then was, and it was one of a number which foreshadowed his meteoric rise through the judiciary to the various national and international tasks he has undertaken since. Besides the questions of law, the dispute required intricate calculations on three different bases, one put forward by one side, and two put forward as alternative choices by the other. When the respective barristers had completed their arguments, the judge leaned back, gazed into the middle distance, and gave a precise analysis of the three alternatives, and his conclusions, without apparently checking his memory on a single detail. The whole thing was over before the court rose for lunch. We won, too.

One cannot help contrasting some of these urbane and conscientious gentlemen with a judge who handled one of our cases in one of the lesser South American republics. An action was started against a certain ship, which was not allowed to sail until twenty thousand dollars was deposited in court. I wrote some months later to enquire what progress had been made. The apologetic answer reported no progress. The judge had disappeared into the hills with the twenty thousand dollars.

We have to be ready to control legal proceedings in many countries. In one collision action in Brazil, the court reserved judgment in 1921, and it has not yet been given. The explanation must be that both sides thought they had lost, so that neither reminded the judge.

I had the responsibility for the first collision action ever to be fought in Mexico. A Canadian ship broke adrift in a hurricane in the port of Vera Cruz, and sank a Mexican naval vessel. The British consul there recommended a good lawyer. I asked him to act for the Canadian shipowner. The reply said: "I shall be delighted to act, but I must warn you that I have no experience in Admiralty law. On the other hand I do not know of any lawyer in Mexico who has. You will have to explain to me what legal principles and procedure should apply." We did this, with the help of London solicitors who did have experience in Admiralty law, and included notes on the usual approach to a defence of 'force majeure' in Latin countries. With this help, our candid friend fought and won the case (against the Mexican navy) up to and including the Supreme Court in Mexico City.

The first collision case fought in the courts of South Korea was only marginally my concern. I wrote one or two of the letters. We achieved a decision whereby our vessel was two-thirds and the other one-third to blame. This we considered very satisfactory, since the other vessel was at anchor at the time.

This naturally leads on to a case in the United States. I think that the ship was the *Pan Massachusetts*. Certainly, it arose in Savannah, Georgia, and the ship knocked over a railway bridge. In the lower court, we were successful in obtaining a finding that the bridge was alone to blame for the accident. It sounds ridiculous, but our lawyers were allowed to introduce evidence that the bridge was an obstruction to navigation. This was so well known that the U.S. government had for years been insisting that the railroad remove the bridge. The railroad, however, put it off and put it off, in an attempt to get a Federal grant for the cost of a new bridge.

So far, so good, but the railroad appealed. In the United States, there are a number of Circuit Courts of Appeal, each of which serves a certain area, usually a group of states. For this appeal a Texan judge headed the panel of judges, and I was very disappointed when they reversed the judgment. It was almost enough to prejudice me against Texas.

On the question of appeals, one of my cases produced a situation I have never heard of before or since. It occurred in Newfoundland and involved cargo damage on a small fast motorvessel which, I was told, had been used in prohibition days as a rum runner. This was when Newfoundland was an independent dominion, before it became a province of Canada. We won the case in the first court, and the judge certainly went to great pains, including a personal inspection of the holds and engine room of a sister ship. The claimants appealed. The Court of Appeal had to consist of three judges. There were only three in Newfoundland who were qualified to sit, so the judge in the first court had to be one of them. After legal argument, the three delivered judgment, the most junior giving his decision first. It was no surprise when he agreed heartily with the opinion he had already expressed in the court below. Unfortunately for us, the other two disagreed with him.

I have often wondered why this happened. Could it have been that the young judge bored his elder brethren so much with his enthusiasm that he made them negative about the whole thing?

This raises in an oblique way an interesting question. What qualities in a lawyer make him a successful advocate? I once asked a London solicitor why my respected senior partner Cyril Miller had been so successful in his twenty years at the bar. He looked very thoughtful, and then said, "There are many good lawyers at the bar. He was one, but the main thing was that the judges liked him." It must be a great art, when faced by an authority as near absolute as that of a judge, to know when to be blunt and when subtle, when to thrust hard and when to circumnavigate.

I heard a story recently of a young barrister now in practice. After he had carefully expounded a complicated point to the court, the judge said, "Might I suggest that your argument could be expressed as folows?" and he compressed it into one sentence. "My Lord", said the barrister, "that would be a travesty of my argument." My informant's comment was that the young man would go far, but it was a toss-up in which direction.

An older story was told me as true, but I have never asked Cyril Miller if it is. He was instructed in a case, and against him was W.L. McNair, later Mr. Justice McNair, and now retired. The judge was Lord Goddard, a very vigorous judge. When he delivered judgment, all his reasons were in favour of one party, but either by a slip of the tongue or a momentary lapse he pronounced the other party the winner. The court then rose for the weekend.

When the first confusion and consternation had subsided, Willie McNair and Cyril developed what can only be described as a conspiracy, but a conspiracy to effect justice, not to subvert it. They discussed the character and foibles of the judge, with which they were very familiar, and rehearsed their action carefully. Before the judge began his first case on Monday morning, Cyril Miller rose to make an application. "Yes, Mr. Miller, what is it?" "In the case your lordship decided on Friday, a small error seems to have arisen towards the end of the judgment. In fact, your lordship entered judgment in favour of the wrong party, and (with tremendous emphasis) my learned friend Mr. McNair says you cannot correct it." "What?" said the judge, his attention at once diverted from the error to the miscreant, "who says I can't correct the error?" McNair rose, put up one or two feeble arguments which were promptly overruled, and the matter was put right.

I hope it is a true story. It deserves to be.

The virtuosity of the barrister of today is remarkable. He can master a subject entirely new to him in a few days or weeks, with the help of his client and expert witnesses, and talk about it as if he has known it all his life. I went to see one barrister about a shipping matter, and as I was leaving he pointed to a pile of papers in the corner and said, "Those are the thalidomide cases." I'm told that most of these men have the trick of forgetting all the technicalities of each case, once it is finished. Then there is room in their minds for the technicalities of the next.

My main criticism is that they tend to go on too long, in their passion for exactitude and thoroughness. Here are two contrasting examples of court work. One was told to me by an Australian solicitor and, like the one above, it deserves to be true. The other happened not long after I arrived in the City.

The Australian case was admittedly a very major affair, but it still exhibits the dangers of over-elaboration. Leading counsel on one side made an opening speech which lasted for seventeen days. According to my informant, the judge had stopped listening long before the end of it, and was patiently waiting until he could give judgment which in due course he did — adversely. Appeal followed appeal until the dispute arrived before the Judicial Committee of the Privy Council. The then Lord Chancellor presided. Before the hearing, he informed the other four judges that one of the counsel engaged in the case was notoriously long-winded. He suggested, and they agreed to, a pact that none of them should interrupt or question this barrister, so that they at any rate would not be blamed for the length of the trial. But alas, human frailty even appears on the Bench, as, before the day was out, had been demonstrated many times. The long-winded counsel was gratified to see the Lord Chancellor making copious notes. What he was doing, as he listened, was to record every interruption by his colleagues, and when the court rose he fined them at the rate of half a crown a word. The Privy Council's judgment was also adverse. I would not suggest that it was a reaction against the gentleman criticised, but he was certainly making it more difficult for them to accept his arguments.

The other case was an English one. The National Steamship Company in London chartered a ship to Louis Dreyfus and Company to load a cargo homeward from South America to Europe. By the charter-party, Messrs. Dreyfus could use "the full reach and burthen of the vessel". Antique phrases such as this are relished by the City. They have been used for centuries, some of them, and everyone in the trade knows just what they mean. Or so they think. This ship, although a fairly standard type of cargo vessel, had accommodation for twelve passengers. The charterers wanted the right to sell passages for the voyage, and keep the passage money. The shipowners disagreed. They mutually decided to have a friendly action brought before the Commercial Court. There was a brief but vigorous argument before the judge, and the whole matter was decided, only four days after the action was commenced, and before the ship had completed loading.

The longest case I ever had to do with was before the American Courts for twenty-one years. I was responsible for the conduct of it throughout. It involved cargo damage, a type of claim so frequent in a P. and I. club's files that it is second only to personal injury. The case's origins were in November, 1940, when the tide of war was about to roll over Greece. The Greek Navy considered the Mediterranean route so dangerous that they ordered ships leaving Greek ports for western destinations to be diverted through the Suez Canal and round Africa. Four of them were in course of loading large quantities of tobacco for U.S.A. The Latakia type of leaf grown in Greece, Bulgaria and Turkey (as well, I suppose, as in Latakia) was popular for blending with Virginia tobacco in cigarettes, and the big companies wanted to be sure of their supplies. The four ships were allowed to go, but only by the southern route, and in the knowledge that tobacco was apt to heat if it was too long in a confined space.

This was amply proved. All four cargoes heated badly, and two of them actually caught fire. I dealt with two of the cases, the more troublesome being the *Ioannis P. Goulandris*. She had an unlucky voyage. First, nasty noises and vibration started coming from the stern of the ship when she was off the coast of Somaliland. She turned round and went back to Aden. There were repair facilities there, but no drydock. All the cargo in the aftermost hold had to be discharged ashore, to bring the stern tube opening above the water. The propellor and tailshaft were removed, and the lining of the stern tube was found to be damaged. After it was replaced, the cargo was reloaded and the ship went on her way, only to develop trouble with the condenser which converted seawater into fresh water for the boilers. She was again delayed for ten days at Durban for these repairs.

While she was crossing the Atlantic towards New York, the cargo began to heat; off Bermuda it caught fire, suffering damage estimated at over one million dollars. She was by then only a few days off New York, so that if the cargo owners and their insurers could show that the delay of thirty-three days at Aden and the further delay at Durban were due to causes for which the ship was responsible under the contract of carriage, it looked as if the shipowners would be paying a huge claim.

A blow-by-blow account of the ensuing litigation would be a book in itself, and probably a monumental bore. But a few unusual features may be touched on. Part of the delay was due to the other three cases being dealt with first, but this did not, as was hoped, help with the *Ioannis P. Goulandris*. Evidence was collected from no less than twelve countries. Affidavits from Greece and Bulgaria, both of which countries were under German occupation, were smuggled out through neutral Turkey. I had to go to the Trading with the Enemy Department to get permission for this. Later, John Monroe, the club's claims adviser in New York, came over to London, and he and I spent days questioning a Dutch surveyor who had carried out the detailed classification survey on the ship early in 1940. (This survey established that the ship was what the public calls by the old formula of 'A1 at Lloyd's'.) I became a considerable authority on ships' tailshafts and condensers.

The legal work was done by James E. Freehill who liked to describe himself as a 'trial lawyer'. Dawson Miller cnce described him as "a tough, but a likeable tough". I got to know him very well, and often quote some of his racy stories. Thickset, with a New York accent you could cut with a spoon, Jimmie loved a legal battle, and he certainly enjoyed this one. Yet he dutifully sought what chances he could for compromise, and reported them to us. At one point, we could have settled for $225,000. I wavered, but consulted with Dawson who unhesitatingly said no.

When the trial eventually arrived, Jimmie's defence tactics were typically unconventional. His first expert witness was the commodore (most senior) chief engineer of the United States Lines. He had probably never seen a tramp ship like the *Ioannis P. Goulandris* closer than half a mile, but his appearance in the witness box, covered with gold lace, to answer some general questions, was purely designed to impress the judge. He was followed by the shipowners' own superintendent engineer, a hard-bitten Welshman named Bill Richards who had mothered this and other ships for years and knew them like children. He told the judge, for example, just how many thousand miles the ship had covered without tailshaft trouble between the classification survey and the trouble off the Somali coast. Moreover, he was almost impervious to cross-examination, since a hearing aid reinforced his native Celtic stubbornness.

Enough of detail. When the dust finally settled in 1962, we had won the case for the shipowners. To lose it would have meant paying over two million dollars, including the interest on the damages. The legal costs came out at about $350,000.

Jimmie Freehill was one of many colourful characters I have known in the legal world. In London, one of the greatest was certainly Russell Stokes. He started practice as a solicitor in 1919, after leaving the army. Finding progress unsatisfactory in a firm identified with his family, he joined an active young man, E.S. Richards, who already had a good City practice, especially with the grain firms. Six weeks later, Richards went abroad on business for a period, leaving Russell in charge. He told me that when the first client came in with a shipping problem, he took copious notes, and then looked up 'demurrage' and various other words in a dictionary before he knew what the other man had been talking about. He went on to build up a huge practice, particularly in the shipping field. At one time, we in Miller's felt he knew more about the branches of law we dealt with than any solicitor or barrister in London. These included marine insurance, a subject which few lawyers study deeply, since actual litigation over it is rare. (Mr. Justice Donaldson, when he was at the bar, was one of the few who included this in his far wider field of study.) We first encountered Russell as an opponent, acting against shipowners. It was because he was so formidable against us that we took to instructing him to act on our side.

He is still, I hear, enjoying his retirement. I remember the many times I walked with him into the Temple, or faced him across his desk, a vast man, but with the fitness of a golfer who played down to handicap one, and a fine tennis player, too. A deep voice to match. A razor-sharp mind. Occasionally testy, but with enough humour, and a certain shyness which seemed quite unnecessary for a man of his ability and achievement. If I as his client was wrong, he told me so straight.

Many times I went to see him on cases with Sidney Fowler, when we shared a room. At a smaller table at right angles to us and to him would sit one of his two assistants, Bill Wilson and George Hardee, with a stack of reference books. Russell would expound: "The first case bearing on this point is . . ." and without removing his gaze from us across the table he would stretch out his left hand to George (or Bill). The book would be put into it, open at the appropriate page, and he would look down, and read out the passage. "The next case is . . .", and he would repeat the process. On the way back from one of these conferences, Sidney said with his usual irreverence, "You know, Frank, that drill with the books. That alone is worth the money."

One of the rare times I remember him astray on a point of law was when I took Michael Summerskill over to him, just after Michael left the bar to join T.R. Miller. It was such an urgent matter that he had no time to prepare. We explained the problem. He gave an off-the-cuff opinion. Then Michael asked (a little nervously to a man twice his age) whether he thought a certain precedent applied. He pondered a moment, and then, with an apparent rage which did not wholly mask a grin, threw down a book, saying, "Yes. But that's the last word. Not only do we have a barrister coming to a solicitor for an opinion, but he throws precedents at him, too."

He told me once of a case in which he had instructed Eustace Roskill when that judge was a Q.C. (Now Lord Justice Roskill, he has had, among other heavy tasks, the conduct of the long official enquiry into the question of a third airport for London, an enquiry wittily referred to by the *Guardian* as "the four site saga".) For some reason Russell called at chambers before Roskill had left for the Law Courts, to find him in a thoroughly depressed state of mind. He was sure the case was a loser. Would it not be better to settle it, even at that last minute? And so on. Russell, according to himself, told him not to be an ass. They had been over the thing very fully, and Roskill had written earlier a confident opinion on the case. The only thing still to do was for Roskill to go into court and prove his opinion right. Which that fine advocate duly did.

One of the many cases in which I was concerned and in which Eustace Roskill was instructed was a small claim put forward in the name of Mrs. Evgenia John Chandris, whose two sons operate the large group of family-owned vessels. It went as far as the Court of Appeal, where counsel's opening speech began something like this: "Your lordships may perhaps be wondering why you are called upon to consider a dispute over such a small sum of money, a sum which might in the circumstances be referred to as the widow's mite." He went on to explain that this was one of fifty similar cases, and its result would decide them all.

Maître Leopold Dor of Paris and Marseilles was a man whom anyone who knew him would regard as a ripe character. His flamboyant attitudes would sometimes lead you to underrate his keen mind and wide knowledge of law, of which his editorship of the international review *Le Droit Maritime Comparé* was only one indication. He enjoyed litigation, and also the good fees it brought him.

Once I was talking with him, and had just agreed his fee with a promptness which obviously made him wonder if he had set it too low, when the telephone rang. It was Colin Mitchell, the head of the Admiralty department of a large firm of City solicitors. Was Maître Dor there? Could he speak to him? I handed the instrument across the desk. As occasionally happens, I could hear both sides of the conversation. Mitchell was acting for a ship in trouble in Algerian waters. The French navy was making a salvage claim, and said that Dor was acting for them. "No", shouted Dor into the mouthpiece, "I am not acting for the French navy. They are only saying that to frighten you. Do not be frightened by them. I will take your case. Just tell me the facts." How could Mitchell refuse?

Dor once gave me a splendid lunch in London, and I had to drop him somewhere on my way back to the office by taxi. He had an English wife, and prided himself on knowing London thoroughly. He kept sliding back the window behind the driver and calling out: "That's not the way." "It's quicker if you turn right here." "Why don't you go along the Embankment?" The driver's neck got redder and redder. After we had dropped Dor, and went on, the driver slid open the window again and said in the broadest cockney: "Excitable old gent, that." I agreed. "Some kind of furriner, ain't 'e?" I said yes, he was a celebrated French lawyer. "Oh" (pause) "I fought 'e must be a celebrated London taxi-driver." To do Dor justice, I think he would have enjoyed that.

As a lawyer, he can best be shown by a comparatively small thing, a written opinion. A very serious claim arose out of a collision off the Belgian coast. The government were insisting that the wreck of the Swedish ship (the *Nippon*) should be removed by her owners. Belgian lawyers gave definite opinions that the shipowners must accept this ruling. I mentioned it casually to Maître Dor. He said, "Did you know I was also a member of the Belgian bar? French and Belgian advocates have given each other the privilege to plead before each other's courts since the war of 1914-18. Would you like me to study the point?" I gladly assented. He wrote a twenty-four page analysis of the Belgian and international law which convinced the Belgian lawyers into reversing their opinion and their government into withdrawing the claim.

Angary is a word known by few, and not even by all lawyers. But I once initiated an action based on angary, which is the right of a belligerent to seize and use the property of neutrals, paying reasonable compensation. It was 1941 or 1942. In those days very few ships flew what we now call flags of convenience, flags other than that of their owner's country. Those that did were in a privileged position. Ships owned by the countries at war were requisitioned by their governments and employed at a bread and butter rate of hire. The few 'free' ships could bargain for all they could get.

Shipping was scarce. A small steamer, Greek-owned but under the Panama flag, was making good profits when she called at a port in what was then Palestine. The authorities there decided to exercise their right of angary. They took over the ship, loaded her with petrol in tins, and sent her to Tobruk, where she was promptly sunk. The lamentations of the shipowner were loud and long, and the defence club had to help him recover proper compensation from the Palestine government. So I had to study this little-known pocket of international law.

At this time, Palestine was administered by Britain under a mandate from the League of Nations. The legal situation was curious. Statutes (known as ordinances) enacted by the mandatory government came first in authority. For matters not covered by these, English common law ranked next, if I remember rightly. If this was not enough, the lawyers had to go back in history, and apply the legal principles of the Ottoman Empire. I believe it is still more or less like that today, except that laws enacted by the new state of Israel have moved into the position of first in authority before all the rest. Anyway, an action was brought in Jerusalem, claiming the value of the ship, plus something for the few days she had been used after the seizure, and a reasonable recovery was made.

Another case I handled for the United Kingdom defence club is sometimes reported as "Adamastos Shipping versus Anglo-Saxon Petroleum Company", and sometimes by the name of the ship, the *Saxonstar*. The facts were involved, and the law more involved, but two factors in it stand out in my mind.

It started as an arbitration, and the arbitrator Mr. John Megaw (now a judge) gave an award against the shipowners. His conclusions of law were challenged in the Commercial Court, where the judge again decided against the shipowners. In the Court of Appeal, all three judges were against, but we went on to the House of Lords, who decided in favour of the shipowners by three to two. Seven judges (if we include the arbitrator) had decided one way, and three the other, but they were the vital three. And to my extreme pleasure they decided the case in the way I predicted at the start of the case.

The key issue, legally, was the proper construction of a charterparty for the use of the ship for three years. Certain provisions had been added to the printed form of contract by an attached clause. By an error, this clause began, "This bill of lading shall have effect . . ." instead of "This charterparty shall have effect . . .". One party argued that as it was not a bill of lading, the clause was nonsense and should be disregarded. The other said the intention was clear, if the words were not. There were other issues, but this was the main point.

In the House of Lords, the then Lord Chancellor, Lord Simonds, gave judgment first. He argued forcibly that commercial documents should be looked at from a commercial angle, in a broad way, and not necessarily with the lawyer's passion for exactitude. The next two judgments were adverse to the shipowner, but the fourth and fifth followed the Lord Chancellor. I heard the judgments delivered, and went to congratulate our leading counsel, Ashton Roskill. He showed me a handwritten note he had just received. It said, "Congratulations on your speeches, which were amongst the best I have heard, especially in reply. You must have had a breathless morning. Simonds."

I have left this case until the end of the chapter, because there is something in it which illustrates what I feel about the law, although it is hard to define. Perhaps it is the search for justice or at the very least for order. (Lord Simonds' comments on how to construe a commercial document must have been quoted hundreds of times since.) Perhaps it is the search for truth.

12

Arbitration

Disputes can be settled in a third way that is neither negotiation or litigation, viz: arbitration. There are two salient differences between this and a formal lawsuit. First, the parties do not have to accept whatever judge is assigned to the case. They choose their own arbitrator or arbitrators instead. Most commonly, each party appoints an arbitrator, and the two arbitrators agree on an umpire. The second is that the proceedings are private.

These two things make arbitration attractive to the business world, which is not anxious to have its troubles publicised. Moreover, in a technical dispute, it may be much better to have it adjudged by someone who knows the commercial background. London is the great centre for arbitrations, especially for the shipping industry.

Fairly early in my business career, I got involved in arbitrations. There seemed to be a flood of them. I had to learn how to appoint an arbitrator, how to instruct him, and sometimes how to prepare the case to put before the arbitrators.

It is impossible to overrate the help I was given in this by two well-known arbitrators of that day. One was W.H. Vernall, whose office happened to adjoin ours in the Baltic Exchange Building. His office boy, whose many duties included typing out the boss's awards, was Clifford Clark, later president of the Institute of Arbitrators and chairman of the London Maritime Arbitrators' Association.

The other was H.C. Brewer, later Sir Henry and several times chairman of the Baltic Exchange. In his basement office in the same building he already had 1,800 awards filed, showing him as arbitrator or umpire, and he went on arbitrating for another twenty-five years after that. He was a considerable figure, in every sense of the word, yet he would always make time for a helpful chat, usually surrounded by his imposing array of files.

And what is a commercial arbitration like? This depends on the parties. At one extreme it can be simplified to the laying of correspondence and other documents before a single arbitrator, with a request that he decide who pays how much to whom. At the other extreme, you can have a 'full-dress' arbitration, where there are three arbitrators, solicitors, counsel, properly drawn pleadings, and all the other trappings necessary for a court action. This has only one procedural advantage over a court action — privacy; with the disadvantage that the parties must pay the arbitrators, whereas the judge is paid by the State.

I have never considered myself suitable to be an arbitrator, and the few cases in which I did agree to act were decided on documents alone.

The first occasion was when a Greek shipowner complained that he had been overcharged by a British liner company which had acted as his agent at a port in Asia. I had to agree that there had been an overcharge. When I met in the Axe the liner man who was on the losing end, I was surprised to find him jubilant. It had given him the chance he had wanted for some time to send a stiff disciplinary letter to the particular branch in Asia which had caused the trouble, and he felt that this was worth the monetary loss.

Another occasion involved a triple collision, rare as such incidents are. I reluctantly accepted the responsibility of allocating blame among the three ships. It was a 'dragging' case, where three ships were at anchor off Staten Island, New York. Two of them dragged their anchors, colliding with each other and with the third. I apportioned the blame 60 per cent, 30 per cent and 10 per cent respectively. The owner of the ship to leeward was most upset. Why should he accept even part of the blame? I pointed out that in the statement of the Chief Officer in charge (the Master being ashore) it was recorded that he saw the ships drifting down on him, took no action, and went below for his lunch. Even if there was no time to raise steam on the engines, he might have lessened the collision by letting out his anchor chains at the right moment, or putting out more fenders.

One of my early attendances at an arbitration included a memorable incident. A ship had been sold by one Greek owner to another, the price being paid partly in sterling and partly in dollars. The dispute arose over the rate of exchange to apply between the two currencies. It was a fairly informal arbitration with Henry North Lewis the solicitor as umpire,

H.C. Brewer and, I think, F.C. Lohden as arbitrators. The parties were represented by solicitors, in our case the formidable figure of Russell Stokes. The buyer of the ship wanted to be present, and brought his accountant with him. The war had begun by then, and Russell called as a witness a bank manager who explained how the exchange control worked. In the middle of his evidence, the Greek accountant suddenly broke in, "But that is not how we work. The way we go about it is quite different . . ." Russell Stokes drove his elbow into my ribs and muttered savagely out of the corner of his mouth, "Shut him up". I dug into the arm of the shipowner and said quietly but just as forcefully, "Shut him up". The shipowner snapped out something in Greek which stopped the accountant in the middle of a word. "What a pity", sighed North Lewis, "I was so interested". I never enquired what the man was trying to say. Was it a way of evading exchange control, or was it a pure misunderstanding?

It was not unusual in commercial arbitrations then to have a solicitor to present arguments. Counsel were not employed so frequently as now, but often a barrister was agreed upon as umpire. I suppose the three legal umpires most frequently called upon in shipping cases in the 1930s were Patrick Devlin, Cyril Miller and Sir Robert Aske. Aske, a Liberal member of parliament, was a man of whom it could fairly be said that he was greatly loved. Only a few weeks before he died, well over 80 years of age, he was on his feet for three days straight off arguing a difficult point of jurisdiction before the Court of Appeal. I went to a conference with him once, which he ended by saying, "I am very sorry, but I cannot see a single reason for taking this to court. Is there much money involved?" £23,000, we told him. "Well, that's a reason," he said with a twinkle.

He was sole arbitrator in a dispute between Moss Hutchison Line and the Ministry of Supply, Timber Control, shortly after the war, over a question of mysterious short deliveries of railway sleepers carried from France to the United Kingdom. Junior counsel (as they then were) Messrs. Eustace Roskill and John Donaldson, did all they could in examination and cross-examination to get information from the master of one of the ships on the circumstances surrounding the shipments. Then, in a few questions, Sir Robert extracted further facts which gave a far clearer picture, and showed that the cargo could not have been lost while in the ship's custody.

He was of the same family, and perhaps a direct descendant, of that Robert Aske of Yorkshire who led the Pilgrimage of Grace, the ill-fated attempt to resist Henry VIII's oppression of the Church and its monasteries. Henry's venal minister, Thomas Cromwell, described it as "the most dangerous rebellion". It was put down with great cruelty, and that sixteenth-century Robert Aske ended his days in the Tower. One could imagine his twentieth-century namesake in the same setting. For all his ruddy face, white eyebrows, gentle manners and twinkling smile, there was a simple directness about him which would take some stopping.

Walking away from an arbitration held in that dingy Arbitration Room A in the Baltic Exchange Building, after Freddie Lohden had struggled unsuccessfully to make something of a hopeless argument, Bob took my arm in St. Mary Axe. "What a pity", he said, "that they couldn't give the old gentleman a better case to argue." The fact that the "old gentleman" was probably ten years younger than Aske himself was irrelevant to his youthful spirit.

He also presided on an occasion which for more than one reason I remember very clearly. The hearing was somewhere in the Temple. The other arbitrators were T.B. McNabb and H.C. Brewer, shipbrokers, and the parties were represented by solicitors. Ours was T.S. Wilding. (This was before he resigned his partnership in William A. Crump & Son to become a P. & I. club manager with A. Bilbrough & Co.) He was a tall thin figure, elegantly turned out, and with a hawk-like profile. I found him a little daunting.

The case concerned a ship which had been damaged by 'ranging', bumping against the quay at which she had to load, under the action of wind and waves. Wilding opened the case, and after a little said to the three arbitrators, "As you know, gentlemen, the quays at Constanza run north and south." McNabb intervened and said, "Surely not. The quays at Constanza run east and west." "Don't be stupid, Tommy", said Brewer, easily roused, "I've been to Constanza. I've seen the quays. They run north and south." "Rubbish, Bung", replied McNabb, using the nickname universally adopted by his co-arbitrator's friends on the Baltic, "I've been to Constanza, too. I'll lay you an even fiver they run east and west." Sir Robert restored peace, and the matter proceeded in a more normal manner.

Then suddenly Tom Wilding erupted. He threw his papers down on the table and poured out a torrent of words. "Sir

Robert, I can't go on. This is ridiculous. I can't present my case properly, in the way it should be done. My client has hopelessly prejudiced my position and his own. Before I was instructed, he agreed that no witnesses would be called. I don't know what to do. I must ask for an adjournment." I felt a complete fool, and wished the floor would open to hide me. Wilding had said nothing to me of this before.

Aske said courteously he was sorry Mr. Wilding felt like that. They all agreed to an adjournment for a day or two. As Wilding and I left, I nervously said I was sorry if I had made it difficult for him. He hooted with laughter. "Didn't you realise?" he asked, "That was pure play-acting, and everyone there knew it, except you. I simply wanted a little time in which to discuss a compromise." The arbitrators did not meet again after the adjournment, as by then the case had been settled fifty-fifty.

Sir Henry Brewer figures again in another memory-picture, in this case as umpire, sitting with a Buddha-like dignity on a very interesting charter-party dispute. The ship in question was chartered by a French liner company for a voyage from one or more ports in "U.K./Continent" to Madagascar. The port of destination sticks in my mind, because of the freak effect of a common error, the failure to delete a word or phrase in a printed form when it does not apply. This contract insisted that the voyage should end at an ice-free port in Madagascar. No prizes are offered for guessing the word which should have been struck out. There was also a clause which allowed the charterers to keep the ship for the return trip at the same monthly payment for hire, provided they declared their intention of doing so before the ship left her last loading port on the Continent. No Baltic Exchange member needs to be told that such an option can be valuable for a charterer, especially if the market for ships rises, while if the market sags, they could hire another ship at a lower rate, provided there is one in the area at the time.

The ship loaded at two or three ports in, I think, Belgium and France, completing at Tarragona, on the Mediterranean coast of Spain. At about the time she was due at Tarragona, charterers claimed the right to the return voyage. The shipowners protested. "The Continent", they said, was a technical expression in chartering that meant a range of ports on the northern and western coasts of Europe, but did not extend into the Mediterranean. Charterers were too late to exercise their option. And, as both parties knew, the market had improved. A ship free for employment at the time discharge of the outward cargo would be completed in Madagascar could expect to earn some £6,000 more for a homeward voyage than she would earn under the charter.

This is the sort of situation which can produce a violent dispute if the parties are ruthless and difficult. The ship-owners may decline to let the ship load, and contract her for a different voyage; the charterers may then get a court to arrest the ship on a claim for damages; and so on. These shipowners were however a Greek firm long established in London and with a reputation as good as that of these very good charterers. They agreed that the ship could do the homeward voyage, without prejudice to an arbitration as to whether charterers had made a technical breach of contract by their late declaration. If the arbitrators decided in the shipowners' favour, they would be paid the extra £6,000.

So we found ourselves before 'Bung' Brewer and his co-arbitrators, to present what we felt was a very straight-forward case. As it was being unrolled, as it were, before him, Sir Henry suddenly intervened. "Do I understand", he asked, "that you are arguing that these words have a special meaning by a custom of the trade?" We agreed. "Then I presume you intend to call evidence to prove the custom." Well, no, we had assumed that this would not be necessary when the arbitrators were all experienced Baltic brokers. Sir Henry then proceeded to point out that in law it is not permitted to plead a custom of the trade without offering proof of it, and several points must be established. Among them, the alleged custom must be unambiguous, and generally accepted. He would allow us an adjournment of twenty-four hours to give us an opportunity to call evidence on the point.

Our solicitor was that same Bill Wilson who used to sit at Russell Stokes' elbow. He and I looked at each other in some consternation, but we set to work at once. We scurried from office to office, from interview to interview, and when the twenty-four hours expired we presented five witnesses, all of great experience, to give their understanding of the cus-tomary meaning of 'Continent' in charterparties. One of them was Theodore Layman, who had been a member of the Baltic Exchange for no less than sixty years. Another was Jack Dean who, besides being an experienced broker, taught shipping subjects to young men studying for the examina-tions of the Institute of Chartered Shipbrokers. Brewer gave them a testing time. Their evidence was generally sound and consistent with each other, but they could not be as precise as we and the shipowners had hoped. In some trades, 'Continent' meant a range of ports from Hamburg to Le Havre. In others, it was Hamburg to Bordeaux, or even to Gibraltar. They agreed that the expression never included Scandinavia at one end, or the Mediterranean at the other. But they also had to agree that it was usual to state the range precisely, as for example "Continent, Havre/Hamburg range", although this was sometimes omitted. When Sir Henry gave his award, he dealt sternly with the "alleged custom". It was held to be void for uncertainty. But I do not think the shipowners were greatly put out at not getting the extra £6,000.

A small matter illustrated how effective and simple arbitration can be. It involved a vessel loading at an anchorage off Cyprus. A storm came up, and she had to put out to sea very suddenly and lie off the land for a couple of days, with seventy shore workers on board. The shipowners wanted to recover the expenses and delay from the charterers, on the basis that they had ordered the ship to load at an unsafe place. The parties agreed that the documents should be submitted with only a written argument to A.M. Conybear, at that time the best-known maritime arbitrator in London. In a few days and with no expense except for his fee, he decided that the claim failed. There was no evidence that the ship was actually in danger.

The quickest decision I ever experienced was also over a question of the safety of a port. Here, the ship was bound for a port in Eastern Nigeria just after the outbreak of the civil war. The shipowners said it was not safe; the charterers, who wanted the cargo, said it was safe. Each side appointed an arbitrator, and the facts were quickly put before them as a preliminary point. The evidence included the daily reports from *The Times* and *Lloyd's List*. The two arbitrators, R.A. Clyde and Clifford Clark, agreed on an interim award. Ships had already been endangered. The port was not safe. The vessel was therefore diverted. The award was given one day after the arbitrators were appointed.

It is the duty of two arbitrators to issue an agreed award, if they can. In fact, they should not appoint an umpire until after they have disagreed. Naturally, it is not easy for an arbitrator who has been appointed by one party to join forthwith in making a decision in favour of the other party. The fact that this is quite often done is an indication of the real independence and sense of justice of arbitrators.

A court of arbitration is one of Her Majesty's courts, even though its proceedings are private and may be informal. The same law, the same principles prevail. I have written of maritime arbitrations, especially on the subjects which concern the clubs, but the same system is used in many other fields. Lloyd's has an internationally famous procedure for assessing rewards for salvage of ships at sea. The grain trade arbitrates on allowances for condition of grain cargoes. Many of the professions have arbitration provisions in their contracts of service. The same is the case in the rules of P. and I. clubs and other mutual clubs, in case questions arise between the club and one of its members.

New York also has a well-developed system of arbitration which is much employed in the maritime field. The U.S. statute which governs it differs in one important point from England's Arbitration Act 1950. In England, arbitrators must follow legal precedents set by the courts, and their decisions on points of law may be the subject of appeal to the courts, unlike questions of fact, on which the arbitrators' decision is final. In America, however, precedents need not be followed and every award is final, unless an aggrieved party can show bias or misconduct on the part of the arbitrators. With no system of precedents to follow, it is possible for two identical disputes to be decided opposite ways. I handled one New York arbitration where the arbitrator I appointed to represent the shipowner was a lawyer, John Crandall, and the other two were 'laymen', that is to say commercial men from shipping offices. The award was two to one against the shipowner. Mr. Crandall explained in detail why he thought his view was right, and referred to the fact that an authority as high as the Circuit Court of Appeals had given judgment to that effect. The other two signed a decision to the contrary, without reasons. When asked, off the record, why they did it, all they would say was, "We never liked that decision of the Appeal Court." One of our New York lawyers, when asked for an opinion on the prospects of an arbitration, always used to start: "It is impossible to predict what New York arbitrators will decide. Subject to that, we would advise as follows." Notwithstanding this, many sound and sensible awards emanate from New York, and the standard of care and consideration given is high.

Moscow also has a highly developed system for maritime arbitrations, capable of dealing with collision cases, cargo claims, salvage, and more arcane subjects such as general average. I can remember when this was first introduced, somewhere about 1930. Shipowners of other countries were very hostile to it, doubtless as a reflection of the political feelings of the time. Our impressions of Moscow decisions in early years were not favourable. One severe critic said he could not understand how they arrived at their decisions at all, unless perhaps the small cases were decided in favour of the foreigner, and the big ones in favour of the Russian interests! In recent years the position has been very different. The Moscow Arbitration Commission has built up a considerable reputation for integrity and expertise. All its decisions are based on Russian Law, and they sometimes surprise those unfamiliar with that law. There is, however, strong evidence that they follow their own principles strictly. One case I handled was the subject of legal proceedings both in Russia and in another country which need not be named. The proceedings in that country were very unconvincing and appeared to be biased. Those in Russia were exactly investigated and carefully argued, and the findings seemed to me to be eminently fair.

The People's Republic of China is the latest country with maritime interests to arrange local arbitration of claims. At the time of writing, shipowners of other countries are reluctant, as they are unfamiliar with the principles which will be applied. But doubtless more and more cases will go to arbitration in Peking (China is reported to have bought thirty ships in 1972), and we must hope that an international reputation will soon be established for fair and well-informed decisions.

Naturally, I cannot avoid a preference for London arbitration against all others. As an example of the standing it has internationally, I remember a Swiss shipowner coming to me for help with an arbitration in a claim under a contract with his own government. (Switzerland now has a thriving merchant marine, and its own college for training officers.) I pointed out that there was no clause in the contract providing for arbitration of disputes. "We know that," he replied, "but now a dispute has arisen, we have both agreed on arbitration in London."

Another indication can be seen in the annual dinners of the London Maritime Arbitrators Association. These are great occasions, when those who accept appointment as arbitrators mingle with solicitors, barristers, judges and even a few of the shipowners and others who produce the disputes which need deciding. It is an impressive sight but also a gay one. The company is good, and the after-dinner speeches far better than is normal. I remember Sir John Donaldson replying to the toast of 'The Guests' just after he was made a judge. With great humour he compared his life and surroundings in his new job with his experiences as counsel or arbitrator on many occasions in the City. He even alleged that the lunches he used to have during arbitrations were much better. One cannot re-create such an evanescent thing as an after-dinner speech, but I can remember my sides aching with laughter at his mock description of what a judge has to suffer.

An arbitrator may be almost anyone, provided he is thought capable of analysis and judgment. Some of the best are some of the busiest of men. The financial rewards are slight and the burden great, but there always seem to be men who will take it on, for the sake of their friends and of the business community as a whole.

13

Legislation

The making of laws is not a matter just for politicians, but for all people. That is my conviction as a result of nearly fifty years of business life.

We tend to take the law for granted, but it is worth imagining what society would be like without it. There would be no rules. Strength alone would decide. There would be no property, personal or corporate, except what could be taken or defended against all comers. There would be no recognised obligations to spouses, to families, or to anyone.

Law of some kind must have come very early to mankind, before herding, houses, or the use of fire. As soon as some group of people set up some right as superior to one person's demands, law existed. It regulated relationships.

One person on a desert island needs no laws. He regulates his own life. A community must have laws. It is no chance that we speak of 'law and order' in one breath. And, when millions of people are grouped together in a nation or in a city, there is no way in which they can live in unity and peace without laws which are either willingly accepted or enforced.

We all realise, though perhaps rather dimly, how the laws of the land affect what we do and don't do, every day of our lives. We grumble about them. At least, I do. But we rarely do what we should do to see that we get the right laws. I say this despite the fact that the firm with which I have spent my days has had a good deal to do with law-making, and I've even had some hand in it myself. Yet none of us has been in any significant sense a politician. We are not the governors but the governed, the taxpayers, the people who have to obey the laws.

The first time I began to realise what could and should be done was in 1927, although in fact evidence of it was under my nose earlier. Victor Lofts and I in the filing room had to put away in the appropriate file the correspondence and lawyers' bills relating to a new American law, the Long-shoremen's and Harbor Workers' Compensation Act. It is curious how stupidly bizarre details stick in one's mind. We filed one long cablegram on this subject from America, in which the telegraph operator misspelt the same word over and over again as 'longshortmen'. But of course a long-shoreman is an American term for a docker – another example of what Bernard Shaw called two nations divided by a common language.

The thing which made Victor and me discuss this matter with some vigour was that the English P. and I. clubs had paid lawyers to 'lobby' members of the U.S. Congress to persuade them to pass this act. We wondered if this was a proper thing at all. The idea of pressure groups has a nasty taste in an English mouth. To use them in another country was even more distasteful. I forget how we resolved the problem. Possibly it was just by reading all the relevant correspondence, and then arguing it out between the two of us. This was not an unusual occupation. Anyway, we came (or I did) to the firm conclusion that in such a matter it was the motive that mattered, not the method, provided of course the method was legal. In those days, as now, anyone lobbying congressmen or senators in Washington on behalf of interests outside America had to disclose who their principals were, and this had been done.

The Act was quite openly promoted by a group of British insurance associations because they thought it in the general interest as well as in their own. Until it was passed, a longshoreman injured at his work of loading and unloading ships might get some payment in respect of his injuries, or he might not. If he could show that the accident was the fault of his employer, or of someone else such as the shipowner, he could claim damages, if necessary through the courts. If he could not show this, he got nothing at all, and there was almost nothing in the way of what we now call 'welfare state' arrangements to ease suffering. The result was a flood of lawsuits of a speculative nature, with men taking a long shot at proving damages against someone. Certain lawyers special-ised in such suits. Some of them who would go to great lengths to solicit from injured men the right to sue on their behalf, were and are called 'ambulance-chasers'. Juries were notoriously favourable towards claims by badly injured men, who were often given verdicts on the flimsiest of evidence. Doctors were also over-sympathetic when giving evidence, and occasionally even dishonest. At about that time a San Francisco longshoreman was awarded $30,000 (a lot in those days) when a doctor swore that he was totally and permanently incapacitated from working. A year later he was injured working on another ship, and received an award for temporary incapacity.

The P. and I. clubs felt that if all men injured working on the docks were guaranteed some income whilst unable to work, however the accident came to happen, this would be a big check on the speculative and even fraudulent lawsuits. It might even reduce the total amount of the claims. This was unlikely, as far more claims would be paid, but at least the money would be more equitably distributed. It would not gravitate so much towards the most litigious claimants. or those with the most active or unscrupulous lawyers. The law was passed, and men became entitled to two-thirds wages whilst disabled, and other benefits. The general view was that the undesirable lawsuits did diminish, at least to some extent.

We therefore found that there had been a valuable social advance, as well as a move towards justice on the question of claims, which concerned the club financially. I was to find that this was typical of this sort of action. The aim was to help in an orderly progress towards a juster world. The clubs did not make a great crusade out of it, but when there was a chance to use their influence in that direction, use it they did. It may not have been quite so definite as that. Sometimes it may have been more a matter of protecting the club's business interests, but this was always done with an eye in the direction of responsibility towards the shipping industry as a whole and the general interest of the community.

Even before 1924 the P. and I. clubs had taken part in promoting the Hague Rules, a code internationally agreed between merchants, shipowners and insurers with the intention of ending the continual bickering regarding responsibility for loss or damage to cargo. The rules stated with some clarity what the shipowners should and should not pay for. They became law in the United Kingdom with effect from 1st January 1925, and within the next year or so throughout the British Commonwealth and Empire, a very extensive chain of territories in those days. Some other countries acted with equal swiftness, but the United States did not pass the rules into law until 1936, and, in the years between, the clubs had spent a good deal of money in pushing the idea there.

Similar action was taken in Argentina later. It is probably fair to say that the issues were not fully understood there until the clubs sent a distinguished lawyer, a member of the Spanish bar and of the English, to Buenos Aires for a period. One can well imagine that explanations in elegant Castilian Spanish would be far more effective than anything an Englishman might say.

My personal involvement in law-making began during the war. One of the many unusual side-developments of the war was that Canada suddenly became an important maritime power. The almost desperate need for merchant ships resulted in the Canadians building and operating, in addition to the few pre-war ships and a few seized as prizes from the enemy, a fleet of 170 ships. Most of them were of three standard types, and all of them were insured with us. It then transpired that Canada, a country mainly concerned with her land resources, had a gap in her legal provision for the needs of seamen. The different provinces all had Workmen's Compensation Acts (rather like the U.S. Longshoremen's Act), but they applied only to accidents occurring on land or within territorial waters. Thus, when a one-eyed seaman on a Canadian ship lost his remaining eye in an accident in Trinidad, all he got was medical assistance and his fare home — no compensation at all. Worse still, an ocean-going tug disappeared with all her crew on a voyage from Montreal to Halifax. The families could not prove a right to compensation, as they could not show that the men lost their lives in territorial waters.

It was hardly possible to follow the same tactics as we did in Washington over the longshoremen. There was a war on, and neither the legislators in Ottawa nor we in London had time to deal with things in that way. I got Dawson Miller's approval to a simple programme. In the cases referred to above and in others which followed, we made it plain that the shipowners were not liable to pay anything, but nevertheless paid gratuitously the bulk of what would have been due if the appropriate compensation act applied. At the same time, I complained bitterly to any Canadian body involved in each case regarding the injustice and uncertainty which prevailed, and pointed out how wrong it was for a highly developed country not to make legal provision for its nationals. After a series of these pinpricks, we had an official approach made to us through the Canadian Shipowners' Association. They said that their government was considering new legislation to deal with the point, but the government wanted to know if it would affect the cost of insurance. I replied that no increase would be made in the first year, and afterwards the increase would only represent the actual cost of the new liabilities. Legislation was enacted, and Canadian seamen thereafter received compensation for injury on the high seas, as well as in coastal waters.

Over the last twenty-five years two of my partners have worked steadily for a sane and constructive development of law throughout the maritime field. Much of this has been through the British Maritime Law Association and the Comite Maritime International, of which the British association is one of the constituent bodies. These are privately organised bodies representing a wide range of business interests, and in Britain and some other countries some of the judges take an active part. Broadly, they discuss and investigate legal issues, and do preparatory work for new laws. The international consideration at government level of possible laws is done by diplomatic conferences and sometimes by different agencies of the United Nations, whereas enactment of laws is of course a question for the sovereign governments concerned. To these international affairs, British government delegations often take one or more P. and I. club managers as advisers on the technical questions involved. To varying degrees, therefore, they have the chance to contribute to new developments every year.

Oil pollution is the field of maritime law-making most in the public eye in recent years. My colleagues have been deeply engaged in this in various ways. Apart from assisting our own government, they have travelled several times to Washington and Ottawa, by request, to give evidence to Senate, Congressional and Parliamentary Committees considering new legislation. The problem throughout has been to make laws which are strong enough to prevent the abuses and restrain their effect on the environment, but not so strong as to be unworkable. There was a real prospect at one time of some laws being absurdly harsh. One draft would have made the owner of a ship from which oil escaped liable without limit for the consequences, whatever the cause of the pollution. This would have included leaks due to damage to an anchored oil-tanker by another vessel running into her, or war damage, or other accidents over which the shipowner would have no means of control. And no shipowner can obtain unlimited insurance against such risks. One state in the

U.S.A. enacted a local law which was so extreme that the Supreme Court ruled that it was unconstitutional.

But this is only one of many fields. I myself had a certain hand in shaping a particular law recently. In the last months of the first Wilson Government, a bill was introduced to make it compulsory for every employer to insure his liabilities towards his employees for injuries at work. The first draft was so unsatisfactory that it would, for example, have forced a doctor who used his wife as his receptionist to insure his possible liability towards her. It would also interfere with the well-established practices in the shipping industry as regards seamen and port employees, an aspect which concerned us directly. I found out which officials in which government department were dealing with the matter. They were good enough to come down to St. Mary Axe to discuss it on more than one occasion. Not all of our ideas were accepted, but most of them were reflected in the greatly improved version of the law which was ultimately passed by Parliament. The whole operation was a most agreeable one, and I feel confident it gave the civil servants a better understanding of the City and its ways. Certainly, it was good for us to learn more of their problems, and to do what we could to help to solve them.

This exercise renewed my conviction that the man in the street should take much more interest in what laws are made. It is folly to leave it entirely to the politicians, and then to criticize what they do. In a democracy like Britain, every citizen has access to 'the corridors of power' through his member of parliament. In addition, it is both a right and a duty that matters be brought to the attention of the ministers, politicians and civil servants specially involved in an issue, by anyone who has information or views which should be helpful.

Towards the end of 1972, Mr. Rajmohan Gandhi, grandson of Mahatma Gandhi and editor-in-chief of the Bombay news magazine, *Himmat*, was in London and made an important speech to a large public meeting. In the course of it he referred to the discussions which had been going on between the Government, the Confederation of British Industry, and the Trades Union Congress. He noted the disappointment in Britain because no agreement was reached, but said that in Asia this disappointment was completely outweighed by the fact that the conference had taken place at all. It seemed to people in Asia (including him) a marvellous thing that such powerful organisations, who often have divergent views, should sit down together to debate what are the right economic policies for the country as a whole.

In theory at least, Britain is governed by Her Majesty's Government, assisted, challenged and stimulated by Her Majesty's Opposition. There is a third party which should take a much more positive part — Her Majesty's subjects.

14

Early Journeys

In Chapter 4 I said of the new ingredient which entered my life in 1933 that it affected everything I did thereafter. One difference was that I often initiated a course of action earlier than might otherwise have occurred, or started something which would otherwise not have happened at all.

My father never left England in his eighty-odd years of life. His idea of a holiday was a stay at Guildford, Shanklin, Ramsgate or some equally distant and exotic area. In early life, I did not see myself as a likely traveller overseas, either for business or pleasure.

My first moves of this kind were directly to do with Moral Re-Armament. In 1937 my wife and I went with a British group of 100 to an international gathering in Utrecht.

In 1946 we went to Switzerland, for the opening conference at Caux. A large disused hotel had been acquired there by Swiss who saw Europe's need not merely for material and financial rehabilitation but also for moral and spiritual rehabilitation. They saw Moral Re-Armament as the means whereby Switzerland (which had been spared most of the horrors of war) could make a great international contribution. Caux, the village on the mountain overlooking Montreux and Lake Geneva, quickly became a symbol of hope in many countries. Some Germans were present in that first year. More came later, and the hate and prejudices of Germans, French and others were healed. It was here, not long after, that Konrad Adenauer and Robert Schuman first began to develop the ideas which took form in the European Economic Community. For both of them it was not basically an economic plan, but a way to end the divisions and wars which had plagued Europe for hundreds of years. Schuman, foreign minister and then prime minister of France, felt acutely on this subject, for as a man of Lorraine he had been conscripted into the German army in the 1914-18 war to fight against France. Here also the Mayor of Hiroshima, the first city to suffer the atomic bomb, found the ability to apologise for the suffering which Japan had caused to other nations.

Although we knew about the conference, Constance and I had no thought of going, and no money to pay fares. But a Scottish friend wrote from Caux, asking us to join him as his guests, and other friends offered to look after the children. There remained the question of the business. I had used up my entitlement of leave, and, even with those who had been away in the Services back in their jobs, it would mean a stretch. I went to Dawson Miller who at once said I must go, and said he would do part of my work himself while I was away. But who would do the rest? I suggested Reggie Meyer, the manager of the department which examined and passed for payment all the claims we received. He agreed to try, and did well enough to be put full time on to dealing with correspondence with the members.

This was one of a number of examples of how a step which I seemed to have been guided to take produced a series of after-effects in other spheres. My two weeks' absence in Caux also resulted in a new approach by the management to the manner in which the firm should be run. From then on the contacts with the shipowner members, by letter and interview, were not dealt with almost wholly by the partners, but spread out wider. And there was great emphasis on the development of all the possibilities of individuals on the staff.

Caux also gave me more confidence in meeting people from other countries. It was not long before I made my first trip abroad for the firm, to Holland and Belgium. I spent a week in Antwerp. The immediate object was to spend time in the office of the club's correspondents there, but I also met all the shipowners we dealt with, lawyers, and others, including the Minister of Justice.

One lesson I learnt then was of value throughout my business life. The shipowner members were not merely glad to see someone from 'our club', as they called it. They had a somewhat proprietorial attitude towards me as its representative, and were ready to drop into my lap any problem which might be on their minds at the moment. As far as the insurance with the club was concerned, they might want to talk about the rate of premium, a claim which had been refused, a lawsuit that was pending, and so on. They assumed I knew all about their affairs. If the point was entirely new to me, they would show me one or two letters, confident that I could reconstruct the whole question from a quick look at them. If I was really stumped, it was permitted to say that I would look into it when I got back, and write. But it was far better to be well primed on every subject they might bring up, and fully familiar with every current issue in which they and the club were concerned.

I also set a useful precedent on this first journey. I had taken my wife with me, because we planned to break away for a few days' holiday with friends in Holland. She proved of immense value in our business contacts. Somehow, the dual effect produced by her presence developed a much deeper relationship with people than I ever did by myself. We were sometimes invited to people's homes, instead of to restaurants or nightclubs. What started as formality quickly became friendship, which in many cases continues until the present day. The practice developed of her always accompanying me, unless I was going to do some particular job in which she would have no part. If it was an expedition to 'show the flag', she invariably came.

We notched up an average of a new country a year for twenty-six years.

15

Australia

My first major tour abroad for the firm was in 1956. The decision made to go to Sydney to help prepare for the trial of the *Wagon Mound* opened up a chance to visit the Australian shipowners. We had several in the club, James Patrick and Co., Wm. Holyman, Huddart Parker, H.C. Sleigh, Ampol Petroleum, and no one had ever been out to see them. It would also be good to see the lawyers and others who represented the club at the various ports. Some of these had visited us on their occasional visits to London. Others we knew only by correspondence.

Then we looked at the routes. It was still a question of piston-engined planes, and the minimum time for the journey was some two and a half days. So we elected to go by way of America, which meant three days, but made it possible to sleep on the aeroplane, either on a bunk let down from the ceiling, or on a seat which adjusted to a fully horizontal position. As I had a big claim pending in New York relating to a disputed general average on an American ship, I arranged also to stay over there for a few days on the way home.

In these days of fast, long-range jets, it seems a long and clumsy journey. The Boeing Stratocruiser which took us across the Atlantic refuelled at Shannon and again at Gander. We slept pretty well in our descending berths, and had time for a brief visit to the Boeing's little downstairs lounge, similar to but smaller than the upstairs lounge in the Jumbo jet of today. At New York my wife firmly walked in by the wrong gate to the immigration control, as her sub-conscious mind told her that an Englishwoman could hardly be an alien.

From New York, American Airlines took us to Washington, to Tulsa, to San Franciso. I began to suffer from the time-zone effect, so well known to the more frequent air traveller of today, and applied the obvious cures of minimum eating, and maximum sleeping. As a result, I failed to see the

Rocky Mountains by moonlight, which my wife got quite poetic about in a rather aggravating way when I awoke. A short and troubled night in a San Francisco hotel. A drive to the airport with a cabdriver who for these 'first time' visitors, drove at 70 miles an hour with one elbow on the wheel as he pointed out all the sights. Then by Pan-American Airways to Honolulu, Canton Island, Fiji and Sydney. At Honolulu airport, a ludicrous incident occurred. As a beginner in water-colours, I was enthralled by my first tropical sunset. I whipped out my brushes, spread a sheet of paper on the bonnet of a handy car, and in a couple of minutes it was pitch dark.

Canton Island is a coral island needed in those days as a refuelling stop, but not today. We did not bother to get out of our blankets, but at Fiji we went ashore for a meal. Everything there attracted us, the lush foliage, the dignified dark giant Fijians with their white kilts, and the food, including our first pawpaw or papaya. We are still hoping to go back. And then came the late afternoon drive in to Sydney from Mascot, with a barrage of chat and questions from a cheerful taximan. We told him we were on business and planning to tour the ports, beginning with Fremantle, and he replied, "Well, I'm a Sydney boy meself, but I always say that the West is the best."

We had a detailed plan, with flights and hotels booked, to visit all the major ports, and to attempt total coverage of the men we wanted to see, but there were two other factors which seemed essential to any visit to Australia. One was to see my relations in Western Australia. The other was to keep in mind our conviction that change for the world through change in people was valid in any country. We knew there were others in Australia who shared this conviction. In fact it so happened that Dr. Frank Buchman, the initiator of Moral Re-Armament, was in Australia with an international group which included English friends of ours, and we hoped to see them during the Easter holiday when we would be in Melbourne.

Within a quarter of an hour of arriving in our hotel bedroom, there was a telephone call from Christopher Prescott, one of the British with Dr. Buchman. They were in Canberra. He thanked me for my letter, and said, "If you want to see us, you'd better come quickly, for we are off to New Zealand on Tuesday." We were due to start next day for Perth, but some quiet thought convinced us that it was right to change our plans, rebook flights and hotels, and go first to Canberra. As it turned out, this was also a great improvement on our original plan from the business point of view, although it took a considerable moral decision, after three days of travel, to get out of bed at 5.30 to catch the 7 a.m. plane for Canberra.

The twenty-four hours there were crowded in the extreme. Canberra was only partly built, and had been referred to as "six suburbs in search of a city". Hotel rooms were at a premium and we doubled up with friends. Dr. Buchman and the rest gave us a great welcome. We had brought with us the first copies printed of a speech on Moral Re-Armament given in Berlin by Peter Howard, the sportsman and journalist, entitled "An Answer for East and West," and I remember Buchman receiving this as if it were a gift of untold value. Perhaps it was. We met a wide range of Australians. A Labour member took us into parliament to hear Dr. Evatt, opposition leader, speak on the budget, and we heard Prime Minister Robert Menzies speak at a public meeting in the evening. We also met a distinguished American lady, Mrs. Henry Hammond, a descendant of Commodore Vanderbilt, who insisted that we stay in her home when we reached New York. Our friends told us in detail of their experiences in Australia, and their impressions of the people and the country's needs. The result was that we left next morning far better prepared for our tour, with as much reliable information on the country as could be assimilated in the time. It left us eager and open-minded, ready to appreciate all that was good, without poisoning the atmosphere with that patronizing attitude which we British have so often adopted, to the fury of our friends. It was an invaluable introduction to Australia.

The next five weeks figure in my memory rather like a film run too fast through the projector. I came back with a list of 150 people I had seen on business, apart from other contacts. We also had an overall picture of an almost incredible country, and of a robust and adventurous people. It was good that we began in the west, with palm trees in the gardens outside our Perth hotel, swans and yachts sailing in the lagoon, and the thousands of wild flower species unknown elsewhere because of the barriers of sea and desert. After the first of our battery of business visits, we took off for a weekend with my relations at Albany and Napier, down on the south west tip of Australia. Two of my father's brothers had landed in 1913, with their wives and the two year old son of the younger of them. They lived in a bell tent until they had cut down enough trees to make a hut. The jobs promised to them fizzled out, but they established themselves as fruit farmers. Now, forty years later, Uncle Frank, from whom I was named, was dead, as was his wife. They left no children. Fred was still sturdy, with four children and a number of grandchildren, all of them in the neighbourhood except my cousin Terry, who owned a restaurant in Melbourne. The rest were still farming the two original farms, and Bill, the eldest, had a shop in Albany town. They were a self-reliant lot. Bert, for example, had built his own house, including casting the concrete blocks. Bill came in for a lot of ribbing for his allegedly English ways. (He had been the two-year-old referred to.) They urged my uncle, still a leathery giant, to write his reminiscences. "Call it The Last of the Pioneers, Dad" they said.

Albany itself was an extraordinary place. Our hotel, the Freemasons', looked a little like one in a Western film, with its long fretted balconies. We were shown the 'ancient' stone church, built in 1801. For Australia it was a historical relic. The harbour was a huge expanse (as big as Sydney Harbour, they said) but in this town of 10,000 people there was of course no need for vast port installations. In fact, the week before there had been two ships in at once, and workers had been taken off the roads to load them. Over to the west, beyond the whaling station, we scrambled over huge rocks to see the breakers of the Indian Ocean send up towers of spray. Inland there seemed endless miles of sand and scrub. They cleared the bush for a farm by dragging an 8-foot steel ball through it with two bulldozers joined by ship's anchor-chains. The momentum was enough to uproot fair-sized trees and all smaller stuff. Due to the small population, contractors did all the main jobs on the farms, the ploughing and sowing, as well as harvesting. The farmer and his family kept things going between times.

Flying back to Perth in the 8-seater De Havilland Dove, we saw the long lines of red where for many miles they were burning off the bush. And I should have mentioned our arrival, too. Our taxi into Albany from the little airport, driven by the mayor (he was the airline's agent) pulled up violently some miles outside the town. Focussed in the headlights was a 6-foot kangaroo. It turned, cleared the fence with a huge bound, and went soaring away across country.

"Have to be careful with those fellows", said the mayor. "If you scare them, they're likely to jump through the wind-screen."

Most of our time was spent in cities, necessarily. Big, bustling, well-equipped cities not so very different from those in Europe. Two things which impressed us most were the passion for sport, and the confident and almost aggressive way in which Australians faced the future. In Melbourne, a city of under a million people, there were forty golf courses and 4,000 tennis courts, as well as cricket grounds and fields for five different varieties of football. As if this was not enough, there were the beaches, miles and miles of them, where very many families had small beach homes, too. And it was not far by car to the mountains for ski-ing. As regards the future, development was rapid, especially in minerals. Farming, too, was expanding by drilling for deep subter-ranean water, and by adding the missing chemical elements which could cause apparently barren soil to bear good crops. This was done by blowing the powder with a fan from the back of a tractor. Restriction on immigration was considered necessary, as education, housing, and all the other services needed could only be provided for an increase of population at a certain rate. Over this rate, there would be a great drop in living standards for everyone. However, there were already the first signs of the new outlook which became official policy when Mr. Harold Holt was prime minister, and now seems to be happily irreversible. Certain people, of whom Mr. K.E. Beazley, a prominent opposition M.P., (now Minister of Education) was one, were already saying in 1956 that Australia's future was bound up with that of Asia. The country was not a little bit of England at the end of a long line of communications. It was not a dependency of the United Kingdom or of the United States. It was a nation in its own right, and must work out its own destiny.

It is interesting to reflect on how much has since developed in this direction. Most Australians and some others remember the dramatic visit of Prime Minister Kishi of Japan. Originally planned as a trade development tour, he made it instead an occasion for formal public apology for Japan's war crimes. Until then, public opinion in Australia was violently anti-Japanese. Australians had been so maltreated in the prison-camps that this was not surprising. Mr. Kishi's apology changed the atmosphere overnight. What is not so widely known is that three Australians had to some extent opened the way for his move, when they went to Japan earlier, with the avowed plan of starting a new relationship between the two countries. One of them was Gil Duthie, the member of parliament who took Constance and me into the debating chamber in Canberra.

There have been many other moves on various levels. The Australian Dairy Products Board sent a special development officer, Stanley Barnes, to help local interests in Thailand, Malaysia and Indonesia to start milk products factories in each country. The aim was primarily to help nutrition in countries where protein was in short supply, and a dairy industry difficult to develop. The milk powder and butter fat was supplied by Australia under her aid programme.

Shipping has developed new links between Australia, Hongkong and Japan. One of the first of these involved two passenger-cargo ships bought by H.C. Sleigh Ltd. of Melbourne. Alleged humorists said this would be a good move as long as they remember to put the business men in the cabins and the beef in the refrigerated chambers. Mr. Paul Hasluck, then Secretary for External Affairs and now Sir Paul and Governor-General, publicly commissioned a large group of young Australians to go to help with a national Moral Re-armament programme in India, telling them they would be doing an essential task which was beyond the power of governments. Another very significant move was when the Australian government vetoed the sale to Japan at cut prices of vast new iron ore deposits, because of the damage it would do to India's export trade for ore.

Australia is indeed becoming a significant force in the whole Pacific basin. When we were there, most of this was still in the future, although it is only eighteen years ago. We saw the vigour of the people, the energy of women who could run a large house without help, play tennis and golf and still find time for many other things, the bronzed life guards on the beaches, the casual competent farmers and the hurrying crowds of the cities. We saw the expanding steelworks and oil refineries on Botany Bay, the heavy rutile sand being shipped in Queensland, the coal mines of Newcastle, New South Wales, the sheep fattening under the apple and peach trees on my cousins' farms, the sugar cane, the avocadoes and the wheat fields, the rolling breakers at Surfers' Paradise. We met shipowners, lawyers, the Minister of Customs, the chief secretary of the Ministry of Transport, clergy, architects, one of the best-known artists. In the hotels the staff were often "New Australians", the immigrants who in many cases came from Central and Eastern Europe. They were proud of their new country and anxious to get on. My restaurant-owning cousin's best friend was an immigrant from Hungary, a tailor. In a year and a half he had worked up to owning two cars for his wife and himself. The arts were beginning to flourish. In Sydney we saw a successful play by a new Australian dramatist. There seemed to be nothing this people could not do, if they wished.

We won no immediate new business in Australia. That was not the aim. It was a time of bridge-building. In us it created a feeling for the country and its people which has never faded, and I know something was created, too, in some of them.

16

Yugoslavia

Our contacts with Yugoslavia went back at least to 1927. At first, they were with the private shipowners. During the war, they continued with the Royal Yugoslav Government in exile. After the war, they were renewed with the new authorities under President Tito, which acquired control of most of the remaining Yugoslav ships, and set out to acquire more.

The post-war arrangements were made through the new insurance monopoly in Beograd, commonly called DOZ, and some of their representatives came over every year to discuss terms. At first, Dawson Miller dealt with them. Later, he asked me to take it over. They kept pressing me to visit Yugoslavia, but for some time the firm was reluctant, and so was I. This was partly due to the pressure of work in the office, and partly to the general anti-communist feelings provoked by the Cold War. Perhaps anti-communist is not the right word in this case. The feeling was much more suspicion, and the fear that a visit would be exploited in some way which we could not foresee. Fear is usually not based on reason, and there was little reason in this, although it was known that some western business men's visits to communist countries had produced very undesirable side-effects. Against this was the fact that we found the Yugoslavs we dealt with agreeable and straightforward.

Eventually, it was decided that we should go. The insurance broking firm which was once part of Thos. R. Miller & Son's business and was still associated with us in friendship also had business with the Yugoslav shipowning and insurance men, and one of their seniors, H.B. Tiley, decided to come, too. We mutually agreed that our wives should accompany us, as the social side of things would be important.

The scope of the visit came in for some discussion. Decentralisation of merchant shipping had been decided on some years earlier and there were shipping companies (or 'enterprises', as they were called in this non-capitalist society) from Piran in the north to Kotor in the south. Later, another was established at Bar, right down on the Albanian border. All these really needed to be seen, so we decided to visit them all, beginning and ending in Beograd. It proved to be an exacting programme.

Yugoslavia in 1957 was only twelve years away from the war, which in that country had been of a bitterness and intensity we British find it hard to imagine. No enemy landed on our soil. Theirs had seen fierce fighting with the Italians and the Germans, and between Yugoslavs fighting each other. More than 10 per cent of the population was killed, including a very large proportion of those between twenty and thirty. You rarely saw a man of young middle age. There seemed a gap between childhood and late middle age. In Croatia there seemed to be only women working in the fields. The men, or most of them, were dead. Every village and town still bore the marks of gunfire and bombs. A Yugoslav friend, well-known to be no communist, told me that the chaos after the war and civil war was such that only an authoritarian central government could have got the country working again. It was a spartan regime. There was nothing, or almost nothing, of the tourist industry so many Europeans know today. The essentials of life, food and housing, were looked after, but everything was tightly controlled, and most non-essentials were simply not there.

We were very cheerily received in Beograd and taken to the Hotel Metropol, the only luxury hotel of international standard. It was imposing and comfortable, and the food was adequate. (It has since become very good.) I was told that it was run as a co-operative with all the workers sharing in the profits, and that this accounted for the good service. A couple of days of meetings, a dinner party for us by our friends from DOZ, and we were ready to leave for our tour of the ports. Then came the shock. We were asked to limit ourselves to a small suitcase for each couple, as we would all go in one car. The top man of DOZ was a communist party functionary, whose primary function was to see that operations were in accordance with national policy. He had arranged for the two most senior men under him, Jankovec and Tomasic, and a senior woman, Grlica Ilic, to go with us. With the driver, this meant eight people, plus luggage, in one car (even if it was a large Russian-built Zim) for 1200 miles and eight or ten days. They did indeed have a spartan approach to things. So Bertie Tiley and I went on strike. We were not prepared to go on this basis. The Yugoslavs were rather surprised. I suppose a degree of discomfort was nothing to people who in some cases had spent years in the mountains with the partisans. They quickly agreed to our terms, and at short notice produced another driver and a second car, a Chevrolet.

As I recall it, cars were not all that numerous then. Imports were not allowed, and the only cars built in Yugoslavia were small Fiats made under licence. Buses and trucks predominated. The roads were bad. The great trunk road from east to west had been built (without much refinement) between Beograd and Zagreb, but not extended at either end. The fine coastal road since completed was, I think, barely started. Some hotels were slowly reviving but accommodation around the country ranged from the middling by English standards to the very primitive. On the other hand, every possible effort was made for us by our three escorts, and by all we met, who gave us the best the country afforded.

Ivo Jankovec in particular proved to be a magician in producing good food and wine, of which Bertie Tiley was a connoisseur. Jankovec was the top insurance technician in the country, a plump jolly man, not too tall, with a personality which makes me think a little of Harry Secombe. He was a tremendous worker, and was known to put in more hours than anyone in DOZ, but to listen to him you would think he thought of nothing but pleasure. On one of his visits to London, I asked him how things were in Yugoslavia and he answered with jets of his staggering English (he was better in French or German), punctuated by puffs at a cigar, "Very good grape harvest. Plenty of wine to come. Very good plum crop. Plenty of slivovic. Only trouble is, not many girl babies. Not many pretty girls to come later." On our tour, I particularly remember how in Zagreb and again in Split he disappeared into the kitchen, and returned with the head waiter bearing a fine fish for our approval before cooking. And in Senj, a tiny port which progress had passed by, he quartered the whole place before ushering us into a little bar. Here, a scrubbed table was soon covered with plates, with cheese, sardines, salami, olives and sliced bread, a simple meal which was quite delicious. There was red and white wine and the marvellous Yugoslav lemonade, which is the juice of a large lemon poured into a tablespoon or so of sugar, and topped up with water.

The whole tour was full of startling differences. In Ljubljana our first business date was at 8 a.m., and they brought out coffee and slivovic, the national drink of plum brandy, as soon as we sat down. They of course had been at work two hours already. The usual hours were 6 to 1 in summer, and 7 to 2 in winter. Then lunch, then recreation, although management personnel often went back to work in the afternoon for a few additional hours. At Postojna we stopped for a couple of hours to see the astonishing limestone caverns. The Piran shipping enterprise then had as general director Boris Snuderl, later taken into the central government as deputy minister for foreign trade. He joined the partisans at the age of fourteen and had some gruelling experiences. He was now about twenty-nine, and had just returned from leading a national trade delegation to Japan. At the lunch they gave us, he found that he shared a regard for the Japanese with my wife, who had met a number of them at Moral Re-Armament conferences. When we said goodbye, she gave him a deep Japanese bow. He responded in kind, and the courtesy was, as is proper, repeated. I can still picture the Adriatic sunlight on the huge man and the little woman bowing and bowing in a ring of laughing Yugoslavs.

Many of the roads were earth and stones. Once the two cars over-ran an unmarked crossroad, and stopped. Our driver ran back, looked around, and returned with a remark which made the Yugoslavs laugh. 'He says,' translated Tomasic, "that this is clearly the international road, because they have been shovelling stones into the holes." A lot of road-building was going on, but this did not always make it easy. If a bridge over a stream needed replacing, the method seemed to be to knock it down first. While the new one was being con-structed, all traffic bumped down the hillsides, splashed through the stream, and ground up in bottom gear to rejoin the road. In that rocky country, it was quite exciting.

The scenery was superb, with islands floating on the deep changing blues of the Adriatic, and the mountains inland getting more and more spectacular as we followed the coast south. In Slovenia, it seemed that every rounded hill was crowned by a church. Dubrovnik was a fairytale place with its mellow red tiles and great medieval walls. They showed us there the shipyard where the galleys were built (now a yacht basin), the first quarantine station where goods and immigrants from countries hit by the plague were kept in isolation for forty days, and told us that the archives included a thirteenth-century marine insurance policy written in Latin. The Kotor Gulf in the south is like a warm water Norwegian fjord, with limestone mountains rising straight out of the water. We turned inland there over the pass of Lovcen, on which the upper part of the road comprised twenty-eight consecutive hairpin bends. The Montenegrin driver flung his car round them with abandon. The Serb driving the Zim was more cautious, and his car radiator boiled badly, a signal for witticisms at the expense of Russia by the Yugoslavs.

Near the crest of Lovcen, we met the general director of the shipping enterprise at Kotor, returning from Titograd, and had an impromptu business conference at the roadside, always afterwards referred to as our 'summit conference', even though America and Russia were only represented by their machinery. It seemed quite normal to the Yugoslavs to talk business at the roadside, and go over again the matters we had dealt with that morning in Kotor. In fact, all through the tour, we seemed to have three or four meetings a day.

Veljko Tomasic was a charming companion, quiet, helpful, and with a fantastic flow of comic stories. The Yugoslavs excel at this. Many of them are regional jokes in this federal republic, about the superiority of the Serbs, the laziness of the Dalmatians, or the independence of the Montenegrins. Others are at the expense of the Russians or Americans, but never (to an Englishman) at the expense of England. Some are 'black' humour, about war and concentration camps. Tomasic said one day, "Do you know why DOZ is so successful as an insurance company? We have a system of rewards. We insure the farmers' flocks, so we give £1 to everyone who brings in the tail of a wolf. We insure the fishermen's nets, so we give £8 for the tail of a shark. And we give £100 to anyone who brings in the head of one of our pensioners." Now that Ivo Jankovec is dead Tomasic must be the most experienced insurance man in Yugoslavia, and certainly he has the greatest knowledge in the marine field. For his doctorate he wrote a thesis on collision liability. Educated partly in France, he is fluent in several languages. He has specialised in all forms of transport insurance, and in international reinsurance contracts from Moscow to London.

Miss Ilic was always called by her Christian name Grlica (girl-itsa), which means 'dove'. She was neat, reserved, but in a quieter way also helped to entertain us. When we returned to Beograd, she asked the two ladies to tea in her home to meet her parents, an unusual privilege.

We found that our first experience of a communist country gave us much food for thought. It was easy to accept the real kindness and fun, the desire to please and help the foreigners, as being everything, but now and then the bare bones of the totalitarian state showed through. Driving in Beograd, I asked idly of my companion, "How many Yugoslavs are members of the Communist Party?" He looked at the back of the driver's head, and said nothing. In one town a senior party official, member of parliament and other things, with whom we had business, provided us with a full explanation on how their system worked. He claimed that Yugoslavia practised true communism, and Russia state capitalism. In one, the means of production and distribution were owned by the people; if a factory burnt down, those responsible for the factory had to replace it. (So they insured it.) In Russia, everything was owned by the state; if a factory burnt down, it was replaced out of the national budget. However, it appeared that in Yugoslavia also every business with more than three workers had to account for itself to the Ministry of Finance. It was expected to show a profit, part of which would go to the workers, including the management. Any reserves or capital expenditure had to be approved, and any balance left after that went to the Ministry. Basic foods and housing were strictly controlled in price, and wages were low. Someone told us that the general manager of a shipyard then got £600 a year. On the other hand, if you were lucky or important enough to get a flat in the centre of Beograd, it would only cost £6 a month.

Another incident seemed to us significant. We arrived at Split about 6.30 p.m. on a Saturday afternoon. At the hotel there was a message that Jankovec was wanted at the Ministry of Finance on Monday morning. (Suppose insurance were a monopoly in the United Kingdom, run by one inclusive Prudential or Commercial Union Insurance Company, then Jankovec's position would be that of chief general manager.) He left within the hour with one of the cars and its driver, drove night and day across several ranges of mountains, surmounted punctures and mechanical trouble, got in at midnight on Sunday, and reported at the Ministry at 6 a.m. on Monday morning.

This tour was the first of five business trips to Yugoslavia. I like and admire the people, and have many friends there.

After a while you can often tell from quite a casual conversation who is a dedicated party member, and who is not. In some ways I am drawn most to those who are the most convinced ideologically. One couple had been two and a half years in the mountains during the war with Tito and the partisans. Sometimes they had only grass to eat. Like the other partisans she swore an oath of chastity, and kept it. After the war the two married, had a family, and he rose to positions of great trust in the party and nation. When the children were old enough, she took an economics degree, so as to be of greater help to her husband. I find such dedication touching, and a real challenge.

In my view, a lot of nonsense is talked about the nature of Communist ideology in Yugoslavia, (and Russia, for that matter). On the surface there has been much liberalisation, especially in the way of freedom of speech. There was even a cartoon in the party's own paper *Borba*, showing the shade of Karl Marx watching two Yugoslav party leaders playing chess and saying, "I don't understand the rules you boys are using." There has also been much decentralisation (DOZ was broken up into eleven insurance companies), and some western practices were introduced at the expense of the hard centralised and dogmatic methods associated with Moscow, especially in Stalin's time. But the one thing a Yugoslav must not and cannot do is to cross the line of national policy and national interest. If he does, he is slapped down. Often, he is jailed, whoever he may be.

When one observes the chaos and self-seeking which are so common in the democracies, one wonders whether the Yugoslavs are wholly wrong. They still claim, I believe, as they did in 1957, to be nearest to true communism. But the question remains: "Who is to decide what is the national interest?" Is it what is laid down by an authority which is at a pinch all-powerful, or is it decided by some other method? The non-party member avoids discussion of such matters, but this is not always so with the party men. After all, they are in power with no effective opposition, and have been so for nearly thirty years. They have achieved, at a cost, great progress for their country. A communist in power has a radically different attitude from that of one in a country where he is part of a revolutionary minority.

My host at dinner on one occasion in Yugoslavia was a senior party man, and talked freely. I felt I had to say that despite my friendship for the country, I did not believe in communism, for I considered it was based on wrong premises, and actually did not work. He admitted it had not been entirely successful. I then said that I believed that the system which we needed would be just as much better than what we now had in the capitalist world as it would be better than communism. At once he said, "Now that is a very interesting idea." It is my deep conviction that the only hope of a bridge between the communist and non-communist world is on this level. Change is needed for everyone.

17

Italy

Later in 1957 we went to Italy. Partly, it was to be a holiday, partly a move to see all the shipowners we knew and all the club's representatives in one go. We took a month over it, so that there was time for relaxation and sightseeing, but we saw fourteen club representatives and twenty-four shipowners, so it was by no means unproductive. We had now got the hang of this kind of visit. It was good to see people in their offices, as it gave you a better chance to sum them up. I remember telling Captain Callisto Gerolimich of Fratelli Cosulich in Trieste that his was the best organised shipping office in Trieste, because the coffee appeared quicker than anywhere else. One club representative had a large, liberally staffed, but dusty and untidy office. Another was the opposite, tiny and active, but there was no indication of anyone competent to take over if the principal was away.

Entertaining was important. I always tried to entertain the people I met, but when (as frequently) they insisted on being hosts, it was important to submit. We were, after all, guests in their country. And again, as before, one had to be ready to cope with any problem. The club correspondents might complain about a delay in paying fees, or a misunderstanding with some shipowner. One shipowner plumped in front of me a problem to surpass all others, or so it seemed. He had bought an old ship in Denmark, and immediately loaded a cargo of cement in Poland for the United States. The engines broke down, and the ship put into Flushing. They broke down again and she put into Falmouth. They broke down a third time, and she put into Lisbon. They could not be repaired there, so the shipowner had her towed back to Italy. Part of the engine was taken out and taken to a shipyard at another port for repair. The shipowner had quarrelled with the repairer, who refused to give up the engine part until he was paid. When I was first told of the trouble, the ship was still lying immobile with the cement on board, nearly as far

from America as when she started some eighteen months
earlier. That was one problem I left over to deal with when I
returned, and it took several years before it was sorted out.

I tackled a good many grievances and difficulties, gained a
little new business, formed plans to drop one of our
correspondents and appoint a new one, collected some
money owing to us, and made a lot of friends. Most of the
journeying we did by sea, a Greek passenger ship from Genoa
to Naples and an Italian passenger/cargo ship from Naples to
Palermo, Messina, Malta, Catania, Bari, Ancona and Trieste.
We also saw the shipping men in Rome and in Venice.

Italy was a great contrast to Yugoslavia. Although some
industries were nationalised, including some of the shipowners and some of the banks, Italy's society was carefree
compared with the disciplined, regimented country across the
Adriatic. Road-traffic was hair-raising, and the squeal of tyres
became known to us as 'Italian noises' to describe a certain
way of driving. One of our hosts and escorts was Aldo
Mordiglia of Genoa, a notable lawyer and a very happy
companion. He had a way of thrusting out an arresting arm
into a stream of traffic and marching behind it across a street
while everybody stamped on their brakes. If you had the
courage you followed in his wake. If not, you stood on the
kerb and marvelled, for the river quickly swirled between you
again.

As a holiday, too, it was most recreational, time to relax
and much to see — the Church of Christ the King at Messina
overlooking Scylla and Charybdis, with its memorials to
seamen of both sides lost in the war; a wild drive up Mount
Etna with a young Sicilian shipowner, who, between his
enthusiasm to show us everything and his affection for his
bride-to-be alongside him, spared occasional glances for the
road as it looped through the lava fields. In Trieste,
Constance bought a hat, despite the language difficulty, amid
cries of "*Modello1 Molto elegante!*" and so on. And we had
three exquisite November days in Venice, with hardly a
tourist to be seen, and misty sunsets over the lagoon.

The high point for me, however, was a single incident in
Rome. Of the Italy we saw, and I realise we missed a very
great deal, Rome seemed a sort of quintessence. Here, more
than anywhere, you seemed to live simultaneously in the
remote past and in today. There was the roar of the streets,
the luxury, the poverty, the feeling of life lived to the full,
and there was also an incredible antiquity closely mingled

with it. One little thing stands out more clearly for me than the Colosseum or St. Peter's, the medieval walls or the catacombs. Many miss it.

On the Capitoline Hill, rather tucked away, there is a church, and under it is a prison. You pay your few lire, go down some steps, and you are in the Mamertine Prison. But this bare stone square apartment was only the guard room. At one side more steps go down by the wall to the prison proper, a noisome cell hewn out of the rock. It is damp and the smell is horrible. A small hole in the corner seems to lead direct to the sewers. It contains two things only, both revealed by spotlights, the rest being in shadow. One is a wooden board which lists the prisoners who, among many others, were imprisoned there. Here lay the Gracchi, the Catiline conspirators, one of the early popes, Vercingetorix the Gaul, and many more, through hundreds of years of suffering. Against each is recorded the manner of his death, beheaded, strangled, or starved to death. A small altar is now let in the opposite wall. It carries the inscription: "This altar commemorates the imprisonment here before their martyrdom of Saint Peter and Saint Paul, during which imprisonment they converted twenty-eight of their jailers." Ten minutes was about all I could stand in that cell, but it left an indelible impression of horror and of hope.

18

India

The first of three visits to India came about in a curious way. A proposition was put to me on behalf of our own firm and two of our friendly rivals, managers of other P. and I. clubs. All three had a certain amount of business from shipowners in India. In addition, matters arose there requiring assistance in connection with ships of all flags calling at Indian ports. For some time it had been felt that better provision should be made for dealing with these matters; and a joint approach had been made by the three clubs to the New India Assurance Company, a large company closely connected with the great Tata industrial group. They had said they were prepared to act as general representatives, but only if some senior person were sent to India to train their men in work which was unfamiliar to them. Would I take it on?

I found myself in a state of acute conflict. It was flattering to my ego to be told they felt I was the best person to do it. I'd long wanted to see India. It was a challenge, and I usually responded to a challenge. Yet there was also a reluctance which I did not understand. Was it to do with the heat? A bad dose of sunstroke years before had left me subject to headaches and dizziness after a few minutes of direct sun. I asked for time to think it over. Sometimes my time of quiet and mental listening in the early morning is spent disentangling what seem to be right decisions from a mass of irrelevant thoughts. It may include quiet consideration about specific people. Occasionally, as on this morning, a clear and arresting thought comes into my mind. "You are afraid to go," I thought, "because you are afraid of being ill. But this is something you can do for India."

Both thoughts clicked with me at once. At this time India, where so many lived on the edge of starvation, was receiving massive aid from many countries. A large proportion of her imports consisted of food grains given by other governments. Without expert knowledge, I had a strong feeling that this sort of aid was, in the long run, the wrong answer. No nation should be accepted as being permanently in need of charitable handouts from others. It was demoralizing. It seemed to me more important to find the way for a nation to meet its own needs. For one man to teach a few Indians some new insurance skills might be a small thing, but it was a small thing of the right kind. As for the possibility of illness, that might come or might not. So I agreed.

The plan duly worked out. I was to spend four months in India in the winter of 1964-65, when temperatures would be lower, and out of the monsoon season. My wife would go with me; I would need her support in many ways. It was not really long enough to warrant renting a flat, so we would live in a small hotel suite. I was very ignorant of what the whole thing would entail, but I asked S.N. Vakil, a New India Assurance man then in London, what language they used in business in Bombay. "Oh, English", he replied, and then added airily, "but we put in a few words of Hindi, Urdu, Marathi and Gujerati to make it easier." I also learned that the normal business wear was a dark suit, with a tie, so I got a couple of lightweight suits in dark colours. And, fortunately, we knew a doctor who had spent many years in India, who not only gave us the usual injections, but spent a long time detailing the precautions we should take to avoid dysentery and other likely infections. This was time well spent. My wife was pretty fit the whole time we were in India. My own fears were realised. I was unwell, on and off, for about ten of the sixteen weeks we were there. The trouble, however, was not what the doctor taught us to guard against, except once or twice when I got slack on the precautions advised. It was continual sore throats and feverish colds, possibly due to the heat of the streets, and the cold of the airconditioning in some of the buildings. I seemed always to be having a day in bed, or wobbling up again, but it was never so bad as to put me out of action for any longer period.

Our base was Bombay, though not in the great sand-coloured headquarters of 'New India' in Mahatma Gandhi Road. They had overflowed into an older building, so I found myself in a more typical Indian office building, with its little shops along the front, its erratic creaking lift, its crowd of workers, dirt, and spatters of betel juice on the stairs. My Indian colleagues were apologetic about the condition of the building, which they attributed to the tight control on rents, and the landlord's consequential refusal to spend any money on upkeep above the absolute minimum. I was luckier than most, for they installed an airconditioner for me, a luxury not present in the general office, but the first piece of equipment provided for me was a set of paper-weights, to stop the overhead fans from blowing papers all over the room.

Nearly the whole of those four months was spent working office hours, usually without a European (which to an Indian may also include an American or an Australian) to be seen, though we did meet a few socially. The office was wholly Indian; and so, with a few exceptions, was the business world in which I moved, the shipowners, ship agents, lawyers, surveyors and occasionally government officials.

The main task was to create a department in New India Assurance to deal with the business of the three P. and I. clubs, and to train the personnel for this, at least on an elementary level. The work centred on Bombay; but the other ports were of some importance, especially Calcutta. We therefore did four trips lasting an average of about a week, to Goa, Calcutta, Delhi, and to the South. At each place I had to cover all the tasks I had carried out in Italy, and in addition to try to cram all the technical knowledge I could into the New India staff, and with it our rather special attitude to the business, which is by no means the same as that of an ordinary insurance company, even a good one. In the main, the instruction was on an ad-hoc basis, taking the incidents which arose each day, and explaining the background of them, as well as how to deal with them. But before I left in March 1965, I did conduct a week's seminar in Bombay, including men from Calcutta, Madras and Cochin. About thirty attended, some of them men from shipowners' offices. The course aimed at giving a complete outline of P. & I. insurance. It was voted a success, although my average temperature that week was around 102 degrees, and I lost my voice once or twice. Each session began with a summary of the previous session, prepared by a volunteer (or someone who had been told to volunteer). One of these summaries was delivered with great flair, and I was interested to note that the report of my talk included a number of things I had not said. Reflection showed that they had been copied from something I had written earlier for another purpose. Our friend's enterprise amused me so much I hadn't the cruelty to expose him to the class, or even to let him know privately that I had seen through it.

Bombay, the commercial capital of India, was fascinating in itself. Like every first time visitor from Britain, I was shocked by the overcrowded clutter of shanties on the way in from the airport, where people live in the extreme of poverty and squalor. There were, too, the families squatting on the city pavements, even outside our hotel. They cooked, fed, washed and slept on a few square feet of paving, and I read one day of a man knifing another for intruding on the area he regarded as his own. Yet, by contrast, the throngs in the street had a dignity and a degree of gaiety which you do not see in London streets. Many of the poor seem to accept the position naturally, and almost gracefully. The beggars also seemed horrible, and it seemed to be true that it was a profession in which some parents deliberately mutilated their children to increase their 'earning' powers. We ourselves in one of the main streets, importuned by a girl of twelve or so, saw her attacked by another girl with screams and scratches when in her eagerness she passed the borderline between their two pitches. Indian friends told us earnestly that Mahatma Gandhi was much against giving money to beggars, as it helped to prevent the poor being properly integrated into society.

In our travels, we saw many aspects of the country, including something of village life. By car alone, we went hundreds of miles in northern, western and southern India. It is often and rightly referred to as the sub-continent. Even the currency notes bear their inscription in fourteen languages, plus English, which is more and more inevitably being recognized as the link language. No other is really possible. Half the country speaks languages with some relation to Sanskrit, and writes them in a variety of spiky-looking scripts. These trace back to a general Aryan source. The southern half, however, is ethnically different, stemming from the Dravidian races who were there before the Aryan invasions. Their languages have no relation to Sanskrit, and are written in curly scripts, more like Burmese or Thai. Indians of the south and north differ in colour, appearance, habits and temperament. There is great resistance to any attempt at enforced uniformity. While we were there, official attempts to make Hindi (a northern language, part bazaar patois, artificially enriched by government experts with manufactured words) universal for some purposes produced a violent reaction in the south. Several people in Madras burnt themselves alive in protest. They are deeply traditionalist, however much they accept modern ways. Wherever they live in the world, and whatever citizenship they adopt, they remain Indian, speak their own particular language, and keep much of their own culture. It was interesting to find that New India Assurance Company had branches wherever there was an Indian community, in Singapore, Hongkong, Manila, in Australia, East and South Africa, in Gibraltar and in the Caribbean. Apparently, Indians in all these places felt happier to deal with an Indian insurance company.

There is still poverty and illiteracy in India, but I have been back twice since 1965 and have seen much progress. On that first visit we met in our hotel an Australian engineer, Ivan Syer, and his wife. He had been lent by an international company making farm machinery to help set up a factory to make light farm tractors. The money was part American, more Indian. The first tractors after the factory was built were assembled from parts sent from England. Gradually, over three years or so, the project was to be changed by introducing parts made in India, the tyres, then the batteries, then the castings, until all or nearly all were locally produced. I remember saying that surely the farmers in these thousands of villages could not look after a modern machine of this sort. Mr. Syer looked at me with amazement. That idea, he said, was exploded long ago. Show them just what needs to be done and, even if they cannot read, they will look after the tractors as well as anyone, and better than most.

The skill and adaptability of Indians has since been proved in many spheres. They have a flourishing atomic industry now. In farming the progress recently is such that it is justly called 'The Green Revolution', and the country is expecting soon to be self-supporting in food grains. I found that in insurance matters they were quick to learn, and, when they saw the point of anything, thorough in carrying it out. Admittedly, you could not take the second point for granted unless you worked to see that it happened, but the best men were equal to the best anywhere in the world.

The arrangement I set up with New India Assurance lasted for five years, during which everyone I heard from said that our business was better looked after than ever before. It was then ended by mutual consent, just before their company was taken over by their government. Several of the men I trained were released to work for a new Indian firm which was formed to take over our work.

At the time of that first visit, the general situation in India was chaotic. It was only two years since the Chinese had invaded the north-east, over-run a good deal of territory and then withdrawn. Frontier shootings were reported daily, involving both East and West Pakistan. Nehru was dead. He had forcibly annexed Goa, the former Portuguese dependency. It was not yet decided whether the territory would be a new state, or merged in one or more of its neighbours.

Corruption at the top encouraged cynicism or non-co-operation with the government at all levels. Let me cite some examples. When the chief minister of one of the state governments was investigated on corruption allegations by the speaker of the central government at Delhi, the finding was that it was imprudent of him to award large state contracts to companies controlled by his wife, but there was no evidence he himself had profited. Bombay was in a 'dry' state, where alcohol could be bought only on permits issued to addicts. (Foreign visitors picked up their permits on landing!) But bootleg liquor was so widespread that it was said to be better and cheaper than that in the official shops. Indian friends told us that it was wise to see the stamps on a package or airletter cancelled by the clerk at the counter. Otherwise, he might remove the stamps to sell again, and throw the letter away.

The British had, with a few thousand dedicated officials, maintained a splendid Indian Civil Service and fine quality rail, postal and other public services. In less than twenty years since independence, these seemed to be slowly crumbling away. Commerce and industry made some rich, and in a few cases were operated with a real eye to the public good, as with the Tata enterprises, largely owned by charitable trusts. But poverty and unemployment were on a staggering scale. Industrial unrest was continuous. Every day or two a chanting procession with red flags passed under my office window, holding up the entire traffic.

There were many good things. There was a large degree of religious freedom. Not only Hindu, but also Muslim and Christian festivals were national holidays. The Pope visited Bombay when we were there. Recognised as a true man of God, he was welcomed by crowds ten deep along the seventeen miles from the airport. A Hindu society stuck up bills everywhere saying, "Welcome to the Honourable Pope". We were taken to one of the smaller assemblies, when twenty-five couples were married by five bishops. The nuptial mass was explained step by step over the loudspeakers by the rich Irish voice of Cardinal Conway to a crowd of 'only' 100,000 in the park or maidan. I doubt if five per cent of those present were Christians. There was a free press and a good one. Village industries were reviving; in government-sponsored and other shops there was an astonishing range of products in silk and cotton, ivory, silver, lacquer, marquetry and many other materials. In Trivandrum, for example, we looked for a few souvenirs and were for a time so stunned by the variety of arts that we found it hard to choose anything. And most of all, this was the largest democracy in the world. The machinery might creak, but it still worked, more or less, for some 400 million people.

The overall picture, however, was such that my wife said she would have found it easy to despair for the future, except for one thing. As in Australia, we were naturally in contact with those who were working for Moral Re-Armament. Some were in jobs; others had, like Dr. Buchman's first recruits, made themselves mobile to do whatever was needed. Of these, the Indians had been joined by British, Australians, and a young Dutchman. The work was led by Mr. Rajmohan Gandhi, eldest grandson of Mahatma Gandhi. He was still a young man, son of Devadas Gandhi whom, when he was managing editor of the *Hindustan Times*, I had seen in London with Dr. Buchman ten years earlier. Trained as a journalist on the *Scotsman*, Rajmohan had a fine career open to him in the press world or in government, but refused it on the basis that his real calling was to a moral revolution for India and the whole of Asia. He admitted that this task, which included ending corruption and exploitation, was even tougher than the one his grandfather undertook of ending British rule in India.

His strategy, with associates such as R.M. Lala, whom I had known in London where he ran as Asian publishing house, included some big public moves. There had been, for example, a mass meeting on the sands in Bombay which recalled the great demonstrations in the independence struggle, and a 'march on wheels' through cities, towns and villages from the southern tip of India 1,800 miles to Delhi. Most of all there was the launching of a weekly news magazine called *Himmat* (*Courage*, in Hindi) which aimed to tell the truth on all issues, and work for answers to problems in terms of changing men. This was launched a few weeks before we arrived in Bombay, was an immediate success, and has been increasingly authoritative ever since.

The real basis of the work, however, was steady infiltration of ideas to and through individuals in all parts of society. In the wide range of business people I met, most had heard of it, many approved, and some helped. Many of the elite in the universities, politics, the trade unions had some touch with this work. But the people who convinced my wife and me that there was a real hope for the future were the students. We met some in Bombay, and more in Delhi, when at Christmas we were invited to a conference they largely ran themselves under the title of "World Assembly for To-morrow's Leaders". They came from all over India. The chairman was a girl gold medallist from the faculty of architecture in Delhi. Some universities sent chosen students. Other young people came under their own steam. There had been training sessions for months before, on the general theme of changing society by change in people. In Delhi they were invited to meet the speaker of the parliament, and to visit a leading daily newspaper. This produced a delightful cartoon in the following issue. Scene, a cross-road. One placard, arrowed, showed the way to "M.R.A. Assembly for Tomorrow's Leaders". Another ditto indicated, "To Memorial Meeting for Nehru and Past Leaders". One politician, distinguished by his white Gandhi cap, says to another, "But can you tell me where to find today's leaders?"

Some of these young men and women were really on fire with conviction, and had been prepared to put right things in their own lives to prove it — quarrels with their parents, dishonesties in examinations, and so on. These were matters perhaps of personal significance at first glance, but in terms of pride important to people at any stage of life. Moreover, decisions on such matters could free people to develop character in a way which impressed statesmen and newsmen, and gave authority to what they said and did.

In my later visits it was clear that things were changing fast in India. The last time we were there, in 1970, we had dinner with R.M. Lala, the editor of *Himmat*. What he told us was confirmed by others. At that time the Congress Party, which had provided a government ever since independence, was deeply split. The opposition parties were also split on which part of the Congress Party they were opposing. The Communists, always ahead of the game in some respects, were split three ways. Yet there were signs of definite progress in many fields, including industry. When I asked why, I was told that in spite of the chaos of politics, the ordinary farmer, business men and worker seemed to be carrying the country forward.

Since then Mrs. Indira Gandhi, the prime minister, has succeeded in reuniting her party, and the government is more effective than for many years, perhaps for the whole period since independence. Farming and industry show great advances. Tragic though the events have been in what was East Pakistan, there seems more of a hope of good relations in the sub-continent since the birth of Bangladesh. The violence and political murders seem to have subsided, even in Bengal.* It is hard to say how much is contributed to this by the men and women working with Rajmohan Gandhi, and in any case this is one of many factors. But a number of incidents, at least, are well known. For instance, a direct result of Moral Re-Armament was the ending of the confrontation between hill and plains people in part of Assam, where guerillas were being sent to China for training, and the newpapers feared 'another Vietnam'. It was the change in a prominent politician, Stanley Nichols Roy, which led the way to reconciliation and the peaceful setting up of the new state of Meghalaya. Again, a group of students in Madras (some of them well-known militants) aided by a professor of psychology, of all people, were challenged by Mr. Gandhi to bring together the parties and end a six months' strike at Standard Motors. The *Times of India* headlined it as "Student Power, New Style". It is the only industrial settlement I have read of for which the credit was given by each of the parties (including the intervening students) to someone else. Bouquets all round, as it were.

India is still envisaged by most people as a vast problem. The average European seems to think (and will often tell you) that the only solution is a reduction in the birth rate. In other words, there are too many Indians. I think that argument dangerous rubbish. If it is valid, it is also necessary to consider that the Indian government's huge expenditure on a birth control campaign reduced the birth rate by only 0.2 per cent. If, therefore, there are too many Indians, it is necessary to slaughter some scores of millions, and to keep on doing so. The sheer arrogance of the argument reminds me of an Englishman who in my hearing lectured a very distinguished South African (and a pioneer of humane

* Since the above lines were written, there have been new crises in the Congress Party, in politics generally, and in the economic sphere. I do not, however, feel this makes my general views invalid.

policies) on what was wrong with South Africa and how to put it right. The critic, of course, had never been to South Africa himself. The same applies to Sir Hugh Greene, who heads a committee to put right all he says is wrong in Greece, and declines any invitation to see conditions for himself.

I cannot claim to be an authority on India, but I would suggest an alternative solution to a situation where several hundred million people do not yet produce enough to meet all their physical needs. Could they not be helped to increase their production? Aid should not be a hand-out to a beggar. It should be a welcome into equal partnership. The whole conception of economic relations between nations needs to be re-thought and re-modelled. There has been one move which could be an example. More than a decade ago a French industralist whose outlook on life was radically changed by an experience of Moral Re-Armament, became president of the jute industry of France and later of the European jute industry. Realising the effect that low prices for jute and other raw materials had on producing countries, Robert Carmichael set out to work for a just price structure for the world jute industry. It meant years of struggle and heart-break, but eventually the Food and Agriculture Organisation of the United Nations took up the cause, and agreements were reached between the producers in Pakistan and India and the distributors and manufacturers elsewhere. It produced stability of prices, and a better standard of living for a great army of peasant farmers.

India can solve its own problems and do more than that. What will it mean to China if to the south there is an effective democracy, second only to China itself in population, where social justice is freely accepted and practised by a responsible and talented people? Where there is enough for all, and to spare for others? Where unity and strength make it unnecessary to fear aggression, and natural to offer friendship to all? It could happen. If it did, it would be a useful lesson to us in Europe, to Washington and to Moscow.

19

Management Training

I came back from India to a crisis in the office in St. Mary
Axe. There had been a sort of surge in the work, one of the
sudden increases which occur in an expanding business. In
addition, we had been involved in two very difficult and
important legal issues, which had taken up a lot of time and
energy. My absence had not helped, although there were no
regrets about the course we had taken. Many people were
seriously overworked, and one of the most senior was in a
bad enough state to be ordered away for a month's complete
rest shortly afterwards. The fact was that events had shown
up a weakness in the firm's structure, one I believe common
to many industrial and commercial firms, small and large.

Within a day of my return, I was separately approached by
Sidney Fowler and John Shearer with similar reports on the
trouble, and the same suggestion for a cure. Work was getting
behind, especially at the level of the partners and their
assistants, and it was not being dealt with, in some cases, with
the care and efficiency we considered proper. Wherever the
paper piled up, the stronger was the temptation to cut
corners in dealing with correspondence, to stall on a matter
which should be dealt with decisively and finally, and
otherwise to store up further trouble for the future. The two
men both felt that this was due to inadequate training of the
younger management men. They asked if I would take on
training them, and offered to free me of other work should it
be necessary.

Again I had to consider in the quiet of the early morning
what course I should follow. The answer seemed to be more
than a simple yes or no. First, I should agree in principle, if
the partnership as a whole approved. However, I should do
nothing until we had made a fuller assessment both of the
problem and the cure. It would also be advisable to
investigate further before starting any training programme.
The plain fact was that, although I had done some ad hoc

training both in London and in India, I was ignorant of
training in general, and felt inadequate for it.

The partners approved. Sidney and I set to work. The
more we talked the clearer it became that, although he and
John had been right in their views, the lack of training was
only part of the problem. For example, we got out figures
which showed that the number of staff had increased by 40
per cent in the last five years. The volume of business had
also increased by about 40 per cent an average of 8 per cent a
year. In that period at least three people had overworked to
the point of being sent away for a rest to avoid a breakdown.
So had I, earlier, after the Australian tour. Manifestly, we
were under-staffed, and had been for years. We had sought
extra help only when the burden of work seemed insufferable. It took time for the new people to learn the job; and,
by the time they had done so, the work had increased to the
point where the burden was still insufferable. We needed a
sufficient increase of staff to get ahead of the game, plus the
training we had contemplated, plus expansion by say 5 per
cent per annum for the next few years.

And where would we put new staff? The present offices
were fully utilised. We were already considering whether to
rent one or two floors of a small new building, adjoining. If
we took on the further staff now envisaged, we would want
three or even four floors. This was no light matter. Rents in
St. Mary Axe are among the highest in London. In 1972 I
had the chance to visit New York and find out what was
being paid there. Friends of ours were paying, in a new
airconditioned building in the financial centre (or should I
write center?) of Manhattan Island, a rental at less than a
quarter the rate of ours in St. Mary Axe. And we were not on
the thirty-first floor, with a superb view of the North River!

We put the whole of our findings and proposals before the
partnership. The cost of expansion also had to include wages
and pensions, secretaries, typewriters, everything. It was a
formidable sum, and produced general dismay. It was
questionable whether the firm's income from the clubs would
carry it. But it resulted in a clear example of how to arrive at
decisions. It was, I think, James Wright who said that the
question was not whether we could afford it, but whether
these steps were necessary to give the level of service we felt
we should give to the members of the clubs. If they were
necessary, then they must be taken, and we would work out
the finance of it afterwards. The whole plan was approved. In

point of fact, the improvement in efficiency made possible more expansion, and income increased sufficiently to cover the extra expense.

Back I went to the question of management training. We engaged a well known firm of management consultants, and told them the problem. They asked a lot of questions about the business, and eventually said that it was so highly specialised and different from anything they had done that they could not help. The only possibility might be one or two lectures on psychology in business interviews, and on how to write a business letter. This was not very attractive, so we were back to square one. We did, however, employ them on our recruiting campaign for new executives. The most conspicuous result of this was a bill for several hundred pounds. It produced no recruits. In fact, the only man we engaged was one who applied to us privately, and we redirected him to the consultants so that he would be interviewed by them as well as us and compared with those who wrote in as the result of our newspaper advertisements. Still, it was not all wasted effort, as we learnt more about recruiting.

How does one recruit for management? Some people swear by advertising in daily and Sunday newspapers and technical magazines, so our failure in this field cannot be regarded as standard. For more senior jobs, many employ specialist firms to find a man who will switch employers, the so-called "head hunters". I regard this process with suspicion, although it can be both justified and successful, if the real aim is to get the right man into the right job. In our case, we seem to have settled down to two major methods. One is to keep a permanent touch with certain universities, and in particular with tutors and professors in the appropriate faculties, who know the sort of people we want. If possible, we like to contact suitable students a year before they graduate. It is a time-consuming business. In one year, twenty-eight students were interviewed at the university, eight re-interviewed in London, and two engaged. But you do get some good men this way.

The second method is personal contact, the good old grapevine, passing the word around. This works in many ways. Our friends in the Temple sometimes recommend a young barrister who, perhaps because he has embarked on marriage and raising a family, cannot wait for success at the Bar. One of our men I met in Bombay, another on board a ship in Hull. Both of them were ship's officers with master mariner's certificates who had decided to leave the sea. Another man got talking to one of our business rivals on a train, and was recommended to apply to us. Others are friends of friends. And more and more we have lost our inhibitions about the type of recruits. The basic factor seems to be not age nor qualifications nor experience, but more the quality of the individual. One of our successes was a fifty-one year old company director, displaced by financial reconstruction of a big company. Once, some of us were discussing our recruiting needs with Dr. Arthur Suddaby, principal of the City of London Polytechnic. He asked what we looked for. Was it a specialist, or a man with training in several disciplines? The youngest partner present, himself highly qualified, blurted out, "The first thing we look for is an honest man." I think he meant more than a person reliable about money and straight in his dealings. We need men who are intellectually honest. And they must be much more, too. They need a spark in their eye, a flexibility, a sensitivity to people. Thorough interviewing, preferably by two or more partners, is essential, and many are sieved out. One man spent an hour with me and another partner, and 'sold' himself to us so vigorously that we hardly got a word in. After we had persuaded him to go, we looked at each other and both shook our heads. On the other hand, we have managed to recommend some applicants to more suitable jobs, one with a well-known British shipowner, one back to the Bar, and so on.

My first decisions on a training programme proved to be valid. They were to concentrate on new recruits (others would have to step up their training of those already at work), to give them a daily talk on a prepared plan covering some months, and to put them into constructive work at once, whilst checking closely what they did. I also decided that it should not be a full-time occupation for me, but that I should keep fully in touch with the firm's daily life by continuing to handle current work myself. A couple of years later, we had a general review of our operations made by another firm of management consultants, Urwick Orr, so we got a second opinion on our training problem. They had done a great deal in the field, and openly said that they now realised some of the work had been a waste of time because, whatever an outside firm could contribute, most management training had to be done on the job and by the people immediately senior to the trainee. We were glad to find that they cordially approved our approach and methods.

For that first 'class' of four men, including a Swedish lawyer, a student with us, who just came along for the ride, I had to invent the training course as we went along. In fact the notes for the daily sections of what became my training manual were sometimes running two or three days in advance, and sometimes two or three days behind. That is to say, I would give the talk from rough notes and later dictate a summary to put in the file for use the next time round. The aim was, first, to explain the firm's place in the business community, both historically and today, to give an outline of what it did and how, and then to provide some ideas on which to base the work they would be doing. The original course ran out to forty-eight half-hour talks, spread over ten weeks, but it gradually expanded to sixty-three. It was a great help to discuss the class itself with that first class in 1965. One thing they insisted on was that it was impossible to be too elementary. So I included sections on how to write a business letter, how to conduct a business telephone call, and the proper relationship with a typist or secretary, filing staff and messengers. These proved particularly useful with young graduates.

One reason I included the one about letters was because of a young man we took on for an executive job at an earlier date. He was very talented but his letters were very difficult to understand. Eventually, a day came when he composed a letter which caused one of the partners to ask him what it meant. He replied, "Well, I couldn't understand the question he was asking, so I tried to give him an answer he could interpret in any way he pleased." He was told, sorrowfully, that his undoubted talents were not suitable for our business. He is said to be doing well in a very big concern, but I don't know what his duties are. A public relations officer, perhaps? Among the points in my notes were the need for each letter to have a specific objective, the need to remember that the recipient's mother tongue might be Italian or Arabic, and the need to build a relationship with the recipient.

The telephone hints included the value of using the other person's name once or twice in the course of the conversation and the practice of noting down the main points as the conversation proceeds. Many of such notes may be thrown away afterwards. The rest are kept, or developed into proper notes for filing, what a solicitor calls an attendance note, which may be very difficult to construct if there are no contemporary jottings.

It is important in office relationships to realise that every individual in the office is essential for the running of the business. It may sound pompous to say that each person deserves the respect which attaches to his function and his status as a human being, but it is nevertheless true. And if a man has a secretary, it is his job, not hers, to ensure that she is not without work in the morning and in consequence kept late in the evening.

Most of the course dealt with technical matters — insurance, shipping practice, law — but naturally only in outline, with references to where details could be found. Some of the most important points were considered more than once, from different angles. But I added a further section, after some misgivings and trying it out on several people first. It was called "The Complete Mutual Insurance Man", and it listed some of the human qualities needed, preceded by some of those which were unnecessary. One of the 'guinea pigs' for this section, a newly qualified barrister, observed, "It needed to be said. The course would not be complete without." It was designed to be read out straight, without comment, and the first part was always received with roars of laughter, followed by thoughtful silence for the second part.

The course, as class after class went through it, had a cumulative effect on the executives of the firm as a group. It was rather like the driving test. It was designed to make you reasonably safe on the road, to establish a pattern of driving for everyone, and so to make conditions generally safer and more straightforward.

The second part of the basic training was also of great interest. It is not common for a young man, even a graduate, joining a firm, to be given a few letters on his second day at work, and told to prepare suitable replies, dictate them for typing, and sign them out. It gave him a real sense of being trusted to use his intelligence and make decisions, but for our own protection it was necessary to control carefully very letter which went out. It quickly became apparent that this called for a whole series of checks. First, the name and address of the addressee. So often something was wrong here. I laugh when people call me Leadworth or Sedgwick or Hedwit, but, to be honest, I don't actually enjoy it. And if the letter is, say, to a French lawyer, it is quite obligatory to address him as Maître. Likewise, it is really necessary to send it to the right address in the right town and country. Then there is the grammar and the spelling. Sometimes the secretary cannot spell, and sometimes the man who signs the letter knows no better, or is not alert enough to notice. A distinguished solicitor friend of mine, Sir Roy Pinsent, told me of an error of his own which shows that shorthand has its pitfalls. He carelessly scanned, signed and despatched a letter dealing with some property which said: "We have now obtained the consent of the sub-lessors, and the only point outstanding is to obtain the consent of the headless horse."

Having considered the form of the letter, you also consider the content. Has the man fully understood who are the different people involved, and the way in which they are affected? Has he understood the facts? If there is a legal issue, has he got the law right? (One of our young lawyers once gave an intelligent legal opinion, but I had to point out that in the particular circumstances English law did not seem to apply. It was either Cuban or Bulgarian law he should have been considering.) What is the objective of his letter? Is it the right objective? If it is, is there a better way of reaching it? By the time all these points have been checked, and if necessary discussed, a good deal of training has gone on. In fact, when the class was up to six or even five in number, I simply could not do it all myself and had to share this work with others.

I have dealt with this in some detail because it touches on a matter which I want to return to later — the functions of management. Perhaps one reason why management is often ineffective is that not enough thought is given to selection and training of people for management jobs. Two days before I wrote this, the newspapers carried a story about a man who refused to join a trade union. Because other men refused to work with him, he was suspended, but on full pay. When he called to collect his pay, at 10.30 a.m. on a Friday, he was jeered at and jostled, and 2,000 men left their work to join in or watch. Whatever was the management doing? Apart from anything else, they could at least have sent the money by post.

We give a lot more training besides what I have detailed above — visits to ships and docks; trips on cargo ships; a short weekly rapid-fire session, at which all the junior management can bring forward their problems and discoveries; an arrangement whereby junior management is organised in a team with more experienced people, in daily or hourly contact; and so on. Experts have told me they know of no firm with such a

complete training programme. Some of our rivals openly
envy it. But, frankly, we hope to improve it.

It will be apparent that management training, as I
approach it, tried to deal with character and human
relationships, as well as technical information. Was it successful in this? That is very hard to measure. The seven or eight
years I worked at it certainly affected me, and there were
some signs that it affected others.

It gave me a great regard for the men and women
concerned. Before the formal training course began a casual
incident occurred, which developed into an important permanent factor. The first woman executive we recruited, a law
graduate, happened to be a friend of my daughter. To ease
her introduction to the City, and that of another woman
lawyer we engaged, my wife and I asked them to our London
flat to meet some of their future colleagues over an informal
dinner. Its success was sensational. Relaxed but active
conversation made it a gay and stimulating evening.

Later each 'training class' was asked to a similar function.
Existing staff began to hint that an invitation to the next
occasion would be appreciated, perhaps because my wife's
apple tarts became something of a legend.

One hesitates to try to assess intangibles, but one thing is
quite tangible. So far we have had seven of my trainees invite
my wife and myself to their weddings, a privilege we value
highly. One couple had both been trained by me, and asked
me to propose 'The Bride and Bridegroom' at the reception.
Since I had helped to select them both for the office, it could
be thought that I was indirectly responsible for the match,
though their romance was unknown to all of us until the
engagement was announced — the best-kept secret of the year.

The night before their wedding I woke at about three
o'clock and, lying in the darkness, evolved or perhaps
received into consciousness the following lines, which I duly
included in a short speech:

> Why join a man unto a maid?
> Why join a handle to a blade?
> The firmness, grace and warmth of wood,
> The spring and danger of the steel,
> Combined can cut away the ill,
> Or carve and decorate the good.
> Who is the handle? Who the blade?
> Don't ask; or ask of Him who made
> Them both for purposes which He
> Has planned throughout eternity.

20

Ships and Men

How fortunate I was to have my life cast among ships! Most of my time may have been spent in St. Mary Axe, nose to grindstone, but ships and the sea were in everything I did there, and I took every chance I could to go down to see them for myself. I can remember the first time I went on board a cargo ship, accompanying a surveyor instructed to get particulars of some damage to grain. It was in the Surrey Commercial Docks, a longish bumpy ride in a battered car, through the gates, over the cobbles, and then an uneasy climb up the gangway slung alongside. She was a smallish tramp ship, but seemed big and high close to. On deck, I at once went to the open hatch where they were discharging sling loads of sawn lumber, and looked down. The next thing I knew was a smack across the side of the head from a wire rope. Luckily, the brim of my bowler hat took the shock, so all I got was a broad line of black grease down my face, but I never again leant over a hatchway without a good look round first. I might easily have been flicked over the hatch coaming into the ship's hold, a twenty foot drop.

Although I'd seen sketches and photographs, I found it more impressive to see for myself the ship's equipment, the heavy cleats and eye-bolts for the wedges and lashings, the derricks swinging round, the speeding and slowing of the winches, with puffs of steam, and drippings of oil. Below, in the hold, were the last few layers of planks stowed, as so often in the trade from Vancouver to Britain, over a bottom layer of bulk grain. I had learnt by then that heavy grain and light lumber together made a good way of utilising the full capacity of the ship, both in space and weight-carrying. Plain to the eye, however, was one of the dangers of this practice. Moisture from the timber had condensed on the ship's side plating, and run down onto the wheat at the edges, where the separating tarpaulins did not reach. The 'grass', which was actually young wheat, showed green and a foot high right along the hold.

Not much later, I visited an American cargo liner in the London docks. The captain asked me if there was anything I would especially like to see. I immediately said, "Inside the bilges". He stared at me as if I was mad, and I had to explain that we often received claims for grain which had worked down into the bilge channels, and been damaged there by the drainage water; and I had never been able to visualise just how and why it happened. So he sent the ship's carpenter down the vertical ladders with me, so that he could lever off some of the protecting limber boards, and I could see the smelly gutter below.

Marvellous things, ships. We landsmen forget how big they are. Those of my youth would be 300 or 400 feet long, those of today may be a quarter of a mile or more. The growth in my lifetime has been almost unbelievable. Even in the late thirties it was said that the most useful size of an oil tanker would be the 'triple twelve', carrying 12,000 tons of oil at 12 knots on a consumption of 12 tons of oil a day. The biggest of today are about 500,000 tons; bigger ones have been ordered, and there is no limit in sight. Stavros Niarchos, one of the major Greek owners, was asked by a shipping journalist what was the biggest tanker which would be built. He replied that technically there was no objection to building a vessel two or three miles long, "and it would shorten the voyage a little". Not so many years ago, I was asked down to see one of the 'small' bulk carriers built for J.C. Carras in Japan. Mr. Carras' energetic son Costas insisted on taking me down to the engine-room, and straight up from there to the bridge, the equivalent of at least seven storeys of a building on land. At which point, I collapsed into a chair. Many of the bigger ships have lifts installed, and apparently it is true that the giant tankers have small motorcycles to help the crew get quickly from end to end of the deck.

My wife and I have been to a dozen launchings of new ships, in England, Scotland, Belgium and Spain. I know of no other couple who has attended two launchings on successive days, one at Newcastle-upon-Tyne and the other at Burntisland. I remember old Mrs. Coulouthros saying a prayer over the ship she named, and standing back so that her grandson, in his school cap, could smash the bottle for her against the ship's bow. Another time, the television cameras at Sunderland focussed with enthusiasm on a twenty-month old girl, Miss Chandris, complete with a little Victorian nosegay, naming and launching the ship named after her. In an industrial and workaday age, a launching is always a moment of pure emotion. The words end, ' . . . and God bless all who sail in her'', the great structure stirs, moves, and begins to slide, and everyone catches his breath. Is it an association of ideas? Or is it that ships have personalities, and this is the point at which the personality is born?

Certainly ships mysteriously acquire characteristics which can well be regarded as personality. Any naval architect or shipbuilder will tell you that it is possible to build two ships which are intended to be exact duplicates, and they will behave quite differently when they are in service. One might be a whole knot faster than the other, a big margin in terms of a twenty years' life. One might ride easily in bad weather while her sister, similarly laden in the same conditions, digs her nose into every wave. Some are always in trouble, some never.

Occasionally, one comes across the freakiest characteristics. For example, most merchant ships have a single propeller with a right-handed 'screw'. It is so set (I hope I understand it correctly) that it drives the ship straight forward, but it is axiomatic that when such a propeller is put into reverse, to stop or send the ship astern, it tends to swing the ship's bows to starboard. It is something to do with torque, and the rule is (mechanically) inevitable. But one ship I dealt with, when the engines were put astern, would sometimes pay off to starboard and sometimes to port. Coming into berth at Colombo, the pilot ordered engines full astern. Away to port went the ship's bows. There was a dredger moored on the port side, and the dredger went to the bottom. There was also a heated discussion as to whether the master had warned the pilot of his ship's playful ways. In the end, the discussion was repeated before a judge, who decided that no warning had been given to the pilot.

Another British ship in the same ownership as that wayward beauty was also in trouble at Colombo. Her trouble was a fire. It was so fierce that in two or three minutes the engine-room was evacuated, and in twenty minutes more the crew abandoned ship. There was 150 tons of dynamite among the cargo stowed in the tweendecks. Fortunately, every one was safely clear by the time the ship blew up and sank. Since cargo owners in the United States were threatening a legal action against the shipowners, we had to investigate the cause of the fire. I got the detailed plans of the ship from her owners. She was a 'Doxford Motorship', one of the simple all-purpose cargo ships with a simple diesel engine, of which many examples were built in the forties and fifties as part of the first replacements of the ships lost in the war. Even so, the engine-room was the equivalent of a three-storey factory, containing 24 major items of machinery, and many minor ones.

I also set out to interview all the ship's eight engineers. Four months after the accident, six of them had left the sea. The second engineer was a boiler surveyor for an insurance company. Two others had formed a partnership and started a garage. And so on. The chief engineer was still at sea. So was the eighth or junior engineer, or at least he was supposed to be. I had to wait a while for him to come out of jail at Antwerp, where he had been put after a fight with his new chief engineer ashore somewhere. This junior, although he denied it, was plainly the man who started the fire. One of the items of equipment in the engine-room was a large oil-fired boiler which provided steam for various services when the ship was in port, and the main engines were not in use. One purpose was to power the windlass which lifted the anchors when preparing to sail. The junior engineer had been detailed to light the furnace under the boiler for this purpose. He turned a drainage tap on a fuel oil tank to make some tests, and obviously allowed oil to flow out onto the deck plating, for when he tried to light the furnace there was a flash-back which ignited oil on the deck. What was worse, he must have left the tap running for there was no other way in which enough oil could have been reached by the fire so quickly as to send a sheet of flame right across the engine-room. He was a large fleshy young man, with a face covered with pimples, and I could not help hoping that he was not a fair sample of the engineer officer of the future.

At least, we were able to prove there was nothing wrong with the ship, and on the basis of this we won the case.

Shipowners continually complain how difficult it is to get good crews. In the past, I suppose, it was more often poverty than adventurousness which drove men to sea. It is noteworthy that Greece and Norway, the two countries whose shipping industry produces more than half the national income, are both rather barren, and with little mineral wealth. Their people need first the fish to eat, and then the earnings of the trading vessels, in order to live. Today, there is a tendency for fewer men to leave the comforts of developed countries for a sea career. More and more seamen come from the developing countries, Hongkong and Singapore Chinese, Indians and Pakistanis, Somalis, Syrians and South Americans. But economic reasons are not the only cause for people leaving the sea. Some former merchant navy officers have told me that the modern ships are so easy to run that they are no challenge. In fact, they are a bore. Another complaint is that bigger ships mean fewer ships and fewer chances of promotion. The number of ships afloat is still increasing, but not nearly as fast as the aggregate tonnage increases. Seamen also miss having a normal home life.

I once discussed British crews with a seamen's union man and several shipowners. They all thought that the best British crews are splendid, the worst abysmal. On another occasion, an owner said that he reckoned about one-third of his crews were professional seamen of top quality, one-third young fellows having a voyage or two at sea to look at the world, and one-third the deadheads who are simply shipped to make up the number. How can shipping attract and hold the right type of man? The spreading practice of wives and sometimes children of crew members taking trips with their men is regarded by most people as a good development. When there are a few wives on board, the men generally seem to work better, and enjoy doing so. The Norwegians are trying another way to deal with the objection to a man being separated from his family for most of his life. They are encouraging officers to qualify for a second trade or profession. A man might spend ten years at sea, and reach a master mariner's standard. Then, in the period when his growing family need him most, he could work ashore as a teacher, returning to sea in command when his children are grown and married.

It is hard to prescribe methods to meet the needs of all men. They are such a highly individual crowd. My wife's ideal holiday is a couple of weeks or so on a cargo ship, and we've met some rare characters there. One captain's conversation was a constant flow of quotations from the classics, including Latin and Greek, Shakespeare, the Bible, various poets and essayists. Another was a physical culture fiend. He set up a stationary bicycle on the wing of the bridge and in calm weather pedalled away there, stripped to shorts and shoes. A third, on one of the Scindia Line's ships, had a whole cabin full of ivory carvings he had collected, some antiques, some specially commissioned from the best artists in India. One of these was a big set piece of a scene from the great religious epic, the Mahabharata. The one quality which seems to be common to most of them is the freedom with which they carry their responsibilities. To watch and listen to them you would not think that they live daily on the basis that a single error could destroy many lives and millions of pounds' worth of ship and cargo. I don't mean they are irresponsible. They take it for granted that sleep and rest go by the board if there is even a slight degree of danger, but they certainly don't show their worries. The only time I have seen a captain seriously agitated was when he had some owner's guests on board, and the gin was running short.

The oddest things happen to ships, and in connection with ships. One broke adrift in the River Tees, and was making briskly for the sea, stern first. The chief officer rushed forward and dropped an anchor. Unfortunately, the ship was at that moment very close to the end of a pier and, due to the overhang of the bow, the anchor (a seven ton chunk of steel) fell squarely onto a small building on the pier, reducing it to a heap of bricks. An Israeli captain was fined in London once for allowing the ship's dog shore leave without its having passed quarantine. A British captain was fined in Venezuela for blowing his whistle for a pilot at eight o'clock on Sunday morning, and waking everyone up. Another ship was accused of emitting smoke from her funnel in London, and damaging the food displayed on a coffee stall in the Rotherhithe Dock Road.

Then, there was the ship which got magnetised. Cargoes of scrap iron and scrap steel are often loaded and discharged with large magnets. The magnet is lowered onto the cargo, switched on, lifted up bristling with pieces of steel, swung over the ship's side, and lowered, and switched off. It is routine for a ship's magnetic compasses to be adjusted by an expert after this process is completed, as the normal magnetic field of the mass of steel which constitutes a ship is affected. The process involves putting pieces of soft iron of appropriate size into the supports of the compass, to compensate. In this case, the stevedores were very careless and kept hitting the ship's bridge with the magnets. When the compass adjuster came on board, he could not get any of the magnetic compasses to work, whatever he did. Whichever way the ship was pointing, the compasses unhesitatingly said that the front of the bridge was north. After a week's delay, the shipowners had to buy a gyro-compass before the ship could sail, and it was a year before the condition wore off. I tried very hard to get the stevedores to pay for the consequential losses, but only recovered a small amount.

One celebrated accident we were involved in was the tragic wartime collision between the *Queen Mary* and her escorting cruiser *Curacao*. The *Queen* was homeward bound and, to confuse any submarines around, was doing a complicated zigzag to a set pattern of course changes. The anti-aircraft cruiser could not, however, follow her through the pattern, since she was only a 29-knot ship against the big ship's 32 or 33. In fact, the only way she could keep up at all was to cut across the zigzags. Two or three times there were near misses as the ships converged, and then came the moment when the liner found the cruiser on a collision course across her bows. From the height of the 80,000-ton ship's bridge, the warship of about 3,000 tons displacement must have looked tiny. A momentary confusion, or hesitation, or whatever it was, and the liner rode right over her. 230 lives were lost. We were approached by the government lawyers acting for the Navy, saying that they had no facilities for handling such a large group of claims as those which the dependant families would make against Cunard Line. Would we help? We agreed to do it on the basis of expenses only. George Didsbury did nearly all the work, but I did a little. I can still picture the schedule the Navy sent us, setting out the names of those killed, with their bereaved relatives, and what service pensions were available to them. We kept in touch with all of them, and prepared their claims for them, until the main lawsuit between Cunard and the Navy was decided after the war. The government then took back the responsibility, and all made a recovery.

Another case which filled the headlines for a time did involve me. It began with a fire of mysterious origin in the cargo liner *Seistan*, owned by the Strick Line, last of the many shipowning companies of the P. & O. group to be merged into the great single fleet of today. The company's main trade was the carriage of every conceivable form of general cargo to the countries round the Persian (or as some say, Arabian) Gulf. The fire began deep in the cargo, and could not be reached. Captain and chief officer had quite an argument as to whether it was better to smother the fire with steam, or flood the hold with water. The captain won, and steam was used, unluckily as it turned out, although the captain could not be blamed for something he did not know. The fire spread, there was a violent explosion (one story said

he funnel landed five miles away) and the ship became in
practical terms a total loss. Nineteen people were killed on
he ship and on a tug alongside.

The cargo was a valuable one, and a Pakistani salvage
company was given a contract to salve what they could of it.
t was known that the cargo had included a large amount of
elly explosives consigned to the oil companies, and the
shippers, Imperial Chemical Industries, sent out an expert to
supervise its discharge. When he saw its condition, he insisted
that the ship (or wreck, as she really was) be evacuated
immediately. The stuff was not in the hold where the fire
began, but the steam which had been turned into the cargo
spaces had part-melted the explosives, putting them into a
highly unstable and dangerous condition. After a careful
investigation, the explosives were very cautiously discharged
into a barge, which was towed some miles out to sea. The
expert lit a long slow fuse, and everyone retired hastily. When
the echoes died away, the owners of the barge said, "By the
way, who pays for our barge?" — but that is another story.

The death roll appalled both the Strick Line, and
ourselves. What caused the fire? There was no direct evidence
at all. Indirect evidence appeared a few months later. A sister
ship with a similar cargo had a similar fire, only this time the
crew managed to put the fire out. When the cargo was
discharged, the fire seemed to have originated in some cases
of 'toe-puff', a substance rather like celluloid, used for
stiffening shoes. Research showed that a shipment of toe-puff
was in the *Seistan*, and in the hold where the fire started. The
Strick Line asked the Ministry concerned if there would be a
government enquiry into the accident. There seemed at first
to be a reluctance, even though it was a British ship with
British lives lost from unascertained causes. The shipowners
and we began to talk of holding an enquiry ourselves, and
publishing the results, but luckily the Ministry decided to go
ahead. They wrote to the manufacturers of the toe-puff (a
company no longer in existence, I believe), and asked them
to make a batch of the substance the next Tuesday, for their
experts to test on the following day. They agreed. On the
Tuesday night there was a fire at the factory, and the whole
batch was destroyed. At the enquiry, it was established that
the stuff was prone to spontaneous combustion. Yet it was
not regarded as a hazardous cargo. It was one of the
borderline substances, which could or could not fall into a
category requiring special precautions when carried overseas.

When it was first produced years before, the company got a certificate from the Ministry that it was non-hazardous. Since then, specifications had been changed, but shipments had continued on the basis of the original certificate. After a very long hearing, the official enquiry attached no blame to anyone for this situation.

No comment seems appropriate, but not many years afterwards better regulations for hazardous cargoes were introduced under the auspices of the United Nations.

Ships are big, dirty, troublesome things, but I cannot help regarding them with affection. I remember bucketing along the Dutch coast in the *Tangistan*, when it was so rough that the pilot refused to come out. The captain told us that these were the waters in which Sir Francis Drake learnt his seamanship in raids on the Spanish-occupied Netherlands. What with fogs and the steep short seas in those shallow waters, it must have been a stern school in the fifteen hundreds. I think, too, of the *Apollon*, newly built at Readheads on the Tyne, bowling across the Atlantic with 13,000 tons of coal. With the wind at force 7 to 8 and the swell on the starboard quarter, it was great to sit on the forecastle head looking aft. Dark clouds made a back-drop, but sun sparkled on the spray flung up above the bulwarks, and sometimes green water flooded across the forward hatches just below our feet. I think, too, of the little *Sela*, 1,039 tons, which took us up to her own country of Iceland. Her engine-room was so clean that the chief engineer did not give us the usual handful of cotton waste on which to wipe our hands, and the drums and other cargo on deck were stowed in so seamanlike a manner that when we arrived, I kicked the lashings and found the ropes still bar-tight. We came back from India by the old *Cilicia* of the Anchor Line. Their passenger service now abandoned, she is pensioned off as a school for stevedores in Rotterdam. Then she was still a very friendly ship, and we enjoyed her atmosphere in spite of our prejudice in favour of the cargo vessel pure and simple.

We under-estimate our ships. They are an essential factor in civilisation, and we must never forget that life as we know it is impossible without them.

21

Greek Shipowners

First things first. I do not know Mr. Onassis or Mr. Niarchos. Everybody seems to ask me that if I admit to some knowledge of the Greek shipowners. But I have had a lot to do with their firms and their ships.

There are well over a hundred Greek shipping firms in London alone, some in New York, some in Monte Carlo, and of course many in Greece. I once asked a leading Greek shipowner exactly why so many of them found it necessary to maintain offices in London. He at once said that there were two reasons; one was chartering and the other insurance. "What about finance?" I asked. "Oh, finance is easy," he replied, "You can do finance anywhere, in an aeroplane if you want to." So that seems to be it. The needs are for the daily touch with the freight market, and for personally dealing with insurance (one of the biggest items of expenditure), in the city where marine insurance is most concentrated. Successive Greek governments have done much to encourage their shipowners to operate from Greece. Some have transferred their crew departments, their ship stores operations, and their accounting, but very many of the men who control the companies stay in London, to keep their hands on the key activities of chartering and insurance.

A lot is written about Greek shipowners. Half-truths are served up, at best, and sometimes the stories are quite untrue. I therefore welcome the chance to write something about them. I know a good proportion of those in London, perhaps half or a little more, and some elsewhere. Once on a London underground train I met Captain John D. Pateras, whom I know slightly, and he introduced me to his companion, saying, "Mr. Ledwith is a great friend of the Greeks." I was surprised. I have never set out particularly to be a friend of the Greeks, although quite a number of them have been very good friends to me. Certainly, I enjoy their stimulating company, I respect their achievements and many of their qualities, and I think I am free of the common prejudices against them.

These prejudices are widespread. They come, I suppose, partly from jealousy and partly from ideological roots. The common allegations are that Greek shipowners are disgustingly rich; they are crooked; they put ships under 'flags of convenience' so that they can underman them, disregard safety regulations, and underpay and starve their crews; they deliberately sink ships to get the insurance money.

Is there any truth in these stories? A little, occasionally, perhaps just enough to warrant dealing with them here, but as regards most of the men concerned they are utterly untrue.

Relatively few Greek shipowners are of course extremely rich. They have usually spent many years in building up their fortunes, and maybe several generations of the family have contributed to the process. A certain number flaunt their wealth. More commonly, they plough it back into the business, and sometimes into other ventures such as real estate and farming, especially in their own country. The great majority give liberally to charity and to the Orthodox Church. Not all are a success. Shipping is a hazardous trade. I have had one shipowner in my office in tears at not being able to meet a comparatively small obligation. A number have gone, or taken employment in the industry where they once gave employment. But most of them do well, partly because of concentrated hard work, continued long after financial considerations make it necessary.

Onassis, Niarchos, and one or two others like them are not typical of Greek shipowners. They are a minority, outside the general community, and even more inclined to go their own way. The main difference, apart from their being even more individualistic in a group who are individualists to a man, is hard to define. It could be that they think in terms of finance first and ships afterwards, against the more general tendency to think of ships first.

One cannot begin to understand Greek shipowners without first knowing that they mostly come from the islands. Many of the islands are more or less barren, forcing their inhabitants to the sea as far back as history traces, first for the fish, then for piracy, then for trade. And even in my lifetime, Greece was a bitterly poor country, scraping a living with a few currants, a little tobacco, the remittances of uncles and cousins working overseas, and of course the earnings of shipowners and seamen. For many many years these earnings were small, but they were essential for survival.

In 1971 my wife and I were honoured to be invited to a rather select dinner in London to celebrate the jubilee of Rethymnis & Kulukundis Ltd. It is not one of the largest or the oldest of the London firms, but it has a unique reputation for the number of shipowners whom they helped in their early days, and who have since become entirely independent of that help. The two families originated in Kassos, but early in this century they left that barren spot for Syra, which made a better base. Both the Rethymnis brothers were at the dinner, four of the five Kulukundis brothers, a number of sons, cousins and close friends. The Greek Ambassador was there, and the Mayor of Syra, who presented a gold medal on behalf of the island. Mr. Manuel Kulukundis made the speech of the evening. He recalled how in 1921 Captain Minas Rethymnis and he had opened the office in one room in Great St. Helen's, with a working capital of £75, most of which went on rent and a typewriter. Shortly afterwards, they acquired "a very good office boy to make the tea and run the errands, who developed in due course into one of the best chartering men in the business — my first cousin Basil Mavroleon." I caught a glimpse of B.M's sturdy frame, and his red face smiling from ear to ear. As chairman of London and Overseas Freighters, the public company owning tankers and bulk carriers which is still a part of the group, he is often quoted by the financial journalists. Manuel went on to describe how the two men and their brothers persuaded relations and friends to entrust them with the agency or management of ships, how they acquired part ownership or ownerships themselves, and the business grew. In six years they grew to become in one way or another responsible for twenty-seven ships. It was quite a romance.

Millers' link with R. and K. (as they are called on the Baltic Exchange) dates from 1922. There were some Greek ships insured in the club before then — Lykiardopulo, Michalinos, C. Michalos, Rodocanachi were all firms to which I delivered letters — but it was R. & K. who opened our door to the Greek world generally, and both firms acknowledge a mutual debt. Dawson Miller was at one time a director of London and Overseas Freighters.

But those earlier days were certainly on a hand-to-mouth basis. The first ships were often old vessels, bought from British owners who considered them ripe for the breaker's yard. Some cost less than £5,000 each. Another Greek told me that when he was at the London School of Economics he was asked to explain to the class why Greek owners could make profits out of a ship after they became uneconomic for British owners. He said he "cooked up something" about all the family serving on board, and board meetings being held in the ship's saloon. There was something in this. A ship would often be owned by several members of the family. Sons, brothers, nephews, cousins would be among the officers and perhaps also the cook and boatswain. The rest of the crew could well be neighbours from the owners' own village. It made both for economy and attention to the business.

There were, however, at least two other factors in the Greek success story. First, the Greeks have a deep feeling for the sea and ships. Ships are living things to them, not just a business. Even though nowadays most of the firms have expanded right out of the family and village conception, the men who own the ships are closer in spirit to the men who man them than in almost any nation.

Take a man like Stavros Livanos, one of the big owners, whose daughters married Stavros Niarchos and Aristotle Onassis. He knew every officer of his fleet, something between fifty and one hundred ships. I was told that he had certificates himself as both master and chief engineer, and that on one occasion he bought a ship, superintended a boiler survey himself, and then navigated her to the next port to pick up the new captain. One of his tankers caught fire and blew up in a South Wales port. Next morning, his London director had a telephone call from the boss. He hastened to give him the latest news about the accident. "What do you mean?" broke in Livanos, "I am speaking from a call-box alongside the ship." He had flown the Atlantic and driven to the ship as soon as the news of the fire reached him. At the shipyard in Pula, in Yugoslavia, the management were showing me pictures of ships they had built. "I see you have built ships for Mr. Livanos," I said, knowing that there had been a dispute about them. "Oh yes," they replied, "What an experience! Nothing was good enough for him, the steel, the workmanship, everything had to be better, according to him." They went on to describe how he visited the yard to press his complaints. At the end of a morning's discussion the director of the yard said that lunch had been arranged at a nearby hotel. "Lunch?" said Mr. Livanos, "I came here to talk business. I've got my lunch in my briefcase."

An example (I could give many) of this passionate involvement in the whole business of ships, but from quite another angle, came when I was talking with Antony Chandris at a time of great depression in shipping. Many ships were being laid up. He said, "I don't want to lay up. I can't help thinking that every time a ship is laid up, thirty or forty families are looking for bread." And some, of course, could be from his own island, his own village.

The other factor, besides the passion for ships and the sea, is the passion for business. At this same time of depression, I said to a Greek owner, "Whatever do you talk about when there's no business to be done?" "Oh," he said without hesitation, "we talk about the business we would like to be doing." They do seem to think and breathe business in a way which is rare amongst Anglo-Saxons. They love it. And they also love a gamble. One of them chartered a ship to a Frenchman who, choosing his moment carefully, left suddenly for Brazil with his mistress and the money he should have paid for the hire of the ship. The Greek came round to see me about it, and I said with a smile, "The trouble with you is that you much prefer a risky contract at one hundred shillings to a safe one at ninety-eight." His eyes opened wide. "But of course," he replied. To be a successful shipowner you have to be something of a gambler. After all, a ship's life may be taken at about twenty years. Would anyone like to forecast how world trade will develop over the next twenty years? Yet the willingness to take a risk is, I think, only part of the way in which they commit all of themselves to their business. An insurance broker told me once, "I always know when so-and-so is buying another ship. He tells us to inform the insurers of his wife's diamonds that they have been lodged with the bank as part security for the new ship's purchase price."

As for the view that Greeks are crooked, my own opinion is that there is about the same proportion of crooks among them as there is among the British, or any other nationality. A great number of those I have dealt with I would cheerfully trust with my own money, or even with my reputation. I think of one man who has been many years in Britain. The firm of which he is a director has 'family' ships and also 'clients'' ships. The cash of all the clients' ships is kept in the same bank account, so completely do those hard-headed men trust him. One serious claim I dealt with for him in Holland concerned a ship which damaged a pier and then sank, obstructing the entrance to the port of Rotterdam. The ship was owned by a Panamanian company, and the lawyers pointed out that it would be possible to evade all payment by stripping the company of its assets, and in effect hiding from the claimants. "I wouldn't really like to do a thing like that," he said. Another matter we discussed was a dispute with a charterer. He playfully listed to me and his lawyer all the underhand tricks he might have used against the opponent, and then said, "No. If I am going to play poker, I prefer to play with my friends. We'll do this one straight."

Perhaps some of the misconceptions in many minds about Greek business methods are due to the fact that to many Greeks business is a game. The puritanical English regard this as quite improper. A rather extravagant example of it was when the two Chandris brothers, finding conventional methods a little too conventional perhaps, decided quite amicably to divide the family fleet into two, a bulk carrier for one, a bulk carrier for the other, a tanker for one, a tanker for the other, and so on. The two London companies continued to occupy the same block of offices. Each brother managed the ships in his group, and developed the business according to his judgment. D.J. Chandris, the elder brother, now includes under his group a number of small cruise ships for the Mediterranean, whilst A.J., the younger, has what is said to be the biggest fleet in the world of large passenger ships, mostly used for ocean cruising. And each is still a director of the other's company! I should add that although it may be a game, it is a serious one. The first time I met D.J.C., at lunch on one of his older steamships, he greeted me before changing out of the boiler suit in which he had been crawling behind the boilers. A.J.C. is a qualified engineer, and is noted for acquiring passenger vessels from other groups and converting them into paying propositions.

Sometimes, the game involves point scoring. A man came in to see one of my partners, told him a story about some business matter, and asked his opinion. My partner completely disbelieved his story. After a little thought he said, "Could we imagine, just for the sake of discussion, that events did not arise in the way you have described, but in this way instead?" and he went on to set out what he thought had really happened. The Greek considered the position thoughtfully, and replied, "Yes. But I prefer my version." This attitude is not exclusive to one race. Only yesterday, I was told of one Englishman who bought a house from another. The seller had started by saying, "I originally bought this house for X thousand pounds." The buyer replied, "I happen to know that it cost you half that." "First trick to you," said the seller cheerfully. It is, I think, a little akin to the bazaar approach, when everyone enjoys a good haggle, and most of all when the ultimate price is a fair one. In countries where haggling is standard practice, I have known disappointment to pass over the shopkeeper's face when I gave in too easily.

There is, too, of course, the misleading silence, the half-truth, but are these unique to any group? Can any of us say with confidence that we are absolutely honest all the time, under whatever circumstances and whatever pressure? In my experience, honesty is a thing you have to struggle for. Even more, an honest relationship with someone else is something you have to work to create. And I am glad to be able to say that with more Greek business friends than I can count I have reached a basis where a straight question will produce the truth and all the truth — whichever of us asks it. I remember meeting for the first time an important ship-owner who had got into a major difficulty over a shipbuilding contract. After listening to him for some time, I decided to take a bit of a gamble myself, and asked him (knowing that shipping earnings had dropped severely since the contract was made), "Have you got a genuine grievance, or is it more that you want to get out of your contract?" He was shocked, and showed it, but then said, "I don't deny that it would suit me to get out of my contract, but I do have a genuine grievance." And so it proved.

'Flags of convenience' is a pejorative phrase, used almost as insultingly as 'apartheid'. Someone once suggested to Dawson Miller that the P. and I. clubs should refuse to insure any ships carrying flags of convenience. He replied that if we did, we would have to start with the British flag. Canadian, Australian, Danish and Norwegian interests, to name only four, have found it more convenient to run ships under the British flag than their own. And so have the Greeks. Germans, Italians and others employ the more usual flags of Liberia and Panama, and at one time (perhaps not now) half of all the 'flag of convenience' tonnage was American owned.

The use of the Cyprus flag for merchant shipping was first suggested immediately after independence by the present Cyprus Ambassador to the United Nations. I happened to be there when he did so, and currently some two million tons of shipping wears that flag. And it was a slightly embarrassing experience when, at a dinner in London, the Ambassador of a certain landlocked country asked me to explain to him the advantages of the system. What flag would you like for your yacht, or your super-tanker? Lebanon, Ethiopia, Somalia and Nepal have all provided facilities on request.

The main reason for this development originally, so I have been told, was the Greek restriction on mortgages and re-sale of ships which made it very difficult to borrow money, in order to buy ships. If, however, the ship were to be registered in Panama or Monrovia, the restrictions were so few that an American or British banker would gladly produce the funds. The great Onassis and Niarchos fleets (and others) were built up in this way, together with chartering contracts. The plan was to go to a bank and ask to borrow 90 per cent of the cost of building a new ship of a specific size, showing a draft contract from the builders and another for the ship's employment for some years by an oil company or a big steel company or someone equally stable. If everyone agreed, all the contracts were signed more or less at once. It was rather like a juggler keeping three balls in the air. If all went well, everybody was paid off in perhaps eight or ten years, and the shipowner had a ship fully paid for to operate for the rest of her economic life.

There were other important advantages. Taxation was one. Most of the convenience countries charge no income tax, only a smallish annual fee for each company. Crew's wages make another strong incentive, especially for United States interests, who cannot pay the very high American wages and still compete in international markets for freight. Another factor has been the restrictions by certain governments against ships of their flags trading to some of the Communist countries.

In the earlier years, a few disreputable owners did take advantage of the system, to cut costs on the wages, accommodation, and number of their crews. There are still one or two such vessels dodging round the oceans. They are, however, as unpopular with shipowners as a whole as they are with the International Transport Workers Federation. The great majority of 'flags of convenience' ships today are new, high-class vessels, well kept up, with crews paid at standard rates or higher. On the day when I went round Madras with an Indian master mariner, we both had to agree that the smartest looking ship in the entire port was a Greek-owned tramp flying the Liberian flag.

The last of the allegations I mentioned was scuttling. In 1924 someone in our office in St. Mary Axe pointed out to me an elegant gentleman in a pearl grey Homburg, with flower in buttonhole, and a strong but not unpleasant odour of hair oil, who was waiting in the outer office. An undertone explained that he was Mr. D——; A——, who was accused of scuttling ships for the insurance money. He went inside to see one of the partners, and did not call again. It was understood that his offer to enter his next ship in the club had not been taken up.

There have been cases, several of them. Not all have been Greek. And of course they are scandalous, and indefensible. On one occasion, Millers were about to help a shipowner to sue the underwriters over the loss of a ship, when the underwriters' solicitors disclosed to us an affidavit from a Brazilian lighthouse keeper. He stated that he had observed the ship going up and down the coast for some hours, obviously looking for a spot where she could be put on the rocks without risk to the crew. That was one claim that was not paid.

However, cases like this are not numerous, and my own opinion is that the number of ships deliberately destroyed for the insurance money in the last half-century may well be less than the number of cases which the courts have held to be fraudulent losses. In saying so, I am not attacking the courts, which have to do their best with what is before them. A good example was the *Tropaioforos*, which foundered in the Indian Ocean, and was the talk of the whole Greek shipping community for years. The court dismissed the owner's claim for the insurance money, and feelings about the decision were acute. It was felt to be an unjust reflection on the Greek merchant marine. One of the lawyers engaged in the case told me he was certain that the ship was not thrown away, but on the other hand the court was fully entitled to find that she was, on the evidence as it came out in court. This is always a hazard in legal proceedings. In a different case, years ago, a shipowner lost his head and told a lie in the witness box. The judge, on the basis of this, rejected the whole of his evidence, and the case went against him. He should have won it.

I never went into the details of the *Tropaioforos* case, but if I had been the insurer of the ship I would not have disputed the claim, for a simple human reason. Because of earlier trouble with the ship, her owner had sent out James Douglas, an elderly and well-known consultant engineer, and he was on board at the time of the casualty. I knew Jimmy Douglas, and he was a transparently honest man. At a conference in my office on another matter, where the facts were in dispute, one of the experts present asked, "What are we trying to prove?" Douglas growled out, "I thought we were trying to get at the truth." No man in his senses who had something to conceal would send Douglas out to the ship. If anything was wrong, he would almost certainly see it, and if he did he would quite certainly tell everyone concerned.

Other lawyers have told me of alleged scuttling cases they should never have won for underwriters. Well, that may be the luck of the game. No one can foretell exactly what will happen in a lawsuit. I do take exception when underwriters, Lloyd's and the companies in England, and insurance companies in other countries, dispute a claim on mere suspicion. I dealt with one case where a ship went aground on the Arctic coast of Russia. Salvage services were offered, and the master felt he should not accept the help of a Soviet salvor without a radio message to his owner for permission. It was a weekend, two days were lost, and it was then too late. The underwriters considered this was very suspicious, and the shipowners had to sue to recover. In another case, when a ship caught fire and foundered off the Spanish coast, the only evidence on which the underwriters relied was a story that when the vessel left a French port several days before, the crew's belongings were packed in suitcases and in the alleyways, ready for disembarkation. Rather a fanciful yarn. And, to go farther back, a claim was fought when a ship sank with a cargo of ore off the south coast of Crete. Admittedly she was an old ship, but a heavy ore cargo can put great strain on the hull in stormy weather, and the owners were a reputable firm. But a circumstance which affected my opinion on the matter was that the crew landed on a rocky coast, and had to trudge right over the mountains, with a single donkey between the lot of them. I could not envisage a Greek crew accepting such an ordeal otherwise than by accident.

An even worse thing, to my view, is the fact that a number of these cases have been compromised. If underwriters are prepared to go into court and accuse a shipowner of gross dishonesty, it should be fought to the end, win or lose. But I know one case where a shipowner, without ship or insurance money for more than two years, accepted an offer of 75 per

cent rather than wait more years for a judgment of the
courts. In another case, underwriters' lawyers were authorised to make steadily increasing offers from 50 per cent
upwards, up to 100 per cent but without interest, which was
accepted. It seems to me quite immoral to make an
accusation of fraud, and use it to reduce your liability below
what it should be.

Admittedly it is sometimes hard to judge on these matters.
The bad cases are not very common. I put part of the trouble
down to the centralisation of claims work at Lloyd's, very
different from the days when every leading hull underwriter
had his own claims expert, but this might not have mattered
if Lloyd's central claims bureau were not overworked. It has
seemed to me as an outside observer that if you can get their
full attention, they are admirable, but often they are too
busy to do other than take the advice of lawyers, without
enough consideration of the reputation of the London
market for fair and at times generous treatment of claims.

As far as the Greeks are concerned, the common impression of the public in all these matters is far too highly-
coloured and exaggerated. What are they really like? First of
all, I would say that family means much to them. Usually, a
Greek family is tightly united. If there should be a quarrel, it
is often equally extreme. One very eminent Greek shipowner
is said to have pursued two of his nephews through the
corridors of the Law Courts, shouting and waving an
umbrella, and this was after winning, not losing, a lawsuit
against them. But a Greek will do almost anything for a
friend, and more for a relation. They inter-marry a great deal,
some links between great shipowning families being almost
like a linking of dynasties in the days when royalty was more
customary than today. It is or was common for a bride to be
given a ship for a dowry. The different island communities
are still somewhat isolated from each other in feeling, even if
many work in London or New York. The Andros families,
Goulandris and Embiricos, tend to keep to themselves. A
Lemos is likely to marry another Lemos, or a Lyras, or a
Pateras, all of whom come from Oinoussoi, off Chios. Until
recently, the men of Chios were regarded as newcomers to
shipping prominence, and, there is still a little feeling of this
kind. Almost all go back to Greece for some weeks or months
every year, so that their roots are refreshed, their relations
visited, and their children encouraged to speak Greek.

Individually, of course, they vary in an extraordinary

manner. Compare, for example, the two M's. One of them is slender, soft-voiced, cultured. Originally, he was a lawyer; as a shipowner he has been a little cautious and conservative, but steadily he has built up quite a large business, very strongly based. But despite his exquisite courtesy, he is a formidable opponent to anyone who, in a dispute, tries to beat him down. There is steel under the velvet. The other died prematurely, flying his own plane into a mountain. He was a gorgeous extrovert, round-faced and round-bodied. If you opposed him, he would try to shout you down. (One of my partners always responded by answering in a very quiet voice, so that he had to stop to listen.) Coming back from a launching he did somersaults down the aisle of the private dining car. He came away from the shipbuilders' reception with three bottles of champagne under his arm. When I raised my eyebrows, all he said was, "I did ask." But under it all he also was a very successful shipowner, and everybody liked him.

This, incidentally, raises an interesting question. Why do I find myself drawn to rascals, sometimes even more than to the men of principle? I can only think I must have a lot in common with them.

C. is a very big operator, and would agree with anyone who compared his methods with Niarchos or Onassis. At one time, he would never order a ship unless a lucrative trading contract for her was fixed in advance. I telephoned him once when serious trouble arose in connection with one of his tankers. "Oh, that's an operating matter", he said airily. "Speak to the managing director."

G. is a literary man, and a great patron of the Church. M. plays the violin. A. is a trustee of Covent Garden, and has a deep understanding of opera. Everyone knows of Manuel Kulukundis' pocket box of water-colour paints. Sitting next to him at lunch once, I watched him do three charming sea scenes on the backs of menu cards, pouring a little water into an ashtray for his brush. Usually, his pictures each feature a particular ship which he remembers. On another occasion, he did a Greek landscape with a characteristic windmill, and I borrowed his colours to do a little English farm scene in return.

I met J. in St. Mary Axe the week his third child was born. I congratulated him, and asked if mother and child were well. "Wonderful," he answered. "It was as smooth as launching a ship." Captain N., like so many, spent long and hard days at sea before settling down to manage ships ashore. He said he often wished to be back in the old days, when to be a master of a tramp ship was the nearest job in the world to perfect freedom. "109 days from Buenos Aires to Belfast," muttered one of his co-directors. "Why bring that up?" he growled in reply. His brother, Captain G., told me that his most vivid memory was as a deck boy in the Black Sea and Danube trade — the stink of the fish oil he had to rub into the deck planks to preserve them.

To get to know these men well, you need to see them in action, dealing with a problem or a difficulty. There is sometimes a lot of sound and fury. Matters get a little like a scene from grand opera, but there is also a very liberal supply of expertise and common sense. When the *Lakonia* caught fire, John Goulandris was in our office the next day to discuss what should be done about the passengers and crew. It was a tragic accident, with heavy loss of life. The newspapers, radio and television spilt oceans of words over it. Every kind of allegation was given an airing. The fact was that the ship had passed the British Government's stringent safety tests just before the voyage. The Greek Government enquiry made findings of negligence against certain officers, but there was also a lot of bad luck. Almost at once, the fire reached the oil tanks and produced volumes of black smoke. The confusion was increased by the burning out of the public address system, no small handicap with a mass of passengers, many of whom had never been to sea before.

That first day, we decided to send lawyers to meet and record the stories of all the survivors as they landed. There were 1,100 of them, put ashore in Hamburg, Falmouth, Casablanca, Piraeus and elsewhere. The Greek Line could under English law have defended the claims under the conditions of the passenger ticket, forcing claimants to sue in Greece. It was, however, decided to discuss all the claims amicably, and most of them were settled in less than a year, no mean accomplishment when several hundred claims are involved.

This was an almost unique case. Most of the excitements I joined in with Greek owners were not on this scale, but at least I have seen how they do business from all kinds of angles. I find it not surprising that they have built up between them such a galaxy of business. Their ships together are worth well over 2,000 million pounds. It is true that if you put fifty of these men together, you will find fifty extremely different individuals, but some of their characteristics could well be copied with advantage by others.

22

British Shipowners

It is harder for me to write about the British than about the
Greeks. Probably all my inhibitions come to the top.

There have been times in history when the flag of the
British merchant navy dominated the seas of the world, even
more than the white ensign of the Royal Navy did at the time
of the 'Pax Britannica'. Britain still has a substantial part in
merchant shipping, but proportionately it grows less. The
most recent figures show the number of British ships to be
almost static. The British tonnage grows, but not so fast as
that of the rest of the world. Many of us deplore this, and
some clamour for a means to restore Britain to the top again.
I share those emotions, but reason tells me the opposite.

British shipping was an integral part of Britain's expansion
throughout the world, the creation of the Dominions and
Empire, and the development of something of an economic
empire both within and beyond the countries which became
the Commonwealth. These days are past. In my view, they
held more to be proud of than to regret. Britain still has a
great international function but in a world so radically
different from that of a hundred years ago, Britain's function
should also be radically different. There is no reason (and no
likelihood) that Britain will in future be the workshop of the
world, or the shopkeeper of the world. Likewise, she will not
be the world's carrier. In manufacturing, trade, and transport
she will be one among many.

But what should be the pattern? It is stupid to have every
country in the world trying to do every job that needs doing.
Surely, one task must be to find out which functions in a
world society can best be carried out by which countries.
A.S.G. Hoar, C.M.G., was a close friend of mine for nearly
forty years until his recent death. He was head of the
Overseas and Foreign Department of the Bank of England,
then a loan director of the World Bank in Washington, and
finished his career back in London as managing director of

he Commonwealth Development Finance Corporation. He
often talked to me of national and international economic
issues. He had negotiated the World Bank's first loan to India.
The grant was preceded by a careful investigation of India's
needs, and was given on the basis that priority was given to
three things, agriculture, transport, and hydro-electric power.
At the time, he told me, every person in that newly
independent country seemed to have his pet project which he
considered more important and urgent than any other; but
would anyone doubt now that those three priorities were in
fact the right ones?

Later, when Yugoslavia broke with Stalin and turned to
the west for finance, it was Hoar who led the World Bank
delegation to talk loans in Beograd. The key issue in the
dispute had been the refusal by Tito's government to accept
economic vassalage to Russia. On the rebound, as it were,
some Yugoslavs wanted their country to make one great leap
into full industrialism. It was of course impracticable, and
again Hoar had to sort out, in discussion with a government,
what should be a country's primary tasks. This time the
government was a Communist one.

Some years ago the *Observer* ran some articles which
probed the same ground in respect of the United Kingdom. I
remember a view was expressed that it was crazy to rely (as
some urged) on such exports as coal, from an industry which
was labour-intensive, and which was already declining. It
would be better to concentrate on things like aeroplanes,
which required the full exercise of our workers' inventiveness
and skill, and incidentally required very little compensating
import of raw materials, compared with the value of the
export. I would go further, and say that our 'invisible'
exports of specialised services are among the best things we
can contribute towards meeting the world's needs.

What place does Britain's shipping take in a picture of this
kind? We can still build splendid ships. Sir William Lithgow's
men on the Lower Clyde must have writhed when press and
public ignored their achievements, and harped on the
troubles of the shipyards on the Upper Clyde. Among other
successes, the Lower Clyde has won contracts from Korea
against keen Japanese competition. We can still crew and
manage ships as well as or better than anyone. As an island
kingdom, we need to have a merchant marine sufficient to
keep us fed and supplied in emergency. What is the true
position, and what should be the aim?

The British shipping industry has gone through a series of convulsions in the past thirty years, and the process continues today. The P. and O. upheaval is only one symptom of volcanic action throughout the industry.

I suppose that when I came into the City, British shipowners could be personified in two very different forms. One was the liner owner, solid, conservative, with a conscious air of superiority a little akin to that caricature of an Englishman which so annoys other people. (They used to say that an American would always tell you his was the greatest country in the world. An Englishman never would. He assumed that you knew.) The other type was the hardbitten tramp-owner, usually based outside London, who saved every penny he could in any direction, and fought for and won a large section of the world's trade, in knock-down competition with all comers.

The latter type is now an almost vanished breed. Great inroads have been made into the very tramp shipping market itself, which bred them, by the large-scale operations of today. Bulk carriers and (in times of scarcity of business) tankers adapted to carry grain may lift as much as five or ten tramps do in one voyage. Big bulk contracts partly replace the voyage by voyage, cut-and-thrust bargaining.

Perhaps the seamen of today would not stand for the conditions of those days. A master mariner friend of mine, now in a shore job in Hong Kong, sometimes talks of his days as an apprentice with a Newcastle tramp owner. When the ship was in home waters, the seamen were paid off, and the six apprentices did all the ship's work. The most common cargoes in those days were coal outwards from the United Kingdom to South America, and grain homewards. The ship carried enough bunkers for the round trip. Before she arrived in Argentina, the fuel for the homeward voyage was shifted from holds and tweendecks to the ship's bunkers. It might be 1,000 tons of coal, and this was work for the apprentices, in addition to their normal duties. "It certainly developed your shoulder muscles," he says.

The tramp owner was a tough character. He needed to be, to cope with the economic switchback of booms and slumps. Many of them have names which are still quoted, and in some cases carried on by grandsons. I can just remember the first Sir William Reardon Smith of Cardiff, but only as dodging him in the passage as he arrived for directors' meetings. The Reardon Smiths of today are, I think, the fourth generation.

W.A. Souter of Newcastle founded his firm in 1919 and ruled it for over fifty years, a familiar figure in our office throughout the period. I never discovered an aspect of shipowning with which he was not familiar, or a limit to his rough Tyneside commonsense. Several times on varying subjects, freight prospects, subsidies, ship management, I sought his advice as a sort of touchstone to test or correct my understanding of the point. And I have done the same to his son who succeeded him. Some of the well-known names fell outside my personal world — Lyle, Hogarth, Ropner, Denholm — but on the board of our defence club there was a tight group of Tyneside men who had a flavour all their own.

R.S. Dalgliesh was the archetype of them, the most individualistic of the lot, terse and salty in speech, bullet-headed and pugnacious, though not without humour. At one meeting Souter (not yet Sir William then) had to leave early, but paused with the door half open to give his view of the matter under discussion. Dalgliesh replied with an emphatic and vulgar monosyllable. "Really", grinned Souter sarcastically, "I am amazed that an alderman of Newcastle-upon-Tyne would even know such a word." And the door closed. Another time, in the era when it seemed impossible for a shipowner to settle any point with Russian charterers without legal proceedings, the directors debated whether to support an owner in a fairly minor claim of doubtful prospects. Dalgliesh ended the discussion by growling, "It's the Russians, so I say, fight 'em."

In trading, he was adventurous as well as tough, but his most celebrated and perhaps most characteristic battle was over the minimum freight scheme. In the early 1930s the tramp-owners were almost desperate at the low level of earnings for their ships after a very long slump which drove a number of firms into bankruptcy. The British Chamber of Shipping sponsored an agreement between the owners that they would not charter their ships below certain rates. The levels set were quite low, and there was at once widespread support. The Greeks, Yugoslavs and others were persuaded to join in, and in the end there was a virtually united front. Dalgliesh, however, would have none of it. He was utterly against any interference with complete freedom to trade as he wished, even if (as it was argued, and generally believed) restriction was a matter of survival. Sir George Christopher, chairman of the co-operation committee, denounced him as, in effect, a traitor to his industry. Dalgliesh was completely

unrepentant, and even seemed to enjoy it. He would not an
did not co-operate, and continued to go his own way. As fa
as I remember, a few others disagreed with the scheme an
evaded it. R.S.D. alone stood out as implacably opposed t
it, and insisted on his freedom being absolute.

Nothing could be more different than the stately world o
the great liner companies, some of them one or two hundre
years old, with their schedules of agreed rates of freight an
their sharing out of numbers of sailings among the differer
lines. Some of them seemed to me to operate almost lik
government departments, with a whole range of manager
each responsible for a little pocket of the operations, and
board of directors at a rather Olympian height. Now and the
their world would be ruffled by a 'non-conference' lin
starting up, and seizing business from them by reductions o
freight. For a short time there would be a 'rate war' in on
trade or another, but it always ended soon, either by th
buccaneer being forced out again, or by his being admitted t
the charmed circle where he conformed to the establishe
state of things. Most of the 'conferences' of companies in th
liner trades were (and remain) international, but in thos
days the British mostly dominated them.

To be fair, it is not easy to give frequent regular services b
fast ships in all the liner trades without a structure of th
kind the 'conference' system provides. For the multitude o
traders who want to send periodical shipments throughou
the world, a degree of certainty is worth paying fo
Moreover, the standards set by the best of the line
companies were quite splendid. The Blue Funnel line, fo
example, gave such a frequent service to the Far East tha
they used to have a rule (and maybe still do) that if a ship go
into trouble, salvage services should only be accepted from
sister ship. And there always was a sister ship within a day o
two's steaming. Before one of their vessels left Liverpoo
outwards, the head of each department on board had to sig
a certificate that all was in order, and the captain then signe
for the entire ship.

The trouble, perhaps, was the assumption by some peopl
in the liner business that matters would always run the wa
they knew and wanted, by a sort of divine right. Thi
produced a resistance to change in their rigid order of thing
as dangerous and damaging as the tramp owners' insistenc
on what they considered their right to seek profitabl
business in a freedom which approached to anarchy. Neithe

conception could be unaffected by the growing intervention of governments into shipping, and indeed into international trade.

It is not for me to analyse or provide answers to the world's shipping problems. I have neither the knowledge nor the ability. As an observer, however, I have seen with sadness the failure of some British shipowners to cope with their difficulties (often grave and not of their seeking), as well as seeing with admiration the way others have faced the same challenges.

The chairman of one large group, for example, said not long ago that the only way to restore profitability was to sell many of their ships. The logic of such a statement escapes me, unless it is coupled with constructive plans. What has worried me more has been the complete lack in some men of the adventurous quality which has brought so many of the Greeks to success. One very well-known British figure was a director of several companies. One of them, of which he was chairman, lost most of a respectably sized fleet in the war. His managing director told me, almost with tears, that year after year, the chairman refused to authorise replacements "until shipbuilding prices come down". They never did come down to the level he hoped for, and the company is now down to one ship. A tramp shipowner in a provincial centre said the same thing to me personally. His company is now extinct. I suspect that a number of the others which have vanished in the last twenty-five years did so for the same reason.

Shipping has also suffered from a disease which has affected industry generally in Britain and other countries, the mentality which puts finance before function. In spite of what is said by half-trained ideologists, profits and the building up of capital are essential to a developed society. If, however, they become the aim instead of the means, the operation suffers. It becomes like another kind of operation, the one which the surgeon says was successful, although the patient unfortunately died.

My own view (ill-informed and prejudiced, perhaps) of the P. and O. affair is that something of this sort of poison was allowed into the affairs of Britain's leading shipowning group. It suffered two traumatic experiences in quick succession.

The first, which is less well-known, was the interior reorganisation based on a report by McKinseys, the industrial consultants. The information available to me as a shareholder and a newspaper reader, reinforced by City gossip, suggested that the P. and O. board swallowed the report whole, and followed its recommendations as if it were handed down from Sinai. This may be quite wrong information, but if the story is true, it was a highly dangerous thing to do. The key decision was to merge the fourteen or so shipowning companies in the group into three large divisions, controlling passenger ships, general cargo ships, and bulk shipping, the last including both tankers and the bulk carriage of dry cargoes. This would, it was said, produce great economies although it would mean extinguishing the traditions, house flags and so on, of a number of proud semi-independent companies. My own judgment is that the plan may have been right, but it should have been started earlier and carried out in stages over five years or more, instead of being rushed through in a few months.

What was done resulted in a large number of people being made redundant, in the smooth modern phrase which makes the process no less rough for the people who suffer from it. It involved director level, management and clerical people shore and seagoing staff. The fact that financial arrangements, such as early pensions, were dealt with fairly did little to assuage the bitter feelings of some who went and the insecurity of many who stayed. And in the later stages, it was claimed that some who were in effect down-graded were offered terms too poor to accept. Other employers in the City had evidence of distress in many applications for jobs from those displaced, and from others who did not want to continue with what had been regarded as an employer of the highest quality. Mr. Clive Jenkins and the 'white collar' trade union he operates did their best to develop a drive for new members, which introduced a further element into the confusion.

Thus, a search for economy produced a real loss in 'job satisfaction' and in loyalty, which surely must have affected the running of the business.

Hard upon this, but after some changes in the board of directors, came the Bovis affair. Whether it should have been regarded as a merger, a take-over or a reverse take-over, it was a marriage between a basically shipowning group with a large building constructor. The reasons given were, I think, purely financial, involving the best use of property assets, tax advantages, and so on. The P. and O. owns four large office buildings in the City and another in southern England, and one aim was to use the property knowledge of Bovis to get a more profitable handling of these buildings. There was no indication that the plan would make P. and O. more effective as shipowners, except in so far as it would help to have more money available.

A mighty storm broke. Certain shareholders opposed the plan. Even more important, a split developed in the P. and O. board of directors, three of whom issued a public statement of dissent. A financial group which held a block of shares placarded the City with stickers, "Save P. and O., tell Bovis no". Rival full page advertisements chased each other through the newspapers. Thousands of pounds were spent on circulars to the shareholders, including personal attacks on some of the people involved. It was all very undignified, and hardly suitable for the Peninsular and Oriental Steam Navigation Company (incorporated by royal charter). Worst of all, the P. and O. shareholders rejected the scheme, and the chairman and six other directors resigned.

There is no point in re-analysing the proposals, or what their effects might have been. I can, however, say from personal talks with many people that the shore and sea staffs of the group were deeply demoralised by the whole affair. Many lost confidence in their employers' future, and some set out to find employment elsewhere.

One hopes that the P. and O. will have a great future. The new chief executive, A.R. Marshall, was the leader of the opposition, and is a dedicated man of great integrity and competence. His immediate task must be to show the world that his company is a success as a shipping company. There is a solid basis for this in the company's ships and contracts, and it may be that in a few years the furore will be forgotten. It may even be that some of the benefits sought through the Bovis plan will eventually be sought and found by other means.*

One factor against the link-up seemed to me important, although it escaped the commentators. Companies and their directors have a variety of problems, but all of them have one in common. Business today is conducted in a rush of events, and it is hard for any board to find adequate time to

* Since these lines were written, the P. & O. Company has made good progress in the shipping field, and instituted an energy division and a finance division. Both were logical developments. The Bovis proposal also was revived on a different basis, which may prove to be effective and valuable.

consider, discuss and plan together. A board which had to deal with two such different businesses would in effect be halving its thinking time. Mergers and diversification can be valuable, but not if they are of such a kind as to reduce the efficiency of the greater unit.

This is, however, only part of the more crucial choice — is it to be finance or function as the governing principle? Money and profits are of only brief advantage if the business is not fulfilling a real need, and doing so effectively and economically. For this reason, I shy off plans which are primarily based on financial advantage. They say that when company A is proposing to acquire company B, old hands on the Stock Exchange will sell their shares in company A. Experience shows that the advantages of the acquisition are rarely so good as is calculated in advance.

Does this have relevance to the future of British shipping? I believe it does. The men who matter most to that future are those who assess the real needs, and go boldly out to meet them. There are such men. The chief increase in British tonnage in the last few years has been made by a few large oil companies. Beside the V.L.C.Cs, the 'very large crude carriers' designed to carry 200,000 tons or more of crude oil, they have produced scores of other oil and chemical tankers of different sizes. But there are also men in various fields ordering bulk carriers, containerships, and others on the basis that they think they are needed. There is always a risk in this. Even the oil companies, with all the data they have available, have sometimes over-ordered in the past. But those who will take the risk, and base their decisions firmly on the anticipated needs, are likely to be Britain's shipowners of tomorrow. They face very difficult problems, including finance, manning, and competition (which is often subsidised by governments), but difficulties rarely stop the man who is right and keeps on fighting.

They say that the best British ships and the best British seamen are second to none. I believe it is the same with British shipowners, and I would like to tell some stories about one shipowner. Not everyone shares my appreciation of him, for he is a very unexpected character, and some find him difficult because of this. These stories, however, I have had either from himself or from people who were present.

One of his salient characteristics is a remarkable rapport with the seamen and stevedores who work the ships. He loves nothing more than to meet and talk with them, man to man.

Once or twice, I have been present at informal gatherings of this nature. At one of them, there were several workers from a shipyard who were actually on strike. He asked them what it was about, and they explained in terms which he evidently understood, although I did not. Then he asked what the top management of the yard thought about it all. They did not know. They only met sub-managers and foremen, and suspected that the men's views did not reach the top. He explained that by chance he was lunching with the managing director four days later, to discuss a new ship, and he would like to see if the managing director understood the issues. Whatever happened, the strike was quickly settled. Another time, some stevedores spoke of containerisation. "There's nothing in it for the shipowner," he said, "I've been into the figures. The only advantage is that it gets the ships away quicker from the bloody-minded dockers." But the grin which accompanied it produced a shout of laughter from the dockers.

When in 1966 the National Union of Seamen called the first official strike of British seamen for fifty-five years, he sent radio messages to all the company's ships, asking the captains to report the views of the men. One captain added to his report that the meeting ended with three cheers for the company, on the grounds that for the first time they had been consulted on the matter! The replies were the basis of his approach to the problem. It was a three-cornered situation. The Labour government of the day was operating a wage freeze, so that the employers were able to say that they could not agree to an increase, in any event. He asked friends connected with Moral Re-Armament (in which he took a certain interest) if there was a way of meeting any of the seamen's leaders unofficially. There was, and he spent an evening with four of them at a private house in Bermondsey. His first remark to them was that British shipowners owed a great deal to their seamen. Their last remark to him was that it was a pity they could not make him an honorary member of the union. Subsequent developments involved moves by many good men, but it is a matter of history that the formula on which the strike was settled was first evolved at that five-hour meeting in Bermondsey. By reducing the number of seamen in each watch, it was possible to pay them more and thus comply with the government ruling of no wage increase without increased productivity.

On an earlier occasion, when a modest wage rise was asked

for, he suggested to the shipowners' committee that they gave more than was asked. There was a violent row, and an attempt to exclude him from further meetings. After unofficial strikes, a second increase was given later. One of the men who opposed him at the committee said to me, "Of course, he was right."

Industrial relations are, however, not the whole of industry. The respect he has from many, grudging in some cases, is based on the solid success of his company, and the figures which are published year by year. This springs from a constant flow of new ideas. A co-director told me once, half-seriously, "He nearly drives the board mad. Some of his ideas are crack-brained, but we have to examine them all thoroughly, as a good proportion are winners." One was to build specially designed ships on a fifty-fifty basis with a big importer. He was the first British owner to order two of the new types of ship. When automation in engine-rooms became possible, he took down plans for a semi-automated ship to the union offices to agree the number of crew necessary, before he ordered the ship. When one aspect of his business faded away, leaving a group of men without work, he started a travel service, to which they all switched with enthusiasm.

In many fields, not only shipping, other countries look closely at what Britain is doing. I believe that our people can still lead in the quality of what we do, in originality and farsightedness, and in making an industry which is closely tailored to the precise needs of the national and international society in which and for which we work.

23

A Vocation for Everyone

Before I completed these notes I retired from Millers and left St. Mary Axe. My personal papers I passed over to others or destroyed, and my bowler hat came off its peg for the last time. Forty-eight years with one firm is a fair time. The careerists of today, who argue that every ambitious young man should try three different jobs before he is 35, may curl a lip at it. There is room for more than one opinion on these things.

It was not always easy or agreeable, and sometimes it was dull. A number of times I wanted to get out. Once I nearly answered an advertisement of a vacancy in another P. & I. club (the Britannia). I toyed with the idea of leaving the City to work without salary for Moral Re-Armament (spell it without capital letters, if you wish). I even thought of taking orders in the Church, although I have no idea if I would have been accepted. But my quiet morning thoughts never encouraged these deviationist ideas. It always seemed right to stay.

A number of years passed before it began to dawn on me that the real reason for my being in the job, and continuing in it, was that only in that way could I give a particular service to that particular circle of people. A job is not just a process one carries out, or a way of making a livelihood or a profit. It is more the rendering of some service which is so necessary that people will pay you to do it.

We are used to thinking that certain people have a vocation — for nursing, or for the priesthood, or for teaching. Why should not everyone have a vocation — a calling? It should be just as reasonable to have a vocation for business, or to work in a factory or on a farm. Many women (with all respect to the women's 'liberation' theorists) clearly have a vocation for home-making. Is there a specific plan for every person's life, a true course to follow, or are we just "ships that go bump in the night"?

Certainly, as the years went past, I gained more and more conviction that I was in the right job; and that, if it was handled the right way, it had a significance even wider than its natural outreach to the wide world of shipping. Perhaps the true vocation of every man is not only to do the right job, but also to be a living part of something bigger, a firm, an industry, a conception of society, even "the kingdom of God".

I was once explaining my ideas of management training to one of my partners. It was impossible to cover everything, I said, so I intended to concentrate on passing on to the trainees the basic principles of Protection and Indemnity insurance. But, as I said it, a sheer slip of the tongue made me say, instead of P. and I., M.R.A., the common abbreviation for Moral Re-Armament. I hurried to correct it, but my partner, much amused, said, "Don't apologise, Frank, some of us have realised for a long time that you regard P. and I. and M.R.A. as the same thing." Certainly, if they are not the same thing, in my life they have fed each other. Insurance is basically a means of caring for those in trouble, and our sort of business brought us into a very personal relation with people in this way. It showed the need for initiative towards putting right things that are wrong.

My activities in business and in other fields both conspired to widen my horizons year by year. I had contacts with coalminers and royalty, shop-stewards and a prime minister or two, with the press many times, and once I was interviewed on radio. I saw the peace of Pacific islands and of the glaciers of Iceland, and twice I was in Belfast during the bombings. Through it all, there has been a connecting thread, sometimes seen in advance, sometimes realised afterwards.

It is so easy to forget the repercussions of the ordinary things we do. I have learnt much from my partners and from other business friends, and some may have learnt something from me. Moreover, although we may not think of it as a model (a small imitation of the real thing, says the dictionary) there is no reason why any business, group, or individual should not be an example. Often one is too aware of the failures in one's own sphere to realise the impact of the successes. What is valid in one place can also be valid in a completely different one.

I discussed industrial relations with Mr. W.G. Jaeger, a great expert in this field, well known in the motor factories, the coal mines and the docks, and at the International

Labour Organisation in Geneva. Knowing my convictions, he asked me how such matters were handled in my firm. I told him, protesting that things were so different there that they had no relevance to heavy industry. We counted our employees in hundreds only, there were no trade unions involved, and no industrial processes. What had that to do with it, he asked, this was a human problem, not a technical one. He suggested that I told some trade unionists how my partners and I approached these things.

The idea kept recurring in my mind, and we took action on it when a large number of workers and management from industry were congregated in London for a weekend conference at the Westminster Theatre. My wife and I invited half a dozen Clydeside shipyard workers and their wives to Sunday tea at our flat. A chartered accountant and his wife acted as co-hosts. (He has since been Master of one of the City's livery companies.) It was a lively occasion. One of the men was most anxious to show us how militant he was for the workers, until another broke in to say, "Well, what would you do, Jock, if you were managing director of the yard?" Before he could figure out a reply, a third cut in with the dry words, "Send for the police." After tea, I rather nervously told them how we dealt with questions of pay, and also redundancy when someone proves unsuitable or for other reasons had to go. I made it plain that it was the firm's policy I was talking about, worked out over the years, and that I had only a part in forming the policy. When I ended, there was a moment's silence. I thought I had made a complete gaffe, but then one of them sighed and said, "It sounds like bluidy paradise."

Some of these men were among the first union representatives to sign the agreements which broke down the barriers between the trade unions on the Lower Clyde. I don't think our tea-table meeting affected the issue directly, but it may have strengthened their own convictions about what was needed.

In recent years, again, unemployment has been a burning issue in Britain. When matters were at their worst, I was one of sixty men in management who issued a statement pledging themselves to do all we could to improve the situation, and towards ending the class war which helps to cause it. It was this statement which resulted in my being interviewed on the radio. I also had a letter published in *The Times* on what the ordinary employer could do, citing my own firm's experience and those of other firms. At lunch that day, one of my partners who had spotted the letter said to me, "I see we've been doing a service to the nation."

Men of responsibility should not feel themselves helpless in the grip of circumstances, currents of trade, government policies, and so forth. We should set out to change circumstances. So many evils, including much of the destruction of man's environment, are considered inevitable. They are not.

We underestimate what people can achieve, and the explosive effect of change in the motives and actions of men. Most of all, we underestimate what can be the consequences of seeking correction and direction from what Mahatma Gandhi called "the inner voice".

When people tried to praise Dr. Buchman in his later years, he would sometimes say, "I have been wonderfully led." St. Paul wrote to Timothy, "I have fought a good fight. I have finished my course." I could not make such claims, but I feel something of that would be true. The story is not yet ended, and there may still be time to shape something better. I am certain the plan is there. Only a little of it can be seen and understood by the finite human mind, but, with patience, enough is seen for the action necessary. Those who follow the thread find a life's work beyond their imagining, and become part of the true destiny of the whole creation.

Index